# ALERT

**JAMES PATTERSON** is one of the best-known and biggest-selling writers of all time. Since winning the Edgar™ Award for Best First Novel with *The Thomas Berryman Number*, his books have sold in excess of 300 million copies worldwide and he has been the most borrowed author in UK libraries for the past eight years in a row. He is the author of some of the most popular series of the past decade – the Alex Cross, Women's Murder Club, Detective Michael Bennett and Private novels – and he has written many other number one bestsellers including romance novels and stand-alone thrillers. He lives in Florida with his wife and son.

James is passionate about encouraging children to read. Inspired by his own son who was a reluctant reader, he also writes a range of books specifically for young readers. James is a founding partner of Booktrust's Children's Reading Fund in the UK.

# Why everyone loves James Patterson and Detective Michael Bennett

'Its breakneck pace leaves you gasping for breath. Packed with typical Patterson panache . . . **it won't disappoint**.'
*Daily Mail*

'It's no mystery why James Patterson is the world's most popular thriller writer. Simply put: **Nobody does it better**.'
**Jeffery Deaver**

'No one gets this big without **amazing natural storytelling** talent – which is what Jim has, in spades.'
**Lee Child**

'James Patterson is the **gold standard** by which all others are judged.'
**Steve Berry**

'Patterson boils a scene down to the single, telling detail, the element that **defines a character** or moves a plot along. It's what fires off the movie projector in the reader's mind.'
**Michael Connelly**

'James Patterson is **The Boss**. End of.'
**Ian Rankin**

# Have You Read Them All?

### STEP ON A CRACK

The most powerful people in the world have gathered for a funeral in New York City. They don't know it's a trap devised by a ruthless mastermind. Despite battling his own tragedies, it's up to Detective Michael Bennett to save every last hostage.

### RUN FOR YOUR LIFE

The Teacher is giving New York a lesson it will never forget, slaughtering the powerful and the arrogant. Michael Bennett discovers a vital pattern, but has only a few hours to save the city before things get too close to home.

### WORST CASE

Children from wealthy families are being abducted. But the captor isn't demanding money. He's quizzing his hostages on the price others pay for their luxurious lives, and one wrong answer is fatal.

### TICK TOCK

New York is in chaos as a rash of horrifying copycat crimes tears through the city. Michael Bennett cuts his family holiday short to investigate, but not even he could predict the earth-shattering enormity of this killer's plan.

### I, MICHAEL BENNETT

Bennett arrests infamous South American crime lord Manuel Perrine in a deadly chase that leaves Michael's lifelong friend dead. From jail, Perrine vows to rain terror down upon New York City – and to get revenge on Michael Bennett.

### GONE

Perrine is back and deadlier than ever. Bennett must make an impossible decision: stay and protect his family, or hunt down the man who is their biggest threat.

### BURN

A group of well-dressed men enter a condemned building. Later, a charred body is found. Michael Bennett is about to enter a secret underground world of terrifying depravity.

# JAMES PATTERSON

## & MICHAEL LEDWIDGE

# ALERT

arrow books

1 3 5 7 9 10 8 6 4 2

Arrow Books
20 Vauxhall Bridge Road
London SW1V 2SA

Arrow Books is part of the Penguin Random House group of companies
whose addresses can be found at global.penguinrandomhouse.com.

Penguin
Random House
UK

First published by Century in 2015
First published in paperback by Arrow Books in 2016

www.randomhouse.co.uk

A CIP catalogue record for this book is available from the British Library.

Typeset in 11.5pt/15pt Berkeley Oldstyle
by SX Composing DTP, Rayleigh, Essex

Printed and bound in Great Britain by Clays Ltd, St Ives Plc

*For Sister Sheila*

## Prologue

# THE OLD SOD

# ONE

"MIKE, MARY CATHERINE here said you're NYPD. So you've gunned down a lot of people, then, have ya?"

I raised an eyebrow over the rim of my glossy waiting-room magazine at Billy, the slim, scruffy law-office receptionist typing at his computer.

Like many of the Irish folk I'd come into contact with in southern Ireland over the last week, Billy had a distinctive, mischievous twinkle in his Irish eyes. Akin to hurling and Gaelic football, pulling the legs of dumb Yanks like me seemed to be an Emerald Isle national pastime.

"The land of saints, scholars, and sarcasm," I whispered to Mary Catherine, who was sitting on the leather couch next to me.

"Well, that depends, Billy," I said as I went back

to reading about what Camilla was up to in my *OK!* London celeb mag.

"Oh? On what, pray tell, Detective?" the receptionist said, finally turning from his screen.

I casually put down the magazine and lifted the floral-patterned china cup of Gevalia coffee he'd fetched us when we came in.

"On what you consider 'a lot,' " I said.

The law office was in the city of Limerick, around ninety minutes west of Mary Catherine's family's tiny farmhouse outside Clonmel, in Tipperary. It was in a new modern brick-and-glass building on a bustling street called Howley's Quay that ran along the rippled slate ribbon of the River Shannon. Outside the floor-to-ceiling window behind the wise-guy receptionist was a high-rise apartment building and a ten-story silver glass office tower.

Not exactly midtown Manhattan, but definitely not the traditional thatch-roof rural Ireland I remembered from the last time I had been here with my family to visit relatives when I was fourteen.

The office belonged to a real estate lawyer, and we were there to close on the sale of the small hotel and golf course Mary Catherine's mother had run before she'd passed away. Since it was a quick sale, money was being left on the table, but Mary Catherine hadn't minded because they'd found a buyer who would keep the place running. Twenty-three people worked there, old family friends and cousins, and Mary Catherine needed to be sure that they would be taken care of before we went back to New York.

"Mary Catherine, sorry to keep you waiting," said the real estate agent and lawyer, Miranda O'Toole, as she poked her head out of her office a few minutes later.

I took my coffee with me as she waved us into her bright office. Miranda was a tall, milky-complexioned woman in her forties with dark-red hair. She unbuttoned her elegant tailored navy blazer, slipping it on the back of her chair before turning down the Haydn playing softly from the Bose speaker on her desk. She smiled as she rolled up the sleeves of her cream-colored blouse.

"I hope your writing hand is limber, Mary Catherine," she said, pointing at a high stack of papers on a small conference table by the window. "We have a lot of documents to sign."

# TWO

"BUT WAIT," MARY Catherine said as we sat. "Where's the buyer? I thought Mr. Hart would be here with us. There was a lot I wanted to go over with him. You know—details about the place, the employee roles, and all the different shifts and such."

"Oh, yes. Mr. Hart," Miranda said, smiling pleasantly as she sat down beside us. "Unfortunately, he had a business thing today up in Dublin, so he came in and signed yesterday evening. I hope that's not a problem."

Mary Catherine looked at her, still a little confused.

"I . . . suppose not," she finally said.

"Perhaps you could call him this afternoon," Miranda said, uncapping a red-and-gold Montblanc pen and offering it to Mary Catherine. "Go over everything then."

"Perhaps," Mary Catherine said, finally taking the pen as Miranda deftly turned over the first sheaf of documents and opened it to the signature page.

"Um, Mary Catherine, before you get started, I'd like to ask Miranda a question," I said as Mary Catherine was about to sign the first line. "If that's okay."

"Yes?" Miranda said a tad curtly as she darted her intelligent gray eyes at me. "I'm sorry, what's your name again?"

"I'm Mike Bennett," I said, smiling the most vacant, stupid Yank smile I could muster. "From New York City."

"Oh, yes. Great city, that. Tell me your concern, Mike. I'm all ears," Miranda said impatiently.

"I know it's probably nothing, but what's all this here?" I said as I pointed at the document. "Under Mr. Hart's name. What exactly is Red Rover Services, LLC?"

"Oh, that's just one of Mr. Hart's companies," Miranda said with a shrug. "He wanted to purchase the property through his LLC for tax purposes. It's nothing to worry about. Happens on contracts all the time."

"Oh, good," I said brightly. "I wouldn't want there to be anything out of the ordinary."

"Completely normal," Miranda said, nodding gently. "Any other questions? Shall we get started?"

"Well, actually, just one," I said as she frowned again. "What does Red Rover Services do?"

"You know, I'm not completely sure," Miranda said, biting on a knuckle.

I grinned some more as I slowly took out my iPhone and placed it on her desk with a click.

"Before we continue, why don't I look it up? These smartphones are just incredible, aren't they? Curiosity would have never killed that darn cat if only he'd had a smartphone," I said.

"What is it, Mike?" Mary Catherine said, frowning over at me.

"Red Rover is a construction company, okay?" Miranda was starting to sound impatient. "They build housing complexes. Mostly in Northern Ireland, but they also had a few developments up in Westmeath." Miranda paused, folded her arms. "But you heard Mr. Hart's assurances that he's going to keep the hotel running. You'll not find another buyer, at any rate. Not in this market."

She turned to Mary Catherine.

"You're going back to America, Mary Catherine,

right? So go ahead and sign. Take the money for your family. It'll all work out, I'm sure."

Mary Catherine stared at the lawyer. The Montblanc made a screech as she flicked it across the glass tabletop at Ms. Miranda O'Toole.

"No developers. I told you that at the very beginning. Several times. You're a dishonest person, Ms. O'Toole. Putting my friends and relatives out on the street in order to make a few euro isn't the kind of thing I do. Unlike you."

"And you're a very naive young woman, Ms. Flynn," the lawyer said sharply. "That old place is on its last legs. Has been for a decade, and everyone from around here knows it. That ratty course has more rabbit holes on the fairways than the ones on the ragged greens. Take the money."

"Mike, it's time to leave," Mary Catherine said, standing.

"Thanks for the Gevalia," I said to the grim-faced lawyer as I clicked my china cup on the glass and retrieved my phone. "It was really awesome. Just like the good ol' USA. And smartphones. Bye-bye, now."

# THREE

"WHY DON'T WE just bring the kids here?" I said for the hundredth time as Mary Catherine and I lay on the guest-room bed staring up at the ceiling.

Instead of answering me, Mary Catherine's warm hand found mine. She lifted my hand to her lips. Her lips soft and warm on my palm. Her soft cheek on my shoulder, warm and wet with silent tears.

I listened to the low murmur of rain against the roof. I knew what Mary Catherine wasn't saying. She wanted me to stay. Or she wanted to come with me. One or the other. It didn't matter. As long as we were together. As we'd always wanted to be. Only we couldn't.

The dreaded morning of my flight was here. The real world was back and getting in the way, as usual. There was no way around it. No matter how we adjusted things. We'd have to be apart again.

What a week it had been. Like something out of a dream. We'd never spent so much time together—alone. For three days, we'd tooled around in my little Ford rental hitting bed-and-breakfasts. We'd seen the Ring of Kerry, the Lakes of Killarney. The best was the fabulous sunny day we'd spent at the Cliffs of Moher, enjoying a windy picnic of Champagne and Irish soda bread as we held each other, staring out at the sea and listening to the crash of the surf five hundred feet below.

I'd never laughed so hard in my life as I had in the previous few days. Or allowed myself to be quite so recklessly happy. It had been an unplanned, unexpected bubble of paradise. One we didn't want to end. Ever.

Yet it was ending. Mary Catherine had to stay and sell the hotel to someone who would keep it open. I had to go back to the kids and my job. There was nothing either of us could do. At least not now.

Or maybe . . .

"What if . . . ," I said as Mary Catherine suddenly sat bolt upright in bed.

"What?" I said.

"Shh!" she said.

I shushed.

"No! It's a car! What time is it?" she said as she leaped onto her feet and ran to the window. "Oh, no. She's here! I knew she'd be early!"

"She" was Mary Catherine's great-aunt, Sister Terese, come to take me to the stupid airport for my stupid flight.

"Get up and dressed! Now!" Mary Catherine said as I continued to lie there. "We can't have this! If she sees you come down these stairs, we'll need the coroner!"

"Oh, please, Mary Catherine. It's the twenty-first century," I said. "She's a grown woman."

"A grown woman? She's an eighty-year-old Tipperary nun! It's the thirteenth century to her every day! And the coroner won't be for her! Out the window and into the backyard. Now!"

"Out the what? It's the second floor!" I cried.

"Hang-jump it. I've done it before. You'll be fine. Do it now!"

We heard a door come open downstairs.

"Mary Catherine? Are ye here?" came a voice.

Mary Catherine shoved me toward the window.

"I'm not going out that window in my boxers, Mary Catherine. That's nuts."

"Get!" she scream-whispered at me, and then

suddenly I was hanging off the windowsill, letting just about everything hang out in the rainy breeze. For a moment. My hand slipped, and I landed on my bare feet with a squish in a muddy lettuce garden. I was barely able to catch the pair of jeans that flew out the window after me, followed a second later by my shirt, Top-Siders, and bag.

"Close your eyes, ladies," I said as I ran into the clucking henhouse at the other side of the garden with my bundled clothes.

I'd just gotten my jeans buttoned and my muddy feet into my shoes when I heard Mary Catherine open the back door.

"Oh, yes, Sister. The hotel was nice enough to drop him off about ten minutes ago," I heard Mary Catherine say. "He said he was going to take a little walk. He has to be around here somewhere."

"Hey, everybody!" I said as I finally tucked in my shirt and stepped out of the henhouse. "Wow, you're right, Mary Catherine. Those are some real nice chickens in there. Shiny . . . eh . . . coats on them and impressive . . . beaks."

I turned to Mary Catherine's aunt. She was about five one and stocky. The expression on her face seemed to indicate that she didn't suffer fools well. Which was unfortunate, because she was about to be spending some time with me.

"Hi—I'm Mike," I said. "You must be Sister Terese."

The little old woman, wearing a plain, light-blue dress that matched her eyes, looked even more skeptical as we shook hands. Nothing new there. Skepticism was pretty much par for the course with me.

"Mr. Bennett," she said sternly. "If yer all done with the . . . chickens, I'll be waiting fer ye in the car."

Mary Catherine grabbed me and kissed me as soon as the nun was out of sight. I kissed her back even harder, if that were possible.

"I'm not getting on that plane, Mary Catherine," I said, finally letting go. "I don't care. I'll quit my job. I'm staying here."

But it was too late. Mary Catherine was already running back to the house. The door slammed, and it was just me, the stupid Yank, standing in the rain in the lonely gravel farmyard.

# Part One

# OFF THE RAILS

# Chapter 1

UP, UP, AND reluctantly away four hours later, I sat mid-cabin in my Aer Lingus flight's Airbus A330 feeling pretty darn sorry for myself.

Forgoing the movie on the little TV in the seat back in front of me, I leaned my forehead against the cold plastic window, staring at the rags of dirty clouds and the gray North Atlantic sailing away beneath the long, slender wing.

What I had said to Mary Catherine still held very much true. I did not want to be on this plane. Not without her. Not after the previous week. Every time I closed my eyes, I saw the wind in her hair atop that white-rock cliff The moonlight on the curve of her back in those cold farmhouse rooms night after night.

I mean, was my brain broken? No matter the

17

complications, parting just didn't make sense. You flew toward a woman like that. Not away.

This plane is heading in the wrong damn direction, I thought, shaking my head as I squinted down at the gray sea and sky.

I was going into my pocket for some gum I'd bought at the Shannon duty-free shop to ease the ratcheting pressure in my ears when I found the folded note.

MICHAEL it said on the outside in Mary Catherine's perfect script.

She must have slipped it in my jeans pocket before she chucked the pants out the window. I quickly unfolded it.

*Dear Michael,*

*From the very moment our eyes met in your apartment foyer all those years ago, I felt it in my heart. That you were mine. And I was yours. Which makes no sense. And yet it is the truest thing I know. I saw you and suddenly knew. That I was somehow finally done with all my silly wanderings. I saw you, Michael, and I was suddenly home. This last week with*

*you has been the best week of my life. You will*
*always be my home.*

*MC*

"Dear God, woman," I whispered as I reread the
note.

Dear God, I thought as I turned and looked out
at the world rushing by through my tears.

# Chapter 2

PRETTY MUCH EVERYTHING was gray as we made our final approach to New York City. The city skyline, the raining sky, the depths of my soul. I mean, I guess it was possible that things could have been more depressing as the plane touched down on the puddled tarmac.

But I doubt it.

I hadn't slept a wink, but that didn't matter. What mattered was that Mary Catherine still wasn't with me. What else was there to say? Or think? Or do? Not much. In fact, nothing at all.

"Jet lag and a broken heart," I mumbled as the flight attendant spouted some peppy "Welcome to New York" crap over the plane's intercom. "Winning combination."

Half an hour later, finally having escaped from

the happy people over at customs, I was at a grim JFK-concourse fast-food joint trying to keep down a lukewarm burrito when I remembered to power my phone back on.

I yawned as the message bell went off like a slot-machine win. Then I stopped yawning. There were six text messages and five missed calls, all from HOME.

A dark swirl of panic ripped immediately through my jet lag. Because of the egregious cell-phone charges, I'd left explicit instructions for my family to call only if there was a true emergency. Something was up. I thumbed the Return Call button. Whatever the hell it was, it couldn't be good.

"Hello?!" came Juliana's panicked voice on the first ring.

"Juliana, it's Dad. I just got off the plane at JFK. What is it?"

"Thank God you're home. It's Gramps, Dad. He's missing. He was supposed to come over here last night to babysit around ten, but when we called the rectory at eleven, they said he'd left at nine thirty. He never made it back last night, Dad. Seamus is missing. We don't know where he is!"

"Is the rectory housekeeper, Anita, still with

you?" I said, grabbing my bag and hustling immediately back onto the concourse.

"No. I told her to go home last night, Dad. Don't worry: I'm watching everybody."

"I know you are, Juliana. You're a good girl," I said as calmly as I could as I tried to read the impossible terminal signs to find the exit. "What am I saying? I mean young woman. Don't worry about Gramps. I'm sure he's okay. Probably met an old friend and stayed over with him. I'm going to find him right now. I'll call you the first I hear from him."

"Okay, good. I'm so glad you and Mary Catherine are home," she said.

I decided to leave out the fact that Mary Catherine was still stuck in Ireland for the time being. One catastrophe at a time.

"And don't worry. Things are under control on this end. I love you so much, Dad," Juliana said.

"I love you, too," I said before I hung up.

My next call, as I finally spotted an actual exit sign, was to my buddies at the Ombudsman Outreach Squad on 125th Street.

"Brooklyn, hi. It's Mike Bennett," I said when Detective Kale answered. "I need a favor. You ever do a missing persons case?"

"Sure, plenty of them. Why? What's up?"

"I just got off a plane out at Kennedy. My grandfather, Seamus Bennett, has been missing since around ten last night. He's eighty-one, white male, white hair, five seven, around a hundred and seventy-five pounds, probably wearing black priest's clothes. He left the Holy Name rectory on West Ninety-Sixth and Amsterdam last night around nine thirty, probably heading west for my building on West End and Ninety-Fifth. We're especially worried about him because he recently had a stroke."

"Seamus?" Brooklyn said. "Oh, no. I remember meeting him at Naomi Chast's wake. I'm on it, Mike. I'll check all the local hospitals and precincts."

I finally went through some sliding doors into the cold, grim predawn street. Above the curbside taxi stand, rain pelted off a fading rusted sign from maybe the eighties-era Koch administration.

WELCOME TO NY. HOW YA DOIN'? it said.

Luckily, I didn't have my service weapon with me because I might have emptied a magazine into it in reply.

"I'm stressed-out, New York," I mumbled. "As usual. Fuhgeddaboudit!"

# Chapter 3

I WAS STUCK in my taxi on the 59th Street Bridge staring at the towers of Manhattan in the honking suicide evening rush-hour traffic when Brooklyn called me back.

The good news was that she thought she'd found Seamus, but the bad news was where she'd found him. I had the cabbie take me straight to West 106th between Columbus and Amsterdam Avenues. Brooklyn was actually waiting for me on the sidewalk twenty-five minutes later, when my cab finally made it to the Jewish Home Lifecare facility.

"He's fine, Mike. I was just in there. He's up on eight, and he's fine," Brooklyn said in greeting as I flew from the taxi to the facility's front door.

"He's in a nursing home, Brooklyn!" I snapped at her as I went inside and showed the security guard my shield. "I don't call this fine. What the hell happened?"

"Twenty-Fourth Precinct was called at around ten fifteen," Brooklyn said as we maneuvered around an old lady in a wheelchair and another one lying on a bed in the hallway. "Somebody reported a confused old man on the uptown platform of the Ninety-Sixth Street number one subway line."

I shook my head picturing it. Seamus helpless on a subway platform, wandering around as the trains blew past. Dear Lord, did that hurt. No, please, I thought, not wanting it to be true.

"He wasn't wearing his priest's clothes, Mike. He was in sweats, and he didn't have any ID on him. When police questioned him, he got emotional, so they brought him here. It's the biggest old-age home in the area, so they thought he might have wandered away from here. They also have an Alzheimer's special care unit, so it was actually a smart move," she said as we arrived at the elevator.

"Alzheimer's?" I said, panicking some more as I pushed the elevator's call button about eighty-six times. "Seamus does not have Alzheimer's."

"I know, Mike," Brooklyn said. "I just spoke to him. He just woke up. They sedated him when he came in, but he's lucid now. You'll see."

Brooklyn surprised me by squeezing my hand.

"Listen, Mike. My grandmother is ninety-one. She's usually fine, but every once in a while, she forgets things. Stuff like this is going to happen going forward. It's natural."

"Dad?" called a voice.

I turned around and saw Juliana coming in through the doorway of the facility with her siblings in their school uniforms. Behind her were Ricky, Eddie, Trent, Jane, Fiona, and Bridget, holding Chrissy and Shawna's hands.

"Look! Daddy really is home!" Chrissy said, grabbing Shawna as she jumped up and down.

"Juliana, what are you doing?" I said as I hurried toward the children and convinced the utterly confused guard that they were all with me.

"I thought everybody was supposed to be in school," I said to Juliana.

"They are, but then when you texted me about Seamus being here, I went and got everyone out. Brian just left from Fordham Prep, too. He's on the train now. We all need to be here for Gramps. Is he sick?"

"Is Gramps going to die?" Shawna said, tears springing up in her eyes.

"No, no. He's okay, honey. He just got a little

confused, and they brought him here. He's upstairs on eight," I said as I lifted up Shawna and gave her a kiss.

"Where's Mary Catherine? Upstairs with Gramps?" Juliana said after I thanked Brooklyn profusely and convinced her that I had things under control so she could go back to work.

"Wait," I said, changing the subject. "How did you get everybody out of school?"

"I cannot tell a lie, Dad. I had to forge a note with your signature. Well, actually two of them. One for me and one for all the munchkins. You have to call Sister Sheilah, by the way. She didn't want to release them to me, but I was kind of pushy, I guess, and she finally relented."

Under normal circumstances such chicanery would, of course, be a no-no, but this was a four-alarm Bennett family emergency. Juliana knew as we all did that rule-bending was allowable when it came to being there for a family member in need. Especially Seamus.

I gave my oldest daughter a hug and a quick fist bump as we walked toward the elevator.

"Forgery *and* lying to nuns?" I whispered to her. "Right out of the old Bennett playbook, I admire your technique."

# Chapter 4

"MICHAEL SEAN ALOYSIUS Bennett!" Seamus said as we came through his eighth-floor room's open doorway to find him sitting in a chair laughing with a pretty young black woman in Tiffany-blue hospital scrubs.

"And the whole squad! The Lord save us all, you're all a sight for sore eyes! You'll not believe what's happened to me, gang. I headed to your apartment house yesterday evening and lost my way, and now here I've woken up Jewish!"

We all laughed as we surrounded him in a group hug.

"Well, it's nice to see you, too, Father. Believe me," I said, choking back tears as I hugged this old man whom I loved as dearly as anyone on earth. I could admit to myself now that I was convinced that he was dead. Bonked on the head by a mugger or fallen down into a Con Edison manhole. To see him in one piece was truly a miracle.

"I hope everyone wasn't worried. I must have given you all quite a scare. I tried to call the house when I woke up, but it just kept kicking into voice mail."

"It's fine, Seamus. It's all going to be fine. First let's get you out of here, okay?"

"Mr. Bennett?" the nice young black woman said to me. "I'm Dr. Blair Greenhalgh, head of the special care unit. Can I speak to you in the hall?"

"Sure," I said. "Kids, keep Seamus company while I talk to the doctor."

"Mike, wait. Come here," Seamus said, embracing me again. "I knew you'd come and get me."

A scared look came over his face. I hated seeing it.

"I'm sorry," he whispered. "I don't know what happened to me. I just got confused. It won't happen again. Please don't stick me in this place or any other place, okay? I'm fine."

"I've got you covered, Gramps," I said, giving him another hug. "I promise."

I finally got out into the hallway with the doc.

"I'm sorry, Mr. Bennett. I know this all must be quite a shock," Dr. Greenhalgh said. "I saw from your grandfather's preliminary medical history that he recently had a stroke in the right hemisphere of the brain. Is that correct?"

"Yes," I said. "About three weeks ago."

"Stroke survivors often experience multiple types of memory loss—verbal, visual, informational. They sometimes wander and get lost even in familiar places. Is Mr. Bennett on any medications?"

"Just cholesterol stuff."

"Okay," Dr. Greenhalgh said, nodding. "This could have been an anomaly. Sometimes memory problems just go away as part of the healing process, but in the meantime, you should try to really help your grandfather with establishing routines. Perhaps you could draw up a small notebook with emergency numbers in it to keep on his person in case he gets confused again. Exercise is great, as is keeping him engaged. That's about it. I'll get the nurse to give you my contact info and get you guys out of here."

Oh, he's engaged, all right, I thought, watching him through the glass in the door after the kind doctor left. He and all the kids were standing in a circle holding hands, heads down, their lips moving in prayer. I smiled as I stood there watching them. You can't keep a good man down.

Thank you, God, I prayed along with them as I closed my own eyes. For all of us being safe and back together again.

Almost all of us, I thought, patting the note in my pocket.

That's when it happened. Right then and there in the corridor, jet-lagged out of my mind.

I opened my eyes and was suddenly home.

# Chapter 5

THE FORTY-FOOT-LONG utility truck called a Supervac gave off a low grumble as it weaved slowly through the Broadway traffic in the upper Manhattan neighborhood of Washington Heights around noon.

The size and appearance of a high-tech garbage truck, with a huge hose attached to one side, the fifty-thousand-pound industrial vehicle was used to clean manholes and construction sites. Fully loaded, it was tricky to maneuver in the congested city traffic, especially in terms of braking, which was why the driver was keeping it at a slow and steady twenty-five miles per hour.

The truck itself was about ten years old and on its last legs from wear and use. The newest thing about it was the fake decal on its cab door that said it was from Con Edison, the New York City–area gas and electric company.

The driver was a doughy, vaguely Italian-looking guy in his forties wearing a blue Con Ed hard hat with matching baggy blue Con Ed coveralls. The con was definitely on, he thought, raising his stubbled jowls with a quick grin.

Then, as the truck finally approached its destination at the southeast corner of bustling 168th Street, he suddenly pointed ahead through the windshield.

"Uh-oh. Problem, Mr. Joyce," he said to the man in the passenger seat beside him. "There's a cop car parked right over our manhole. What do I do? Keep going?"

Mr. Joyce glanced up from the cluttered clipboard in his lap. Like the driver, he also wore bogus baggy Con Ed–blue coveralls and a matching hard hat. With the Oakley Sport sunglasses he wore under his hard hat, all you could tell about him was that he was pale and had a dark, reddish-brown goatee.

"Of course not. We're on a tight schedule, Tony. Just pull alongside," Mr. Joyce said calmly.

"Pull alongside?" the driver, Tony, said nervously. "Are you sure we shouldn't just come back a little later? It's the cops!"

"Listen to orders, Tony. Just pull alongside and let me handle it," Mr. Joyce said as he rolled down his window.

There was only one cop in the cruiser. He was a lanky middle-aged black officer, and he looked up none too happily as Mr. Joyce gave him a friendly wave from the truck window. The cop had his hat off and a sandwich unwrapped in his lap.

"Sorry to bother you, Officer, but you're parked over a manhole we need to gain access to," Mr. Joyce explained, trying to make his voice sound as American as possible.

"Gimme a break, would you?" the cop said, flicking some five-dollar-foot-long lettuce off his chin. "Why don't you go and take a nap somewhere for half an hour? When you come back, I'll be gone."

"I wish I could, Officer, honestly. But this one's a real red ball. Apparently there's some kind of power problem at the hospital," said Mr. Joyce as he gestured at the multibuilding New York-Presbyterian/Columbia University Medical Center complex across Broadway.

The cop gave him a savage look, mumbling something about red and balls, as he lowered his lunch and finally pulled out.

After Mr. Joyce hopped out of the cab, it took

them less than a minute to maneuver the massive truck into position. As Tony got the manhole open with the hook, Mr. Joyce removed a blueprint from his clipboard and knelt with Tony at the rim of the hole.

"Start jackhammering right there," he said, pointing into the manhole, a little left of the center of its south wall. "Should be about six feet in. It'll look like square aluminum ducting, the same you would see in an HVAC system. Text me immediately when you see it. Oh, and watch those electrical cables at your back while you're working, if you don't wish to get fried. Half of them are uninsulated, and all of them are quite live."

"You got it, Mr. Joyce. I'm, uh . . . on it," said Tony, repeating an advertising expression that Con Edison had used in their commercials a few years before.

"This is no time for joking, Tony. Just get to work," Mr. Joyce said.

# Chapter 6

WHEN MR. JOYCE got to his feet, the other Supervac truck they had stolen was just pulling up to the curb. His partner, Mr. Beckett, climbed down from the cab in the baggy nondescript Con Ed getup with sunglasses. He could almost have been Mr. Joyce's double, except his goatee was jackrabbit white instead of reddish-brown.

Without speaking, both men crossed the sidewalk and descended the steps into the 168th Street subway station. MetroCarding through the turnstile, they bypassed a sign directing them to the A train and found the concrete corridor for the number 1 line elevator.

"This station is one of the deepest in the entire system, Mr. Beckett," Mr. Joyce said as they stepped off the elevator onto the bridge that connects the uptown and downtown sides of the massive arched number 1 line's underground station. "We're presently ten stories below street level."

Mr. Beckett nodded. He was pleased with his partner's automatic use of their code names now that they were finally operational. All the exhaustive lessons he'd given his young partner about tradecraft had definitely sunk in.

"Why does it say 'IRT' here while upstairs, on the A line, it says 'IND'? What do the initials mean?" Mr. Beckett wanted to know.

"It doesn't matter for our purposes," Mr. Joyce said, frowning. "You will find it boring."

"No, I won't. I promise. We have time to kill before that fool Tony gets to the air shaft. I'm curious. You don't think I enjoy your little history lessons, Mr. Joyce, but I actually do."

Mr. Beckett was right. Science was Mr. Joyce's forte, but history was his true passion. Since he had arrived in the country years before, he had found the history of America, and especially New York City, surprisingly rich and fascinating. He was looking forward to delving into it more deeply at his leisure once all was said and done.

Especially, he thought, since he was about to

make a great deal of the city's history himself in the coming days.

"The abbreviations actually mean nothing anymore," Mr. Joyce explained. "They're just old subway nomenclature, remnants of the time when the city subway system was divided into lines run by separate companies instead of the current unified Metropolitan Transportation Authority. IRT stands for Interborough Rapid Transit, while IND stands for a company called the Independent Subway System. You may have noticed the abbreviation BMT on other lines, which stands for the Brooklyn-Manhattan Transit Corporation. I could go into detail about the three lines and how they fit into the subway system's famous color-coded numerical and alphabetical signage if you wish."

"No, that's okay. I need to stay awake," Mr. Beckett said and laughed.

"I told you that you would find it boring," Mr. Joyce replied with a sigh.

"On that, as on most things," Mr. Beckett said as he clapped his protégé playfully on the shoulder, "you were annoyingly correct, my friend. How does it finally feel to be out of the lab and into the field?"

Mr. Joyce watched as a pigeon suddenly flapped

out and down from a tunnel ledge above them and started pecking at some garbage between the uptown rails. Then he shrugged.

"I wouldn't know. I don't feel. I think."

Mr. Beckett smiled widely.

"That is why you are so valuable. Now, give me damage estimates again in tangible human terms."

"At the minimum, we're looking at massive damage to the tunnel, shutting down service for months, and obviously terrifying this city like nothing since nine eleven."

"And at the maximum?" said Mr. Beckett, hope in his bright-blue eyes behind the shades.

Mr. Joyce folded his hands together as he closed his eyes. Mr. Beckett thought he looked almost Asian for a moment, like a pale, goateed Buddha.

"We collapse a dozen city blocks, destroying the hospital complex, much of Washington Heights, and killing thousands," Mr. Joyce finally said.

Mr. Beckett nodded at this pensively.

"And we go when, again?" he said.

"Tomorrow night."

"So many decisions," Mr. Beckett said, gazing north as a downtown-bound 1 train pulled, clattering, into the station. "So very little time."

# Chapter 7

"DAD, DO I really have to wear this?"

Sunday morning around ten thirty, I waited until I heard the question repeated two more times before I looked up from an open old tin of black Kiwi shoe polish that I was using to teach Eddie how to shine his shoes.

The question was posed by Jane, who stood there in her lavender flower-print Easter dress. Her Easter dress from the previous year. Considering she'd grown about two inches in the meantime, she looked a little like Alice in Wonderland, suddenly enormous after consuming the "eat me" cake—or was it the "drink me" drink?

"It is a tad formal, I guess," I said as I buffed at Eddie's school shoes, "and, um, weird-fitting."

"Gee, Dad. That's really what a girl wants to

hear. 'What a weird-fitting dress you're wearing.' You really know how to pay a compliment."

"Give me a break, Jane, will you, please? I'm up to my neck here. Do you have another nice dress?"

"Um, no. Mary Catherine was supposed to take all us girls shopping before she left, remember? Or maybe you forgot. Like the way you forgot to bring Mary Catherine home."

I winced. I probably deserved that one. In fact, I knew I did. The fact that Mary Catherine hadn't come home with me was still stinging to everyone. To me most of all.

"Figure it out, Jane, okay? Please? You can wear jeans, I guess, if they're nice. We have to look really good, remember? That's the point here. That's the theme. Sweet and presentable and appropriate, okay?"

"Hey, everyone! Dad said we can wear jeans!" Jane shouted as she took off down the hallway.

"Dad, can I borrow your razor?" someone else asked a minute later.

This new query came from a groggy-looking Brian, still in his pj's. I looked at his smooth, pale, sixteen-year-old cheeks. There was no hair to speak of. I didn't say this, of course. Not passing on my observation was a no-brainer. Dad 101.

Maybe his eyesight was better than mine. Make that definitely.

"In my medicine cabinet," I said. "But hurry up. Please. We need to do this for Seamus. We need to pull together, or we're all going to be late."

Ten minutes later, I had everyone ready and gathered in the living room. Jane had actually found another dress and was looking quite spiffy, as was everyone else. Even I was wearing a tie for the special occasion. Everyone was present and accounted for except Seamus and Ricky and Juliana.

Which reminds me, I thought as I checked my watch. I nodded to Fiona, and at my signal she hit the stereo as the clock struck eleven precisely.

The door to the back bedroom opened just as the first strains of "Immaculate Mary" filled the room. Out the door came Juliana, holding a book-marked Bible, followed by Ricky, wearing his altar-boy robe and holding a lit candle, then lastly, Seamus, wearing a surplice and clasping his hands in prayer.

As they arrived at the front of the room, I elbowed a day-dreaming Trent to up the volume or, better yet, actually start singing from the lyric sheet I had printed out.

Since Seamus needed to take it easy after his

stroke, I'd decided to turn the apartment into Saint Bennett's Cathedral this Sunday and do Mass at home. He seemed to be fine enough since we brought him home, but I was still quite worried about him, of course. Not having Mary Catherine here to help me keep an eye on him, I decided to err on the side of caution.

The good news was that Gramps really seemed blown away when he saw the furniture rearranged in the living room and all the kids in their Sunday best.

"Good morning, parishioners," he said, winking, as he stood smiling at the front of the room.

"Good morning, Father," everyone said, smiling back.

Seamus stood there, then suddenly brought a finger to his open mouth as a vacant look glazed his eyes.

"Now, what's next?" he said, looking down at the carpet, confused.

"Seamus?" I said as I stepped forward.

"Psych!" he said to me, snapping out of it after another moment as everyone laughed.

"Don't worry: I'm not ready for the glue factory yet, Detective. Still a marble or two rolling around in this old gray head."

"Very funny, Father," I said, stepping back. "I'll be the one with the stroke next if you keep it up."

"Nonsense," Seamus said. "Now, where was I? I know. Let us begin today as we begin every day. In the name of the Father and of the Son and of the Holy Spirit."

# Chapter 8

THAT EVENING, I was minding my own business, sheltering in place on the couch with a pint of Smithwick's, about to watch the Yanks at Boston—ESPN's game of the week—with Seamus and the rest of the boys, when I made the mistake of checking my phone for messages.

My boss, Miriam Schwartz, had sent a text about an hour before. In it she let me know that during the week I'd been in Ireland, the department had appointed a guy I'd vaguely heard of named Neil Fabretti to be its newest chief of detectives.

Chief Fabretti was trying to get up to speed before officially starting on Monday, Miriam explained, and was requesting a quick informal meet and greet with his transition team at his house up in the Riverdale section of the Bronx. In the next half hour, I thought, groaning, as I checked my watch.

Get up to speed during a New York–Boston rubber game? I thought as I stared at my phone, dumbfounded. I'd been busting my hump all day with laundry and homework and getting dinner on the table. I'd even been to Mass—or at least Mass had been to us. I'd been looking forward to a little Sawx-crushing, male-bonding downtime all day.

Are you sure this guy is the new chief of detectives for the *New York* police department? I almost texted back.

Instead, I reluctantly put down my Smithwick's and stood and found my keys.

"Excellent idea, Michael," Seamus said as I headed out. "We could use some goodies for the game. And don't forget another six of Smithy's."

"Sorry, Father. No goodies tonight. It's all baddies, in fact. A.k.a. work."

"Work, Dad? But it's Yanks-Sox! That's sacrilegious."

"My sentiments exactly, Brian," I said as I hit the door. "Keep me posted on the score. I'll be back as soon as I can."

Chief Neil Fabretti's house turned out to be on Delafield Avenue in a ritzy section of Riverdale called Fieldston. It wasn't a huge house, maybe two thousand square feet, but it had a slate roof and antique stained-glass windows between its Tudor beams. Not too shabby. Especially for a cop. It had to be worth well over a million bucks.

"Mike, I'm so glad you could make it," said Chief Fabretti as he gave me a firm handshake.

Fabretti was a neat and trim fiftyish man in a brown golf shirt and khakis. He looked more like a corporate executive than a cop. I wondered if that was a good thing. A large black curly-haired dog ran around us in the foyer, woofing and sniffing.

"Down, Faulkner. Down!" Fabretti said. "I know—Faulkner? My wife's idea, as is the house and pretty much everything in it. She's the cultured one, an editor at Knopf. I'm just a lovable fool from Brooklyn who married up. Anyway, the other guys just left. I know this is a pain in the ass during the game. I actually have it on in my den. This won't take long, I promise."

He led me into a cozy, dark, wood-paneled room. Beyond a writing table were built-in bookshelves with actual books on them. I spotted a shelf of Hemingway. *The Day of the Jackal* next to Keith Richards's *Life*. A section of military history.

The one thing I had heard about Fabretti was

that he was political. But who knew? A real library was pretty telling in terms of character. Maybe this guy was okay, I thought.

"Can I get you a beer?" Fabretti said, opening a little fridge beside his desk. "Well, if you can call it that. My wife has me weaned down now to Beck's light. It's more like beer-flavored water."

"No—that's okay, Chief. What's up? How can I help you?"

"You can help me by just continuing to do what you do, Mike," Fabretti said as he cracked open a brew and sat behind his desk. "People complain that you're overrated—a hot dog and a headline hound—but I've done my homework, and you're obviously not. You're just flat-out one of the department's best detectives, if not *the* best. I've been following your phenomenal career, Mike. I'm a big fan."

A fan? Hmm, I thought. Maybe the rumors were true. Politicians plus flattery equals what? Nothing good was a pretty sure bet.

"Where am I being reassigned?" I said.

Fabretti laughed.

"C'mon, Mike. It's okay, I swear. I definitely want to keep you at Major Crimes. But I also need you to do what you've been doing. I want you to be flexible in terms of floating to local precincts occasionally to help on extra-pain-in-the-ass cases."

"How can I be in Major Crimes plus be a precinct detective?" I said. "Who will I answer to? The precinct captains or my boss, Miriam, at Major Crimes?"

"You'll answer to me, Mike," Fabretti said after a moment. "You know I'll always have your back. You'll work out of Major Crimes for now. What do you say? This will be a little experiment. One we'll correct as we go."

Or, more precisely, make up as we go.

I definitely didn't like it. A man without a home in the department was a good guy to scapegoat when the pressure got turned up. I didn't want to be that goat, but it wasn't looking like my opinion mattered.

The books had to be the wife's, I finally realized.

"Whatever you need me to do, Chief," I finally said as I turned to the flat screen above the fireplace, where Ellsbury was hitting into a double play.

# Chapter 9

AT 3:23 A.M., the two Supervac trucks turned off their headlights and pulled off the northbound FDR Drive into a junk-strewn abandoned lot beside the Harlem River across from the Bronx.

After he put the first truck into park, Tony took a bottle of orange Gatorade from the cooler they'd brought, cracked its lid, and commenced gulping. His stubbled face was filthy, and he was sweating profusely; he had in fact sweated through the back of his heavy coveralls.

"Hey, you want some of this, Mr. Joyce?" said Tony, coming up for air.

"No. All you, Tony. Truly, you broke your butt down in the hole. I'm proud of you," Mr. Joyce said.

It was true. Tony had some heft on him and could use a few suggestions about his hygiene, but no one could say he wasn't a worker. He'd been going at it hard for the previous three hours, shuttling between the two manholes, really hustling. He'd been Johnny-on-the-spot for every task without a word of complaint.

They were finally done now. At least with the prep work. It had gone off without a hitch. The truck tanks were empty, and the manholes were closed. Everything was set up and ready to go.

"How's the link?" Mr. Joyce called into the radio he took from his pocket.

"Crystal clear," Mr. Beckett, in the other truck, replied.

They had hacked into the MTA's internal subway video feed, and Mr. Beckett was now monitoring the security cameras at every 1 line station from Harlem to Inwood.

"Okay, I see it," Mr. Beckett said over the radio a second later. "It's pulling out of One Fifty-Seventh in the northbound tunnel. There. It's all the way in. You have the green light, Mr. Joyce."

Mr. Joyce took a cheap disposable cell phone from the left breast pocket of his blue coveralls. It was a Barbie-purple slide phone made by a company called Pantech, a simple phone one would buy a suburban girl for her middle-school graduation. He turned it on and scrolled to the phone's only preprogrammed number.

Theory becomes reality, he thought. He thumbed the Call button, and the two pressure cookers preplanted in the train tunnel ten stories beneath Broadway twenty blocks away detonated simultaneously.

# Chapter 10

THE INITIAL EXPLOSION of the pressure-cooker bombs, though great, was not that impressive in itself. It wasn't meant to be. It was just the primer, the match to the fuel that the two trucks had been pumping into the air of the tunnel for the previous three hours.

The tunnel was dome-shaped, seventy-three feet wide at its base, twenty feet high, and a little less than four miles long. Within milliseconds of the blast, a powerful shock wave raced in both directions along its entire length. There were no people on the subway platforms that late at night, but in both stations, the wave ripped apart vendor shacks on the platforms, MTA tool carts, and wooden benches.

As the wave hit the south end of the 181st Street

station, a three-ton section of the vaulted tunnel's roof tore free and crashed to the tracks—as it would in a mine cave-in—while up on Broadway, the fantastic force of the blast set off countless car alarms as it threw half a dozen manhole covers into the air.

South of the main blasts, in the tunnel between the 157th Street station and 168th Street, the shock wave smashed head-on into the approaching Bronx-bound 1 train that Mr. Beckett had spotted. The front windshield shattered a millisecond before the train tore from its moorings, killing the female train operator instantly.

As the train derailed, its only two passengers, a pair of Manhattan College students coming back from a concert, were knocked spinning out of their seats onto the floor of the front car. Bleeding, and still barely alive, they had a split second to look up from the floor of the train through the front window at a rapidly brightening orange glow. It was strangely beautiful, almost like a sunset.

Then the barreling twenty-foot-high fireball that was behind the shock wave slammed home, and the air was on fire.

Back at the abandoned lot near the Harlem River, Mr. Joyce had to wait seven minutes before he heard the first call come in on the radio scanner he had tuned to the fire department band. He clicked a pen as he lifted his clipboard.

"We did it, Tony," he said, giving the driver a rare grin.

"Phase one complete."

# Chapter 11

MORE BLUE AND red emergency lights than I could count were swinging across the steel shutters and Spanish-language signs at 181st Street and Saint Nicholas Avenue when I pulled up behind a double-parked FDNY SUV that morning around 4:30 a.m.

I counted seven fire trucks and an equal number of police vehicles and ambulances. As I hung my shield around my neck, I saw another truck roar up. Rescue 1, the FDNY's version of the Navy SEALs. Holy shit, was this looking bad.

I found the pitch-black subway entrance and went down stairs that reeked of smoke. All I could hear were yells and the metallic chirp of first-responder radio chatter as I swung my flashlight over the tiled subway walls.

The initial report I received from my boss, Miriam, was that some kind of explosion and a subway tunnel fire had occurred. One memory kept popping into my head as I hopped a turnstile and ran toward the sound of radios and yelling.

Don't tell me this is 9/11 all over again!

I went past a station booth and almost knocked over white-haired, blue-eyed fire chief Tommy Cunniffe, thumbing something out of his eye.

"Chief, Mike Bennett, Major Crimes, NYPD. What the hell happened?"

"Massive tunnel explosion of some kind, Detective," Cunniffe called out in a drill-sergeant baritone. "Two stations, One Hundred Sixty-Eighth Street and here at One Hundred Eighty-First Street, are completely destroyed. We have the fire almost under control here, but there's colossal structural damage, a large cave-in at the south end of this station. It's like a mine accident down there. We're looking for bodies."

"Is anybody dead?"

"We don't know. I heard over the horn there was a train that got fried a little south of One Sixty-Eighth, but everything else is still unknown at this point. I got two engine companies down there working a water line that we had to feed seven stories down through the elevator shaft. It's an unbelievable disaster."

"Chief," came a voice from his chest-strapped radio. "We got movement. A heartbeat on the monitor."

"Coming from where?" Cunniffe yelled back.

"Up near you, in one of the other elevator shafts."

"Downey, O'Keefe: get me a goddamn halogen!" Cunniffe screamed at two firemen behind him.

I ran over with the firemen and helped them pry open the door to one of several elevator shafts. When we got the doors open, three huge rugby-player-size firemen appeared out of nowhere and tossed a rope.

"Hey, Danny, what the hell are you doing? It's my turn," said one of them as the biggest clicked his harness onto the rope and lowered himself into the darkness.

"Screw you, Brian," the big dude said. "You snooze, you lose, bro. I got this. Watch how it's done."

I shook my head. These guys were amazing. Tripping over themselves to help. No wonder people called them heroes.

"Send down the rig," said the fireman in the

shaft a minute later. "We got two, a mom and a daughter. They're okay! They're okay!"

Everyone started cheering and whistling as a pudgy Hispanic woman, clutching her beautiful preschool-age daughter, was pulled up out of the shaft into the light.

"Okay, good job, everyone. Attaboys!" Cunniffe bellowed as EMTs took the mother and child up the stairs. "Now get the f back to work!"

An hour later, I was deep underground ten blocks south in full-face breathing apparatus and a Tyvek suit as I toured the devastation that had been the 168th Station with FBI bomb tech Dan Dunning, from the Joint Terrorism Task Force.

"This is unbelievable," he said, swinging the beam of his powerful flashlight back and forth over the vaulted ceiling.

"Which part?" I said.

"This was one of the grandest stations of the whole subway system, Mike. See the chandelier medallions next to the cave-in and the antique sconces in that rubble there? This used to be the station for the New York Highlanders, who went on to become the New York Yankees. A part of history. Now look at it. Gone. Erased."

"Could it have been a gas leak?"

"Not on your life," Dunning said. "Gas and electric are surface utilities. These are some of the deepest stations in the system. Ten stories down. Whatever blew them up was intentionally put here. I can't say for sure yet, but you ask me, these goddamn bastards set off a thermobaric explosion."

"A what?"

Dunning pulled off his mask and spat something out.

"Thermobaric explosions occur when vapor-flammable dusts or droplets ignite. They rely on atmospheric oxygen for fuel and produce longer, more devastating shock waves. As you can see, when they occur in confined spaces, they are catastrophic. They pumped something down here and lit it up. A gasoline mist, maybe, is my guess. Just like a daisy-cutter bomb. I mean, look at this!"

We hopped down off what was left of a platform and walked over the burned-to-a-crisp tracks toward a blackened train. As crime-scene techs took pictures, I could see that one of the train's plastic windows had melted and slid down the side of one of the cars like candle wax. Inside, the driver was burned pulp, and the two other bodies in the front car were skeletal and black, like something from a haunted house.

"Look at that," Dunning said, pointing his light at a half-burned sneaker in a corner.

"Wow, the shock wave must have knocked them out of their shoes," I said.

"Worse, look at the sole of it. It's almost completely ripped off. That's how powerful this bomb was. It separated the sole off a sneaker! Think of the incredible violence that would take."

I shook my head as I thought about it, breathing in the sweet gasoline smell of burning that the respirator couldn't filter out.

What was this, and where was it going?

# Chapter 12

THREE HOURS LATER, our command post shifted four blocks northeast, to the NYPD's new Thirty-Third Precinct building at 170th Street near Edgecombe Avenue.

When I wasn't answering my constantly humming phone, I was busy upstairs in a huge spare muster room helping a couple dozen precinct uniforms set up a central staging area for what was obviously going to be a massive investigation.

Everywhere I looked throughout the cavernous space were stressed-out, soot-covered MTA engineers, FDNY arson investigators, and FBI, NYPD, and ATF bomb techs chattering into phones as they tried to get a grip on the scope of the disaster.

The biggest development by far was the discovery of shrapnel in two separate sections of the tunnel. Preliminary field reports seemed to indicate that the metal shards were from some sort of pressure-cooker bomb placed at the two main blast sites. We hadn't released anything to the press as of yet, but it was looking like this was in fact a bombing, a massive and deliberate deadly attack.

At 6:05 a.m., the mayor suspended the city's subway service systemwide. It was a huge, huge deal. Eight million people now had to find a new way to get to and from work and school. A mega meeting at the precinct command post had been called for nine thirty. The mayor and police commissioner were on their way, as were head honchos from federal law enforcement agencies and the MTA bosses who ran the subway.

I'd managed to get hold of my first coffee of the morning and had just declined a third call from some annoyingly persistent *New York Times* reporter when I looked up and saw the chief of detectives, Neil Fabretti, come through the command post door. I almost didn't recognize him in his stately white-collar uniform. At his heels was a tall, clean-cut white guy in a nice suit whom I didn't recognize.

"Detective, I can't tell you how much I appreciate you being all over this," Fabretti said, giving my hand a quick pump. "I already spoke to Miriam. NYPD has the ball on this, and I want you to head up the investigation. The rest of Major Crimes is now at your disposal as well as any and all local precinct investigators, as you see fit. How does that sound? You up for it?"

"Of course," I said, nodding.

"Do you know Lieutenant Bryce Miller? He's the new counterterrorism head over at the NYPD Intelligence Division," Fabretti said, introducing the sleek dark-haired thirtysomething cop at his elbow. "Bryce is going to be involved in this thing from the intelligence angle, so I wanted you guys to meet. You're going to be working together hand in glove, okay?"

I'd heard about Miller, who was supposed to be something of a hotshot. He'd been an FBI agent and Department of Justice lawyer linked closely to the Department of Homeland Security before being hired splashily to show the new mayor's seriousness in fighting the terrorists who seemed to love New York City for all the wrong reasons. But *hand in glove?* I thought as I shook Miller's hand. I was in charge, but I also had a partner or something? How was that supposed to work? And who was to report to whom? I wondered.

Miller shook back briefly, as if he didn't want my soot-stained jeans and Windbreaker to muss his dapper gray suit.

"Hercules teams have been deployed to Times Square and Wall Street," Miller said in greeting.

I assumed Miller was talking about the Intelligence Division's tactical units, used to flood an area to show any potential attackers the NYPD's lightning-quick response capability.

"The helicopters are up, and there are boats in the water. Just got off the phone with the commissioner. We're going full-court press in Manhattan, river to river."

Weren't such shows of force supposed to *prevent* attacks? I thought.

"Now, what is this thermobaric bomb stuff I keep hearing?" Miller continued. "That's crazy speculation at this point, isn't it? Something like that would take an incredible amount of technical know-how and meticulous planning. We would expect a blip of chatter activity from surveillance before such a large-scale attack, and my team and my contacts in Washington are reporting exactly nada. Couldn't this just have been a utility screwup?"

"I don't know about any of that, Bryce," I said,

eyeing him. "I was actually just with the bomb guys and saw the shrapnel from what looked like pressure-cooker bombs in two separate locations."

My phone hummed again as I took a black piece of something out of the corner of my eye with a pinkie nail.

"No matter how little anyone wants to say or hear it, this was definitely no accident."

# Chapter 13

LATER THAT MORNING, Mr. Joyce and Mr. Beckett and Tony were in a brand-new dark-green Ford F-150 pickup truck rolling south down Faile Street in a heavily industrial area of the Hunts Point section of the South Bronx.

Mr. Joyce took a long, soothing sip of his cold McDonald's OJ and began humming to himself as he looked out at the sunny day. As he watched, a low LaGuardia-bound FedEx cargo jet came roaring in overhead. Mr. Joyce, being an avid plane spotter, took one look at the shape of its purple tail and knew immediately that it was a McDonnell Douglas MD-11F.

Searching for and finally spotting the exact location of the aircraft's aft gas tanks, he vividly imagined shooting them with one of the refurbished FIM-92 Stinger missiles they had at the warehouse. He cocked his head to the left as he calculated the physics of a twenty-two-pound hit-to-kill blast-fragmentation warhead ripping into a six-hundred-thousand-pound plane's fuel tanks at twice the speed of sound.

He took another sip of OJ. They continued to roll. All around was nothing but block after grim block of run-down brick warehouses and industrial buildings. There were no residential buildings or even gas stations in the desolate area, and many of its streets didn't have so much as a sidewalk.

Which was precisely why they were operating out of this god-awful area. With no concerned citizenry for miles, it was a perfect place to base their operations.

After another block, Mr. Beckett, behind the wheel, hit a garage-door opener and they pulled under the rolling steel gate of an unremarkable but dilapidated two-story stucco structure wedged between an abandoned warehouse and a stinking recycling center.

When the steel shutter was closed behind them, they climbed out of the truck and came through the garage door into the lower floor of the small building. The dim, windowless space had black-painted walls and a long, fully stocked pinewood bar. There were neon signs, a jukebox in one corner, a pool table, and even several black-painted circular wooden booths along the far wall.

"Now, this is what I call a hideout!" Tony said, looking around in amazement. "This is awesome! And unexpected. I would never peg you smart guys for living in a dive bar."

"I'm glad you like it, Tony," said Mr. Joyce, going behind the bar and clicking a green neon Rolling Rock sign on and off. "It does have a certain ambience, doesn't it? This building was once an illegal after-hours place. After we moved in, it was easier just to leave everything as is."

"Where do you sleep? On the pool table?"

"Of course not," Mr. Joyce said with a grin. "There's an apartment upstairs. I'm going to hit the restroom for a pit stop. Why don't you let Mr. Beckett fix you a drink? Sit and relax for a bit. I think we all need a well-deserved rest before we start phase two."

Tony yawned and smiled back.

"What is phase two, anyway, Mr. Joyce? Same shit like with the trucks?" he said.

"All in good time, Tony. Relax now. I'll be right back," Mr. Joyce said with a wink as he headed down the hallway.

# Chapter 14

MR. BECKETT SAT Tony in the booth at the far end of the long room and placed a rum and Coke in front of him. Then he went to the floor safe behind the bar and came back with a white plastic Food Emporium shopping bag containing the agreed-upon twenty thousand dollars in twenties and fifties.

"Hey, thanks," said Tony, smiling from ear to ear as he glanced at the money and lifted the drink. "You know, you guys are such gentlemen. I mean, I thought I'd never get a job with my record, but then I look up and there you guys are outside that homeless shelter like some kind of godsend. My whole life I've partnered up with sucker after sucker, and I just want you to know how privileged I feel to finally work with a couple of real smart players. You must have been, like, professors or something, am I right?"

"Well, Mr. Joyce is the real brains," said Mr. Beckett as he headed back to the bar. "He's a genius in mathematics as well as materials engineering. He used to be an actual rocket scientist—well, missile scientist, if you want to get technical. And here's some advice from personal experience."

"What's that?" Tony said.

"Don't play chess against him, especially for money."

"Not a chance," Tony said with a laugh. "Never touch the stuff, Mr. Beckett. Why don't you pour yourself a drink and come and sit?"

"Sorry, Tony. I don't drink. I like to be in control at all times," said Mr. Beckett.

"You don't drink? What do you do for fun?" Tony said.

Before Mr. Beckett could answer, there was a faint, flicking, whistling sound from the dimness on the other side of the room near the bathroom. Then there were two sounds, all but simultaneous. The first was the click of Tony's dropped drink landing miraculously upright on the table. The second was the loud crack of his head as it slammed back violently into the plywood back of the booth.

Mr. Joyce emerged from the hallway with the compound hunting bow after Tony stopped twitching. He stood before the booth for a moment with his dark goatee cradled in his free hand, peering at the fletching and the twenty-seven-inch carbon shaft of the broadhead arrow that protruded from Tony's left eye socket.

"That was just terrible," Mr. Joyce said.

"Come now, Mr. Joyce. I liked Tony, too, but we have to cover our tracks," said Mr. Beckett as he retrieved the bag of money and returned it to the safe.

"Please: you don't actually think I care that Tony is dead, do you?" Mr. Joyce said with a laugh. "I'm just upset about this new bow I bought. I was aiming for right between the eyes, but one of the pulleys must be overtight. I booted it down and a little to the right at the last second."

"Now, now, Mr. Joyce," said Mr. Beckett as he came over. "You have to admit that this light is horrendous, and besides, no one is perfect one hundred percent of the time. Your little toy is quite effective, if you ask me. What's the expression? 'Close enough for government work?'"

Mr. Joyce took a pair of side cutters off the bar, reached behind Tony's ruined skull, and cut away the carbon shaft embedded in the plywood. Tony landed faceup on the filthy concrete after Mr. Joyce kicked him off the booth seat. He slid the arrow out of Tony's eye by the fletching, then lifted the dead man's left hand and checked the cheap digital watch on his wrist.

"Look at the time, Mr. Beckett," Mr. Joyce said. "Grab his ankles, would you? We really need to get going. You know traffic is going to be a nightmare."

# Chapter 15

AT A LITTLE after eleven o'clock, I was back on the streets of Washington Heights. Well, back *under* the streets of Washington Heights, to be exact.

"See? It's over there, Mike," said Con Ed supervisor Al Kott, a few rungs below me on the Saint Nicholas Avenue manhole ladder. He pointed his flashlight at a ruined section of fire-blackened brick in the north wall.

"That wall there isn't supposed to be like that. It's been jackhammered, by the looks of it. And not by my guys. I already checked the records. There's been no maintenance in this hole for the last eighteen months."

"You see anything that looks like an air shaft in there, Al?" I said.

"Maybe," he said, pointing the beam of his flashlight into the gap. "I don't know. It's all burned and wrecked to shit, but I think I see some ripped metal about five or six feet in."

I nodded as I thought about that. More details had been revealed at the precinct meeting by the bomb experts. Evidence was pointing to two bombs placed on the tracks just north of the 168th and 181st Street stations. Massive cratering above the blasts at two air shafts corroborated the thermobaric bomb theory. Some kind of fuel had been deliberately pumped into the tunnel.

That had to be it, I thought as I stared at the ripped-open wall and massively damaged Con Edison manhole. This spot was one of the locations where the flammable bomb fuel, or whatever the hell it was, had been pumped down.

We had our *where,* I thought as I climbed for the circle of daylight above me. Now we just needed to find our *who.*

# Chapter 16

THE BUILDING WAS a new thirty-two-story glass highrise on Haven Avenue overlooking the Hudson River on the west side of Washington Heights.

The man was in apartment 32J. He was a junkie, thin and middle-aged, vampire pale, with long, gray ponytailed hair and a road-worn, angular face. In a wifebeater and once-black but now faded-to-gray pair of jeans, he sat on the gleaming oak floor of the small, high-end condo's living room, his bony knees up and his back flat against a wall.

Despite this spartan sitting position, he appeared comfortable. Like he'd long ago become used to sitting on hard, bare floors.

There was no furniture in the room. Not a stick of furniture in the whole apartment, in fact. The only other object in the apartment was a white iPad, facedown on the floor between the gaunt man's beat-up hiking boots. He sat there, staring at it steadily. As if, any second now, it were about to perform some sort of amazing trick that he didn't want to miss.

Every once in a while, he'd flick a glance around the empty room. The bare white walls. The rectangle of cloudless, cornflower-blue sky showing through the big, curtainless window.

He wondered who owned this place. Would they actually have bought an apartment just for this? Or maybe it was rented.

He yawned, rolled his shoulders, stretched. As if that mattered. He didn't need to know about all that. He only had to make sure his own part worked so he could get the rest of the money.

The instructions couldn't have been simpler. He just needed to do it, leave the apartment, get into the rental car parked in the lot on Broadway, and head straight back to Florida.

He glanced at his watch. Three minutes. Hot damn! Three! he thought. Then he went back to staring at the tablet again.

He was trying to keep his mind blank, stay serene. But as the clock ticked down, it became exceedingly difficult.

He kept thinking about the craziest, most

screwed-up shit he'd ever done in his life. How he'd broken into houses when people were home sleeping. How he'd knifed that kid who tried to take his shit that time when he was living on the beach in Key West. In the back of the neck, too. He had to have killed him. He sure hadn't stuck around to find out.

The worst was in the midnineties, when, during a Christmas visit to his little brother Kenny's house, he up and flat-out stole his brother's new Toyota Echo, which had his two nieces' car seats in the back and a woman's new winter coat in the trunk that couldn't have been anything but Kenny's Christmas present to his wife.

But all that put together, thought the man as he rubbed his sweating palms on the soft, threadbare thighs of his Levi's, couldn't hold a candle to the act of certifiable insanity he was about to commit.

Literally, no one had ever done anything like this. No one. It was going to rearrange people's minds.

Did he really want to be part of that? He didn't know. Half of him was afraid, of course, especially about getting caught. That would not be good. But he really didn't think he would. The plan was pretty much *foolproof*.

The other half of him was excited about it. Not just about the $150K he was due but also because it was so big-time. Monumental. Wasn't like he was winning any Nobel Prizes anytime soon, so what he was about to do would definitely leave a mark.

The alarm on his cheap watch suddenly went off. The tinny blip-blip, pause, blip-blip was like an electronic amplification of his racing heart.

*It was time.*

He flipped over the iPad and propped it in his lap and pressed an app and the screen suddenly showed a live shot of upper Manhattan, to the east. Small buildings could be seen far below with Matchbox-like cars between them moving slowly in the congested streets.

It was the view from the camera he'd already mounted on the high-rise building's roof that was connected to the iPad through Wi-Fi. In the corner of the screen, numbers showed the camera's satellite GPS coordinates to the second decimal point and that its elevation was at 326.8 feet.

On the iPad screen, the tiny buildings began to grow in size as he remotely activated the camera's zoom lens.

Zooming and meticulously searching and zooming again, the man swiped at the screen with his long fingers, zeroing in on the target.

# Chapter 17

A SUDDEN FRANTIC call from Chief Fabretti redirected me immediately from the Saint Nicholas Avenue bomb site back to the command center at the precinct.

I was told that the mayor was about to speak for the first time about the attack to the press, and to the world, and I was needed to deliver an up-to-date briefing to him in person before he went on.

As I turned the corner of Broadway onto 170th, I could see that a portable stage and flag-flanked podium had been set up outside on the street in front of the Thirty-Third Precinct's front door. Standing in the blocked-off street around the stage was a large crowd of FBI people and cops and mayor's-office guys playing cops with coplike

EMERGENCY MANAGEMENT Windbreakers over their shiny suits.

And still they were outnumbered by media people. Everywhere there were camera guys in plaid flannel shirts playing with light meters and tripods while their metrosexual news-producer bosses did that one-finger-in-the-ear thing as they gabbed into their cell phones.

In addition to regular news vans, I spotted a massive trailer-size national news satellite truck, like the ones you see outside events like the Super Bowl. I did a double take as I drove past a startlingly good-looking, tall brunette—a name-network reporter—with her head back, getting her eyeliner touched up by her assistant.

There's a real buzz in the air, isn't there? I thought as I parked and got out. Like we were at a red-carpet event.

I didn't like it. I knew people were freaking out and needed to know what was happening, but this was nuts. It never failed. Every time these things happened, the circus atmosphere seemed to get worse. Less thought and emphasis seemed to be placed on the incredible human pain inflicted on the victims and their families and more on the hysterical contagious excitement generated by the knowledge that Something Big Is Happening.

I found Chief Fabretti with Lieutenant Bryce Miller on the sidewalk near the precinct's front door.

"Just about to call you, Mike," Fabretti said. "The mayor changed his mind about the briefing. He's going on any second now, and he needs to, and I quote, wrap things up with his speech people."

"His speech people, of course," I said, nodding, as I looked out at the media horde. "You think this is the right approach here, Chief? Little on the splashy side, isn't it?"

The mayor's buddy, Bryce Miller, jumped in. "Mayor insisted it be outside," he said. "Not holed up in a bunker somewhere. There's a lot of scared folks out there. We need to project calm. It's important people understand that everything's okay. That we're in control of things."

In control of things? I thought, cocking my head. *We are?* I wanted to say.

# Chapter 18

A MOMENT LATER, accompanied by a barrage of camera clicks and flashes, the mayor, Carl Doucette, came out of the precinct with his five-man police security detail.

Normally a glad-handing, life-of-the-party type, the new mayor—tall, with curly gray hair—looked somber, serious, almost nervous as he stepped to the podium and took out his prepared statement. If he was faking looking shaken up, he was a fine actor, I thought.

"As everyone probably has heard by now, very early this morning there was a massive explosion in the number one train tunnel beneath Broadway in Washington Heights," Mayor Doucette began.

"Three people have been killed that we know of, and I'd like to say first that our hearts go out to those victims and their families. We are still very much in the process of investigating the explosion, but from our initial review, we can say definitively that this was not a utility malfunction, nor was it industrial in nature."

The clicking of the cameras increased as he looked up from his notes.

"At this point, we can only conclude that this was an intentional act, of what exact nature we cannot say. It seems as if a flammable material was pumped into the tunnel at some point last night, and that the built-up material was ignited with one or perhaps two explosive devices, causing catastrophic damage to a large segment of the tunnel as well as to the Hundred and Sixty-Eighth Street and Hundred and Eighty-First Street subway stations.

"This part of the tunnel is ten stories down, one of the deepest in the entire system, and we have engineers still assessing the risk of further collapse. Though we are planning to bring back train service on a rolling basis this afternoon into the evening rush, people can expect that number one train service will be down in both directions for well into the foreseeable future."

He paused again, took a breath.

"But though our train service is shut down," the

mayor said, staring at the cameras now with a calm and steady seriousness and intensity he'd never before displayed, "I want to let whoever committed this cowardly, murderous act know once and for all that the spirit of this city and its citizens will never be shut down."

There was a smattering of spontaneous applause.

"We will continue as we have always done, and you will be found and brought to justice."

"Yeah!" somebody with a deep voice called out from the media pit, and more people began to applaud.

"Try as you will, neither you nor anyone else will ever be able to shut down our city or the American people."

Maybe doing a big press conference like this was a good idea after all, I thought as the clapping increased. I hadn't voted for the mayor, because he seemed soft on crime, but he was surprising me. Watching him operate up close for the first time, I could see he was a natural leader with an ability to lift people's spirits.

The mayor smiled gently as he raised his hands to wave down the applause. He brought the microphone in a little closer to himself as a chant of "USA! USA!" started from somewhere.

The mayor smiled at the chanting and was waving his hands for calm when there was a glow of something pink behind his head.

It was rose-colored, a strange, halolike mist that I first thought was some kind of weird television lighting, because as it appeared, the side of the mayor's head suddenly looked like it was covered in shadow.

But then the tall mayor staggered oddly forward and to his left, and my mind finally caught up to my unbelieving eyes.

I watched in horror as the mayor dropped straight down behind the podium like a bridge with its pilings blown out.

# Chapter 19

THE NEXT FEW moments were beyond strange. Frozen and dumbstruck, I stood there unable to do anything but stare down at the fallen mayor and the blood pumping out of him. My mind must have still been a little shell-shocked, because as he bled out, all I could do was keep looking him over, again and again, harping on the most useless details.

Like how he'd come out of one of his shoes, a new cordovan loafer. How though he was married, I saw he wasn't wearing a wedding ring. How there were little pink anchors on his navy-blue socks.

Though there were more than a hundred people standing around—cops, reporters, photographers, neighborhood residents—none of them seemed to be moving, either. It was suddenly impossibly quiet, as if someone had just called for a moment of silence. I distinctly remember hearing birds chirping in the park across from the precinct, and off in the distance on Saint Nicholas Avenue there was the brief grumble of a passing bus.

Then out of the dead silence, someone in a shrieking voice that was so high and loud it was impossible to tell if it was a man or a woman suddenly yelled.

"Sniper!"

The spell broke instantly. Everyone in the vicinity of the fallen mayor, including me, broke away like a stampeding herd from his body.

I didn't know where Lieutenant Miller had gotten to, but Chief Fabretti and I dove immediately between a couple of cruisers parked out in front of the precinct. I could hear several cops crying out, "Where? Where? Where?" simultaneously over the chief's radio as we crawled on our hands and knees in the gutter.

"Unbelievable! This isn't happening! You hear the shot, Mike? I didn't hear jack shit!" Fabretti said beside me, where he gripped a short-barreled .38 he had pulled out of somewhere. "Damn it! We have a sniper team covering the rooftops. What just happened?!"

I shook my head and was about to take a peek

out at the rooftops myself when there was a loud, thunking crack of wood as another bullet ripped into the podium.

"Down!" I yelled. "We're still under fire!"

I noticed that there wasn't even a hint of a gun crack for the second shot, either. Which meant one of two things—either the shooter was using a suppressor, or he was really far away. I was going with the latter. The mayor's massive wound indicated a large-caliber round probably shot from a rifle with a long range. I shook my head. Like Kennedy, I thought in horror. The mayor had just been *assassinated!*

"That second shot just hit the front of the podium, Chief," I said after a moment. "Tell your men that it seems to be coming from dead west, up a Hundred and Seventieth."

Fabretti was calling it in when I heard a woman's friendly voice.

"Excuse me, Officer. Over here, please. Excuse me."

I looked up and squinted into a painfully bright light above the sidewalk. Next to it materialized a tall, attractive woman. It was the statuesque network reporter I'd seen previously, her painted eyes huge and dark and almond-shaped, her thick pancake makeup a garish, yellowy tan. Her camera guy was a short, stocky, friendly-looking bearded Hispanic guy who gave me a wink with his free eye.

We were still being shot at, and they wanted a sideline report?

I guess I wasn't the only one in full-out shock.

"Get down!" I yelled as I grabbed them and yanked them behind the car.

# Chapter 20

TWENTY MINUTES LATER I was in my Impala, hammering it toward the west side of Washington Heights behind a trio of commando-filled NYPD Emergency Service Unit trucks. The trucks were military surplus BearCat armored personnel carriers; I used to think using them was overkill—at least I did up until I saw the mayor get blown away. The countersniper team in position near the precinct had triangulated the shot with their gunshot echo system, and we were headed now toward a highrise building on Haven Avenue, where it seemed like the shots had come from.

I almost didn't believe it when one of the SWAT cops pointed out the suspected building to me. It was so far away. On the other side of Manhattan. Easily three-quarters of a mile. The chill that had gone down my spine had stayed there. Because only a world-class sniper could have made a shot like that, I knew.

Which raised the question: Who, or what, were we dealing with?

"Dude, I blame the media. It's all their fault, damn it!" cried out an uncharacteristically pissed-off Arturo in the front seat beside me as we roared west toward the building. The young Puerto Rican cop, whom I met on the Ombudsman Outreach Squad, was usually pretty even-tempered.

Along with half the department, my crew had responded immediately to the shooting. I'd grabbed them and taken them with me the moment the decision had been made to raid the suspected building.

And no wonder Arturo was freaking out. The mayor had been rushed to Columbia Presbyterian, but everyone knew he was dead. First a bombing and now an assassination? We were in a new territory of spooky, and the adrenaline couldn't have been running higher.

"What did you just say?" said Brooklyn Kale from the backseat. "The media? What are you talking about, Lopez?"

"Exactly, Arturo," said Doyle, sitting beside her. "When you open your mouth, it would be nice if you maybe made some sense from time to time." Jimmy Doyle, another young cop from the Ombudsman Outreach Squad, had become my right-hand man.

"Use your brains, fools," Arturo insisted. "The media are right now in the process of doing millions upon millions of dollars' worth of free PR work for whoever is doing this. Such over-the-top, wall-to-wall coverage just sets the bar higher and higher each time for the nut jobs and terrorists to get everybody's attention.

"Which means bigger explosions, more bodies, and more atrocities. They should take their cue from the baseball media, which nipped fan stupidity in the bud when they wisely decided to stop showing people who run onto the field."

"So don't tell people there's terrorism? That's your solution?" said Brooklyn.

"How about at least not sensationalizing it so much?" Arturo said. "This is a bloodbath. Stop selling the frickin' popcorn."

"Congrats, Arturo," Doyle said as we skidded to a stop in the driveway of the Haven Avenue building's underground parking garage. "I think you actually might have made your first-ever good point."

"Shut up, people, please," I said, turning up my radio as a just-arriving NYPD helicopter swooped in from the south and hovered over the building.

"There's something on the east side of the building," the pilot said after a minute. "It looks like some sort of a rifle."

The ESU cops spilled out into the driveway and busted out their ballistic riot shields and submachine guns. We stayed behind them as we went across the pavement toward the side door of the building. Having neither the time nor the inclination to find and ask the super for the key, the ESU breach team unhesitatingly cracked the door open with a battering ram.

After dismissing the elevators as dangerous because of potential tampering, the ESU guys left a small contingent in the new building's sleek marble lobby as the rest split up into the building's two stairwells.

My team and I followed the ESU team in the north stairwell. Despite being pumped up with adrenaline, we had to stop twice for short breathers to get up the thirty-two floors.

We were the first team there. An alarm went off

as the lead ESU guy hit the roof door, and we were out in the suddenly cool air with the roaring, hovering NYPD Bell helicopter right there almost on top of us. The pilot pointed to the top of a little structure that housed the elevator equipment.

I ran across the tar paper to its ladder and climbed up and just stood there staring at it.

# Chapter 21

I'D NEVER SEEN anything like it before. I wasn't an expert, but the long black rifle looked huge, like a sniper rifle, perhaps a .50 caliber. It was bolted into two strange, bulky stands that could have been motorized.

But the strangest thing was what was attached to the top of the rifle. Perched where the scope should have been was a bulky device about the size of a hardcover book that looked like a robotic owl. It had a single viewfinder in the sighting end and what looked like greenish-tinged binoculars in the front.

"You've got to be kidding," said ESU sergeant Terry Kelly as he arrived behind me.

"What the hell is it?"

The short, muscular cop spat some chewing

tobacco as he knelt and carefully tilted the gun over on its side.

"One of those damn things!" he said. "On a .50-caliber Barrett! Of course. Why not? It's like the training video said. Only a matter of time."

"What are you talking about, Sergeant?" I said.

"We saw a Homeland Security video about this three weeks ago," Kelly said. "See this scope thing on top? It's a computerized targeting system. It has a laser range finder in front, like rich golf guys have to get exact distances."

I nodded.

"Well, you get behind it and sight your target through the system's long-range zooming video camera and just tag it with the laser. Then the computer calculates all the factors of the shot—the air density, Magnus effect, even target movement—and puts them through the computer. Then the computer—not you—robotically positions the gun and fires it.

"Anyone, a three-year-old child, can become a world-class sniper with it. All you have to do is tag the target. What am I saying? You don't even have to be behind the gun! It has Wi-Fi."

"So this was probably done remotely," I said.

"Without a doubt," he said. "Why expose

yourself on a rooftop when all you have to do is set the gun up beforehand and just do it from cover? All you would need is to be within Wi-Fi range."

"Call the other team and tell them to go straight to the top floor," I told him. "We need to get the super up here and start searching every single apartment."

We rushed off the roof and down onto the thirty-second floor and started banging on doors like it was Halloween for cops. Only three of the residents were home. After we were done searching their apartments, the super, a tall, middle-aged guy who looked like a stoner, finally showed up in a brown bathrobe, holding a set of keys.

"Listen, man," he said, "I'm still waiting to hear back from the management office. I don't even know if I should be letting you into people's apartments. Don't you need a warrant or something?"

"Tune in, bro," Kelly yelled in his face. "While you were busy watching *Harold and Kumar Go to White Castle,* the mayor just got blown away with a rifle we found on your roof."

"What? Okay, okay. Give me a second," he said, fumbling with the keys.

One by one, we searched seven apartments, but there was nothing.

"What about this apartment?" I said to the super. "Where's the key?"

"Uh . . . that one's vacant," the stoner said. "It's for sale, so I don't have the key. The management company has it, I think."

"Don't worry about the key," said Kelly as he led the way, holding the battering ram. "Fortunately, we brought our own."

The ESU men blasted open the door of 32J and rushed inside.

When they gave the all-clear and we went in, the first thing I noticed was the shattered living room window. The second was the skinny guy with a gray ponytail sprawled out in front of the kitchen's breakfast bar with the top of his head missing. There was an iPad beside him.

I turned and looked west, out through the broken window at the Hudson.

On the Jersey side of the river, about a mile away, there was another high-rise.

Where someone else had shot the mayor's shooter with another computerized rifle, I thought. I would have bet my paycheck on it.

This isn't good, I thought as I radioed aviation to hit the roof of the building on the Jersey side to see what they could see.

"Mike, you really think this is the guy who killed the mayor?" asked Brooklyn as she stood over the body.

I nodded.

"And who killed him?" asked Arturo.

I stared out the window as the chopper appeared overhead on its way across the Hudson. The sound of the rotors was almost deafening through the broken glass.

"The nut job who's trying to show us how smart he is," I yelled.

# Chapter 22

AT EXACTLY 1:23 P.M., thirty-seven minutes after the mayor's assassination, a hundred blocks almost directly south, a white delivery van turned west onto 81st Street from York Avenue on Manhattan's famous Upper East Side.

"Dude, four-two-one. That's it. Up there," said the preppy white college kid in the van's passenger seat.

The handsome young Hispanic driver beside him squinted ahead out the windshield.

"That old church there?" he said.

"No, stupid," said the white guy. "The church? How we gonna put it on the pointy roof of a church? *Next* to the church there. That crappy white brick building."

The white guy's name was Gregg Bentivengo.

His handsome Hispanic buddy was Julio Torrone. They were recently graduated New York University students, now roommates and partners in a start-up marketing and promotional firm they'd dubbed Emerald Marketing Solutions.

"A church?" Gregg said again, rolling his eyes. "There's even a picture of the building on the instructions. Didn't you see the picture of it?"

"That's your job," Julio said, coming to a dead stop as a green pickup two cars ahead parallel-parked. "You're the navigator, bro. I'm the pilot. Where should I park us, anyway? This block is jammed."

"Too bad we didn't pick one of those blocks where it's easy to park," said Gregg, rolling down his window and sticking his head out. "The building's got an underground garage. Maybe they'll let us leave the van off to the side in the driveway there for a second while we unload. You know, I would have asked for more if I'd known how bulky these damn things are. Plus they weigh a ton."

"You can say that again. I'm not lugging it across the street again, especially the way you almost let it bail when we were getting it over the curb."

"*I* almost let it bail? I beg to differ, my friend. *You're* the one who didn't tighten the hand truck's strap," Gregg said as he rolled the window back up and removed a small navel orange from the pocket of his white North Face shell.

Gregg was always doing that, thought Julio, annoyed. Grossly hoarding food in his pockets like a squirrel or something. Peanuts, little candies. Drove him nuts all through school.

"Besides, you're the muscle in this little caper," Gregg said as he began peeling. "I'm the sweet-talking, persuasive guy."

"The what?" Julio said. "You were tripping over your tongue with the concierge mama at the last place so much I thought you were doing an impression of that 'That's all, folks' pig dude in that old-timey cartoon."

"Screw you," Gregg said, flicking a piece of orange peel at him. "When she looked up, she was so hot that I got a little startled is all. I was lovestruck. Besides, I recovered quick enough."

"That's true," said Julio, smiling. "I almost pissed myself laughing when you told her it was the new flux capacitor for the roof, and she was like, 'Oh, okay, elevator back to your right.'"

"Hey, you know my motto. If you can't bowl

them over with brilliance, then baffle them with bullshit."

"Hey, traffic's moving now," Julio said. "Let's get this over with."

It was even easier than the last drop. The middle-aged Asian guy at the garage must have been new or something, because not only did he let them park in the driveway, he also let them into the side door of the building with his key without calling the super or even seeming interested in what the hell they were doing there.

It took them exactly eleven minutes to position the green metal box that was about the size and weight of a large filing cabinet on the southeast corner of the six-story building's roof, as per the instructions.

It must have some internal battery or something, Gregg thought idly as they were leaving the roof, because, like the first metal box they'd dropped off at the hotel on Lexington and 56th, it didn't need to be plugged in or turned on or anything.

"What do you think they are, anyway?" Julio said as they got back into the van.

"Weren't you listening? They're carbon meters," said Gregg, picking up the half-peeled orange he'd left on the dashboard. "The clients are environmental activists who want to take readings of this one-percent-filled area but were denied by the city and the building boards. Enter us, underground marketing heroes extraordinaire, to the rescue."

"Carbon meters, my ass," Julio said. "Whoever heard of a freaking carbon meter?"

"Do I know?" said Gregg. "You can call it a fairy-dust-reading meter if you give me five grand cash to sneak it onto some dump's roof."

"Probably some sketchy guerrilla data-collection thing hoovering up the whole block's passwords and data or monitoring people's online porn habits," Julio said.

"I peg this guy for a hot Asian nurses fan," Gregg said as the stupid parking attendant gave them a friendly wave and they began to back out onto the street.

"Who knows?" Julio said after they were rolling. "Maybe our clients are NSA."

"I doubt those two bastards were NSA," said Gregg.

"They were definitely bastards, but smart ones," Julio reminded him. "Don't forget, nerdy NSA types are computer geniuses and shit."

"Right," Gregg said skeptically. "You play too many video games."

"True," Julio said. "Anyway, it's done. What do you want to do now? Hit the gym?" asked Julio.

"Too early," Gregg said. "Pizza?"

"Okay, but then we need to get this truck back or we have to pay for eight more hours."

## Part Two

# THE CITY SLEEPS

# Chapter 23

HOME FINALLY, AND still damp from a glorious hot shower, I plopped my tired carcass down at the head of the dining room table at around 7:30 p.m.

I was clad in a pair of orange swim trunks and a Yankees number 42 Mariano Rivera jersey, which worked better than you might think as a pajamas ensemble. Actually, my atrocious getup was the only thing I could find now that the laundry was piling up at an alarming rate. I was down to the bottom of the drawer and would be staying there, no doubt, for the time being.

My hastily put-together late dinner for *la familia* Bennett was French toast, one of my go-to dishes. I'd offered to get pizza again, but the kids were pizzaed out and demanded a home-cooked meal. They had probably meant a home-cooked *dinner,* but too bad for them—they hadn't specified. They seemed to enjoy it well enough, or at least they enjoyed my wise heavy-handedness with the confectioners' sugar.

I was relishing my French cuisine with a bottle of Guinness, the only adult beverage left in the house. Like the laundry, the whole grocery thing was something I had to work out, since Mary Catherine was still away.

Speaking of Mary Catherine, I'd been jazzed to find a letter—an actual paper snail-mail letter—from her on the hall table when I'd come in. The good news was that there was a new lead on a buyer for the hotel. No definite offer as of yet, but things were looking good.

The bad news was that though she had asked about the kids, there was really nothing about us or our fabulous romantic week together on the windswept Cliffs of Moher. Or about her heart-wrenching note, which I had read on the plane.

What could that mean? I wondered. Cold feet? Buyer's remorse? I didn't know. All I knew was that I wanted her back here with me so hard it was starting to hurt.

But like I said, at least I was home. Finally clean and warm and home, though I wasn't in a real talkative mood after my truly insane day. I was more than content to just listen to the dull roar of the kids all around the table, talking and giggling. Even their teasing was comforting. Their normalcy, their obliviousness to the horror of today's events, was just what the doctor ordered.

I was still sitting in my family's warm chaos, mopping up the stout and syrup, when Seamus came in at speed through the apartment's front door.

"Long day, eh, Mick?" said Seamus, looking a little flustered when he spotted me.

"About a week long, Father," I said. "Make that a month, but I can't talk about it. I refuse to, in fact. Pull up a chair and a plate. How's the nanny hunt going?"

After Seamus's health scare, and down one Mary Catherine, I thought it best to look for some temporary help.

"Been on it since this morning," Seamus said. "That's why I'm here. I think I might have found someone. He was recommended quite highly by a friend down at the archdiocese office."

"*He?*" I said.

"Yeah. He's a bit . . . well, unconventional, you might say."

"Unconventional? How so?" I asked as the doorbell rang.

"See for yourself," Seamus said, blinking at me. "That's him now."

# Chapter 24

OH, I SEE, I thought when I went out into the hall and opened the door.

The young man was tall and Colin Farrell handsome, with spiky black hair and black Clark Kent glasses. Nineteen, maybe twenty. He was wearing a white-and-green tracksuit.

"Hello, there," he said with an infectious smile and an Irish accent. "I'm Martin Gilroy. Father Romans sent me here about a job?"

"This way," Seamus said, ushering him in before I could open my mouth.

The ruckus in the dining room ceased immediately as Seamus and I brought him into the living room. The kids stared at him in dead silence as we walked past.

"Hello, guys," Martin said, smiling.

If he was fazed by the ten sets of wide eyes on him, he hid it well. He actually stopped and craned his neck to look in the doorway.

"Hey, what are ya having in there? French toast, is it? Breakfast for dinner?"

He crouched down next to Shawna and made a funny face. "Then what's for breakfast, I wonder? Let me guess. Steak and green beans and mashed potatoes?"

I smiled along with the kids. This guy was pretty good. I was starting to like him already.

"So tell us a little something about yourself, Martin," I said as we sat on the couch.

"Not much to tell, really," he said, crossing a big neon-green Nike on his thigh. "Me home is a little town in County Cavan, Ireland, called Kilnaleck. Eight of us in the family, not including Mom and Da. Got out of farm chores by playing football, or soccer, as you lot call it, for what reason I'll never know.

"Anyway, I got good enough at it to get a scholarship to Manhattan College. I'm also on the track team. Trying to get a mechanical engineering degree on the side, as I thought it might be good to have a backup plan if my dreams of becoming Beckham don't turn out. I don't drink, so that hampers the ol' social life a bit at school. I like kids and staying busy, and, um, I could use the money."

"Any experience?" I said.

"Plenty, since I was one of the oldest in my family. No one died on me. I also worked at the town camp since I was sixteen, so I got all my first aid stuff and all that."

"Do you cook?" Seamus asked.

"Oh, sure. Breakfast, lunch, dinner," he smiled. "All at the right times, too, if you want. Only kidding. Nothing fancy, but I can keep kids fed."

"You know how to do laundry?" I said.

He took off his glasses and polished them on the edge of his track jacket.

"I can iron a crease in a pair of trousers you could shave with," he said as he slipped the glasses back on. "Actually, that's not true. I read that somewhere. But I've done laundry before. Separate the whites and the colors or something, right? Hell, I'll do the windows, if ya want. Improvise and overcome, that's me motto. Bring it on."

"Martin, there's ten kids out there. Ten," I said. "What would you do with them? What would be your strategy?"

"There's a park around here, right? Riverside, is it? Well, weather permitting, after their homework and whatnot, I'd keep 'em out there, run 'em around, like we do at camp. Get 'em tired, wear 'em down, and then dinner and off to bed while I hit the chores."

I smiled. I didn't like this kid. I loved him.

"When can you start?"

Martin shrugged and smiled again.

"I don't know. When can I start?"

"Tomorrow? Say, six a.m.?" I said.

"See ya then," he said as he stood up.

"Just a second," I said as I saw him off at the door. "The trains are out. How'd you get here from the Bronx?"

He zipped up his track jacket.

"I ran," he said.

"You ran here from the Bronx?"

He nodded.

"And now I'm going to run back. Got to keep in tip-top for track. Why?"

It was my turn to smile.

"No reason, Martin," I said. "See you tomorrow."

# Chapter 25

IT WAS DARK and nasty and raining cats and dogs the next morning. The dim, dreary, churning East River beneath the Brooklyn Bridge looked about as scenic and lovely as a field of freshly poured cement as I crossed over it in my department Impala, heading to work.

Even so, my day had started at top speed. Martin Gilroy hadn't been on time. He'd been early. All the kids seemed excited to see him, especially the older girls, who seemed particularly ready and mysteriously dolled up to go to school.

Seamus had stayed over and was on hand as well to show Martin the ropes. The lovely old codger was looking pretty good, too, I thought, after all he'd been through. Pink and healthy and cheerful. Back in form.

I was pleased. All men are mortal, and Seamus, at eighty-plus, was more mortal than most, I knew, but I doggedly refused to think he was ever going anywhere except to say Mass.

On the other side of the bridge, I found the first exit for DUMBO and took it. My trip to the hipster-paradise neighborhood of Down Under Manhattan Bridge Overpass wasn't because of a burning desire for an ironic beer T-shirt but a work location shift. With all the media hoopla over the mayor's assassination, case headquarters had been changed from the Thirty-Third Precinct to the NYPD's discreet new Intelligence Division building in Brooklyn.

On a dark, narrow cobblestoned street just off the river, I parked in front of the large nondescript old brick building that I'd been to only twice before. I shielded my way past three armed-to-the-teeth SWAT cops manning the plain, dingy lobby and then two more stationed at a stainless steel console in the hall on the second floor.

On the other side of the security checkpoint, through a metal door, the transformation from the nineteenth-century brickwork outside to the twenty-first-century high-tech office inside became complete. There were sleek glass fishbowl offices and flat screens everywhere. Clocks on the wall gave the times of cities around the world. A lot of federal Homeland Security money was on full display.

The office was also packed with cops—dozens of detectives in polo shirts and suits. The way everyone was running around with serious expressions on their faces reminded me of an army on the muster. A tired one that just got its ass handed to it and was trying to figure out what to do next.

"Hey," I said to Doyle as he came out of the men's room.

"Mike, hey," he said, leading me toward a crowded conference room at the end of the hall. "C'mon, we're all down here about to have a briefing."

"What's going on?" I said.

"No one told you?" he said.

I shook my head.

"Brooklyn and Robertson scored some footage of what looks like the bombers from both of the bombing locations. They're about to show it right now."

# Chapter 26

A TIRED-LOOKING Arturo put a coffee in my hand as they dimmed the lights and put the first video up on the smartboard.

On the screen appeared a large industrial-style truck—almost like a garbage truck—with Con Edison markings on the cab door. It stopped in the middle of Saint Nicholas Avenue near 181st, and two men got out of it and popped the manhole cover.

It was hard to see them, unfortunately. It was dark, and they wore dark coveralls and Con Ed hard hats with the peaks pulled down low over their eyes, which were covered with sunglasses. Both were medium to tall in height, five ten to six feet; both were pale Caucasians. One had a dark goatee; the other a white one. The guy with the dark goatee was running the show. He had a clipboard and seemed to be barking orders as the other guy drew a huge air hose–like thing from the back of the truck and climbed down into the manhole with it.

"The truck is a vacuum truck," said Brooklyn, who was running the smartboard for the stunned-silent room of cops. "It's used for cleaning manholes and sewers. Engineers at Con Ed say it can easily be modified to become a large pump."

Brooklyn showed the next video, which was of a much better, less grainy quality. Another pump truck with Con Edison markings was visible out in the street by the 168th Street subway entrance with two men behind it. The same white-goateed guy was there, but the other guy was different; on the short side, tan, no facial hair, a little pudgy. The pudgy guy got into the hole with the pump this time while the older man waited by the manhole up top.

None of the guys had any distinguishing marks that we could really see. No tattoos or birthmarks or buck teeth. Was that on purpose? I wondered. It seemed like it. It seemed like these guys were going out of their way to be nondescript.

"Is that the same truck?" a cop behind me called out.

"No," Brooklyn said. "There were two of them. We found both on a deserted stretch of the Harlem River Drive near the Macombs Dam Bridge early this morning. No tags; their cabs were burned to a crisp. We're still trying to trace down where they might be from through their manufacturer. The good news is that the FBI lab people found traces of the material they pumped into the tunnel in the backs of the trucks. It was powdered aluminum."

"Powdered what?" said someone else near the front of the room.

"Powdered aluminum," Brooklyn said. "It's the main ingredient in flash powder, the stuff they make fireworks out of. We're still trying to track down where you could get your hands on such a massive amount. It's not easy, because it has many industrial uses. Apparently they make lithium ion batteries out of it."

"Unbelievable," I said, gaping at the screen. "So you're saying these three guys got all this expensive industrial equipment together and then just up and went ahead and stuffed that train tunnel with gunpowder like it was a huge firecracker?"

Brooklyn nodded slowly, a solemn expression on her face as she stared with me at the white-goateed man, whose image was paused on the screen.

"And then they set it off," she said.

Everyone turned from the screen as Lieutenant Bryce Miller came in, clutching some photocopies.

"Attention, everybody. This just came from the State Department. We sent the mayor's shooter's prints to the feds, and they just ID'd him.

"His name is Alex Mirzoyan. He was born in Armenia, came here when he was eleven, lives in Sunny Isles Beach in south Florida. We don't want to jump to conclusions too quickly, but Sunny Isles Beach is where a lot of the Miami Russian Mafia live. He has the priors of a low-level criminal: credit card fraud, some burglaries, drug possession. But what's concerning is that last year he traveled to Armenia and stayed there for six months."

"Armenia? Is that near Russia?" said Arturo.

"Sort of," I said. "It's more toward the Middle East. I think it actually borders Iran."

The room absorbed that in stunned silence.

"The Middle East? Iran?" said Brooklyn. "So we're thinking terrorism? All this is Islamic terrorism?"

"Now, wait. Slow down," I said. "We don't know that. Terrorists take credit, usually, and there's been nothing but silence, right? Plus we don't even know if the two things are related yet. The assassination could have been a crime of sick opportunity. Like that nut who sent ricin-laced letters to politicians after nine eleven. We have to treat them as two separate crimes until further notice."

There were some tentative nods, but even I was unsure about what I'd just said.

Like everybody else, I was freaking out and had no idea whatsoever what the hell was going on.

# Chapter 27

ON THE EASTERN edge of the well-heeled Upper East Side in Manhattan, the crowded and busy neighborhood of Yorkville runs from 59th Street to 96th Street between Lexington Avenue and the East River.

Before 9/11, the neighborhood was the site of the largest disaster in New York City's history: in 1904, just offshore of Ninetieth Street in the East River, the steamship *General Slocum* accidentally caught fire and sank, killing more than one thousand passengers.

And now, at exactly 8:15 a.m., Yorkville's dark history began to repeat itself as a mechanical coughing started up in the two metal boxes that had been illegally positioned the day before at 421 East 81st and 401 East 66th.

The coughing, followed by a revving sound, came from small but quite powerful modified gasoline-powered generators contained inside each device's metal housing. As the engine rose in pitch, the generator drove its steadily increasing electrical current through a four-foot-wide tightly wound coil of copper wire that was surrounded by a copper tube of equal length. The movement of the current through the copper cylinder instantly began to build an electromagnetic field. One that mounted and mounted as the engine pitched higher and higher, like an opera singer's crescendo.

Then the explosives packed between the devices' wire and tubing suddenly went off, sending a massive, invisible electromagnetic pulse in all directions at the speed of light.

The volume of the detonation inside the roof-positioned devices was negligible—a loud electrical pop, like a transformer blowing. But the sudden effect was anything but negligible.

The first official sign that something was wrong was the critical-failure alarm in the busy control room of the city's Department of Transportation. The supervisor on duty dropped the Red Bull he'd just cracked open when he looked up and saw on the big board that every traffic light from 59th to

90th Street had just gone off-line, as though someone had hit a switch.

The traffic lights weren't the only things in Yorkville to go offline. At Gracie Mansion and Rockefeller University and Weill Cornell Medical Center and Memorial Sloan Kettering Cancer Center and Bloomingdale's and the moneyed Chapin and Brearley schools and every other building within a hundred square blocks, all electrical activity instantly vanished, and every computer and light and elevator immediately ceased to work. It was like the return of the Stone Age.

People screamed and went flying as a packed southbound number 4 train coming into the 86th Street station jerked to a sudden stop. The same thing happened on a smaller but no less terrifying scale as the Roosevelt Island tram car coming out of its concrete berth over Second Avenue and 59th Street slammed to a halt and swung back and forth above the traffic.

It wasn't just the buildings. In the side streets and avenues and even on the FDR Drive, alongside the East River, the morning rush-hour commute's cars and delivery vans and taxis and dump trucks en masse began to coast out of control and plow into each other as their engines suddenly and inexplicably failed.

As countless car accidents occurred, pedestrians halted, staring at their suddenly fried cell phones. Shop owners opened the doors of their suddenly darkened businesses and stepped out onto the sidewalks, looking around.

On the riverside jogging path just north of John Jay Park, a female NYU student stopped by the river's railing to check what was wrong with her suddenly dead iPod. Tugging out the earbuds, she glanced up at a strange low whining sound above her.

Then she screamed and looked, dumbstruck, at the still-spinning rotor blade from a falling traffic helicopter as it missed her head by less than five feet, a split second before it crashed nose-first into the East River.

At a safe distance away, and above the electromagnetic pulse, on the sixty-fifth floor of the Courtyard hotel on Broadway and 54th Street, a man in a white bathrobe stood in the east-facing window of his room with a pair of binoculars.

Behind him came the sudden hiss and pop of radio static followed by a frantic voice. Then another. Then another.

Mr. Beckett lowered his binoculars and turned and smiled at the police-band radio on the table behind him.

The abject confusion from their latest attack was already starting, he thought.

Good.

He smiled at Mr. Joyce, who was sitting in a soft chair beside the radio, also in a white bathrobe, fastidiously clipping his toenails.

Mr. Beckett lifted the mimosa from the room-service cart at his elbow. He raised it in the direction of his friend.

"What shall we toast to, Mr. Joyce?"

"The power of the human imagination, of course, Mr. Beckett," said Mr. Joyce as he finished his left foot and recrossed his legs and started on the right.

He shrugged.

"What else is there, after all?"

# Chapter 28

AFTER THE CONFERENCE ended, my team and I set up shop at a couple of desks in a far corner of the crowded, kinetic Intelligence Division bull pen.

Although it was early in the morning, everyone already seemed a little haggard. The cops around me were doing their best to hide it, but it was obvious that people were getting scared. A bombing and an assassination were insane even by New York's standards.

An hour later, I was still on the horn with the department public relations office trying to disseminate stills of the Washington Heights bombers to the news outlets when it started.

I had just tucked the desk phone receiver under my chin when I suddenly noticed the rhythmic, low-toned, almost subliminal buzzing that had invaded the sterile white office space. When my hip vibrated, I realized that the sound was everyone's cell phones vibrating.

But why would everyone's phones be going off at once? I thought, hanging up my desk phone and snatching up my cell.

"Mike, did you hear?" It was Miriam Schwartz on the other end.

"No. What?" I said frantically.

"We're getting reports of a massive blackout on the East Side of Manhattan. But it's not just that. The cars have stopped. All the cars are in the streets. They've stopped working."

"The cars have stopped?" I repeated stupidly.

"We just got nuked!" someone called out behind me.

My eyes popped wide open. That couldn't be true. How could that be true? I thought. Yet I remembered from a late-night History channel show that one of the side effects of a nuclear bomb is frozen cars—the bomb fries all their electronics.

A strange numbness invaded my face, my brain. It was a weird sensation that I'd felt only twice before.

The day the doctor told us that my wife, Maeve, had inoperable terminal cancer.

And on the morning of September 11, 2001.

Dear God, my kids! Where are the kids? I thought as Miriam tried to tell me something. The damn bridge! I need to get over the bridge back to Manhattan, then get to Holy Name. But Brian went to school in the Bronx. I needed to figure out how I was going to get him.

"Mike! Damn it, listen to me!" Miriam said loudly. "It's not a nuke. That's what everybody is assuming, but it's not true."

I let out a breath and did my best to refocus.

"I'm listening, Miriam."

"ESU reports on scene at the affected region state that there is no radiation being detected anywhere. Though it does look like a nonnuclear EMP-type weapon or something might have been set off. The power is out for a hundred square blocks, and New York State ISO—the organization that manages the electrical grid—said it isn't a blackout. At eight fifteen, just bam! Everything went off in Yorkville like someone blew out a candle. The FBI's JTTF is heading up to a staging area near the base of the Fifty-Ninth Street Bridge. I already said you'd meet up with them there."

"On my way," I said, and I waved at Doyle and the crew to follow me as I hit the door.

# Chapter 29

IT WASN'T ON the radio news yet as I sped out of Brooklyn across the Manhattan Bridge. Traffic was completely screwed up from almost the moment we arrived in Manhattan. We made it only as far as 44th Street and Second Avenue, a little past the United Nations, when the traffic became literally impassable.

I pulled the car over and double-parked and stood on the unmarked's hood and stared north to see what was going on.

And continued to stand there, frozen and silent and blinking, in the cold falling rain.

It was a sight to behold. Something right out of a disaster movie. Second Avenue was stopped dead as far as the eye could see. On the sidewalks and between the utterly still cars, people were walking south, away from the area.

There were office workers, a lot of schoolkids. The worst were the doctors and nurses in medical scrubs pushing people in wheelchairs. A frantic and confused-looking churning multitude of scared New Yorkers was heading straight toward us.

"How's it looking, Mike?" said Robertson as he got out of the car.

"Not good," I said, hopping down. "Get the others. We need to walk from here."

At Second Avenue and 59th Street, two empty NYPD cruisers and an empty FDNY ambulance stood in the middle of the entrance to the 59th Street Bridge on-ramp ominously silent with their flashers on.

I was silent, too, as I stood and stared above the emergency vehicles at the red trailer-size Roosevelt Island tram car, lightless, with its window broken open, swinging back and forth in the rain like a hanging victim.

We walked east, toward the FBI staging area, along the stone base of the bridge. There were a lot of frozen empty cars in the streets and an exodus of freaked-out people heading quickly past them and us.

At First Avenue, on the other side of the bridge

underpass, I could see that a city bus had sideswiped half a dozen parked cars and was turned sideways up on the sidewalk. A crushed moped appeared to be stuck under its front bumper.

"Not good," Arturo commented.

"At all," Doyle concurred.

The worst sight of all was a block east, on York Avenue. In the distance, in the area known as Hospital Land, a large crowd of emergency personnel beside a line of ambulances appeared to be in the process of evacuating Sloan Kettering and Weill Cornell Medical Center.

"What are they doing?" said Arturo. "Don't they just need to get all these cars out of here so they can get in some temporary generators?"

"To power what?" said Brooklyn. "Everything is fried. This isn't just a blackout, Lopez. Everything electronic is broken. Everything. Every water pump to flush a toilet. Every fridge and stove is going to have to be fixed or replaced. They're going to have to evacuate the area for who knows how long."

"You're right," Doyle said. "We've never seen anything like this."

The FBI's staging area turned out to be at the site of an old concrete dock and helipad jutting out into the East River almost beneath the bridge. A dozen agents, six of them in olive-drab tactical fatigues, had set up tents and tables and a gasoline-powered generator.

We'd just reached the first tent when there was a low, thumping hum, and a helicopter appeared from the fog under the 59th Street Bridge. We stopped and stared at the dark navy-blue Bell 407 with no markings as it slowed and banked and swung around and did a steady, controlled landing despite the wind.

Its rolling door snapped open, and out came four men and a woman in FBI Windbreakers carrying large kit bags. I kept looking at the copper-haired female agent as the whining helicopter lifted off again immediately and headed back the way it came.

I was either hallucinating or the woman was my old pal Emily Parker. With New York City under siege, I could have definitely been hallucinating, but it turned out I was right.

"Mike," Emily said, giving me a grim half smile as I approached. "What's a nice guy like you doing in a place like this?"

# Chapter 30

"HERE, GIVE ME a hand with these radios," she said, pulling some out of her bag. "We're definitely going to need them with all the cell sites fried."

"What brings you here?" I said to Emily after I introduced her to my guys. "I thought you were back down in DC." Emily worked there for the Bureau's Violent Criminal Apprehension Program and lived in suburban Virginia with her daughter, Olivia.

"That's just my luck," Emily said. "I came up this morning on the Acela and was starting a VICAP presentation to some junior agents when the bells went off. You know the drill. Now it's all hands on deck until further notice. With the roads blocked the way they are, they're going to chopper the entire New York office up here from lower Manhattan if they have to."

"Have you heard anything?" I said.

"I was about to ask you the same question. One of the agents with me, John Bellew, was on the horn with some State Department think-tank guy. The initial read is that this was caused by one or several NNEMPs."

"The whosiwhatsits?" said Arturo.

"Nonnuclear electromagnetic pulse weapons. It's a weapon that creates a massive electromagnetic field and then pulses it in a given area, creating an energy wave so powerful that it erases magnetic computer memories and welds closed the microscopic junctions in sensitive transistors and computer chips."

Arturo looked befuddled. Agent Parker had that effect on people, I knew.

"That seems pretty high-tech. Who could pull this off?" asked Brooklyn.

"NNEMPs aren't impossible to build, but it's very difficult. You need someone with high-level technical expertise. Basically, this isn't a homemade pipe bomb. This is the result of a highly intelligent operation that's probably well funded."

"Which points to terrorism—but as of now, there are no demands," I said. "And no claim of credit. The subway explosion, the assassination, and now this. Why keep doing all this? What's the motive?"

"The same as all terrorism," said Emily. "To inspire fear, to cause pain and injury, and induce psychological torture. The rapidity of each act seems to be an attempt to crash the system, to overwhelm our ability to respond."

"They're doing a damn good job," said Arturo.

"Is it Islamic?" asked Doyle. "Al Qaeda? Like nine eleven?"

"They're certainly on the list, but it could be anyone. Iranians, North Koreans."

"Hey, Mike, you hear that? Iranians again," said Brooklyn.

"Why, what's the Iranian link?" Emily asked.

"The mayor's shooter is actually Armenian," I said. "It could just be a coincidence, but he traveled home recently, and Armenia is next door to Iran."

"Or maybe it's some ramped-up American nut job," said Doyle. "A smart one with a real hard-on for the people of New York City."

We all turned as a big NYPD Harbor Unit boat suddenly roared past out of the fog on the river, heading north.

"Whoever it is," I said, "we need to find them. Fast."

# Chapter 31

HALF A MILE southeast of the FBI's staging area, the wake of the speeding sixty-foot blue-and-white NYPD Harbor Unit boat washed up a broken neon-yellow kayak paddle and a Clorox bleach bottle covered in old fishing line onto the rocky shore of southern Roosevelt Island.

Sitting in the rain on an empty bench above the island's garbage-strewn shoreline on West Loop Road, Mr. Joyce looked at the junk and then out at the water. New York was rarely thought of as a coastal city, but it actually had 520 miles of coastline, more than Miami, LA, and San Fran combined.

His reddish goatee was gone now, and he wore his hoodie up over a Knicks ball cap and a reflective orange traffic vest over his black denim construction coat. Beside him on the bench was some construction equipment as well as a fluorescent yellow construction tripod along with a surveyor's graduated staff.

He turned as a car pulled up. It was a big, bulky old '76 Cadillac Calais, a two-door hardtop that was nineteen feet long with a 7.7-liter V-8 and a curb weight of more than five thousand pounds.

Mr. Joyce did not have to look at who was behind the wheel to recognize it immediately as one of Mr. Beckett's many cars. Mr. Beckett, who was a bit of a gearhead, was obsessed with American cars, with a particular and peculiar soft spot for Cadillacs from the 1970s.

"You're late," said Mr. Joyce as Mr. Beckett emerged from his metallic-brown barge, putting on his own traffic vest.

"How is that possible?" Mr. Beckett said, smiling, as he extended his hands playfully. "The boss is never late."

"Was there trouble?" Mr. Joyce said, eyeing him.

"Please," Mr. Beckett said, knocking on the trunk. "You're the brains, I'm the muscle. You do your part, and I'll do mine, okay? Is it time to do our little survey?"

"Yes."

Mr. Joyce handed him the staff and a walkie-talkie as they walked north toward the base of the 59th Street Bridge.

"So they did use the abandoned helipad, as you anticipated," Mr. Beckett said as he gazed across the water and saw the activity on the Manhattan shore of the channel.

Mr. Joyce shrugged.

"With the streets impassable, a dock with helicopter access is the most logical place."

Mr. Joyce stayed back near the street with the tripod while Mr. Beckett walked off a bit with the staff and stood on a patch of muddy grass near the water.

"This is one big bitch of a bridge, eh?" Mr. Beckett said over the Motorola. "How old is it? Give me the tour. I know you want to."

"It was built in 1909," Mr. Joyce said. "Between 1930 and 1955, in that bridge pier behind you, they actually used to have a car elevator to bring people on and off Roosevelt Island."

"A car elevator in a bridge? That's incredible. What an amazing city this is. It's almost a shame bringing it to its knees."

"Emphasis on the almost," Mr. Joyce replied. "Move to your left."

"If I go any more left, I'll be swimming."

"Okay, stay there. Don't move."

Instead of a construction level on the yellow tripod, there was a Nikon camera fitted with a zoom lens. For the next twenty minutes, Mr. Joyce took photographs of the police and FBI agents. It was time in their campaign for reconnaissance. Time to assess the competition, as it were. The police could hardly be called competition, especially at this point, but one never knew. The two partners couldn't get too cocky. Besides, information was like weaponry. Better to have it and not need it than need it and not have it.

Mr. Joyce snapped a photo and sent it through Wi-Fi to the facial recognition software on his iPhone. Michael Bennett came up on the readout with an address on West End Avenue. Mr. Joyce nodded. Good to know.

"Foggy out here today," commented Mr. Beckett when they were done and heading back for the car.

"Yes, isn't it?" Mr. Joyce said, walking with the tripod on his shoulder like a soldier on parade. "And I have a funny feeling it's going to get even foggier."

"What do you think of this honey, Mr. Joyce?" said Mr. Beckett in the car as they did a broken

U-turn. "Rides like a dream, doesn't she?"

"Tell me, how many miles to the gallon does it get, Mr. Beckett?" asked Mr. Joyce.

"City or highway?" asked Mr. Beckett.

"City," said Mr. Joyce.

"One," said Mr. Beckett.

He stopped suddenly another hundred feet up, by an abandoned construction site. The huge car's weight bounced low and soft in the springs.

"Well, what do you know?" Mr. Beckett said, looking around. "Opportunity knocks. Give me a hand, Mr. Joyce, and we'll kill two birds with one stone."

Mr. Beckett popped the trunk, and they got out. Mr. Joyce went to the back of the long car and stared down at the two NYU graduates they had hired to place the EMP devices. The young men stared back up with their empty eyes open and their hands and mouths bound in duct tape. They had multiple bullet holes in their heads.

"Would you look at this trunk, Mr. Joyce?" Mr. Beckett said proudly. "Just look at it. It's bigger than most apartments in this city."

"It is rather roomy," said Mr. Joyce as he bent and lifted the first dead kid up to his shoulder and carried him to the Dumpster and dropped him in.

# Chapter 32

SEVERAL HOURS LATER, Emily and the team and I were just east of East 78th Street and Cherokee Place, alongside John Jay Park.

I'd never been to the park before or even heard of it. The buildings that formed a kind of horseshoe around it were nice ones, I saw. The park and playground were empty, but I could easily see it on the weekends being packed with kids and nannies. It was an upscale leafy enclave that reminded me a little of the famous Gramercy Park.

What wasn't looking very upscale was the silver Volvo SUV that had jumped the curb on 78th and plowed into a fire hydrant and utility box and the wrought-iron fence surrounding the park.

The Volvo was now just a crumpled mass of metal and broken glass. The air bags had all deployed, but the hydrant and a huge dislocated section of the fence had gone through the car all the way to the backseat. Everybody in the car had died in an unimaginably horrible way.

Three more dead, I thought, sickened and angry and getting angrier. I'd heard that an old woman being transported out of Sloan Kettering had gone into cardiac arrest, which made the body count at least four. I thought of all the stores we had passed in our search for the EMP devices. Block after block of owners standing there mute and devastated in front of the darkened doorways of their nail salons and dry cleaners and restaurants and grocery stores, their lives and livelihoods in tatters.

All these poor people. I suddenly felt incredibly tired. And what was more frustrating was that we couldn't help them. We were supposed to prevent these things, protect people, save them. And we weren't doing it. We weren't doing a damn thing.

The search for the NNEMPs had come down to the most basic footwork—i.e., walking to every building in the devastated area and asking supers and staff if they had received any strange deliveries. We'd been doing it all day to the tune of nada progress. The needle was still hiding in the haystack. If there even was a needle.

Emily came over as I sat on the curb by the park's entrance and cracked open a bottle of water.

"How many injured, you figure?" I said up at her after a long sip. "How many dead?"

I suddenly chucked the half-filled water bottle in my hand as hard as I could into the middle of the street.

"And why the hell is this happening?!" I yelled at the top of my lungs.

I was losing it a little, I knew. Maybe more than a little. I was beyond frustrated, beyond worried. I'd been hitting it hard for the last couple of days. Watching the mayor get shot was alone enough to give anyone a case of post-traumatic stress disorder.

This whole situation was just so freaking insane!

"I know you're angry, Mike," Emily said calmly, after a beat. "We all are, but unfortunately, anger will get us nowhere."

"Yeah, well, neither is calm, cool, and collected, Emily, if you haven't noticed," I said. "That's why I'm going to try raging pissed-off for a bit. Feel free to join me at any time."

That's when Doyle ran at me from across the street, hollering into his radio.

"That was from a uniform who knows the area,"

Doyle cried. "He said some super said some kind of device was installed recently on the roof of his building on East Eighty-First, just two blocks from here. He said it's a metal box that looks burned. That's what we're looking for, right?"

Emily and I exchanged a glance.

"That's exactly what we're looking for," she said as she offered me a hand.

# Chapter 33

SITUATED HALFWAY BETWEEN York and First Avenues, 421 East 81st Street was a narrow six-story disco-era white-brick apartment building.

Waiting for us out in front of the building were agent Ashley Brook Clark, an intense FBI technical analyst, and Dr. Michael Aynard, a pudgy, aging hipster in a yellow-and-brown flannel shirt and big glasses who was a physics professor at NYU and one of the foremost experts on NNEMPs in the world.

There were a lot of mirrors in the building's small, low-ceilinged lobby and even more tenants—a tense crowd of mostly older people and a few young moms with toddlers. Several had flashlights to ward off the dimness of the unlit lobby, and some had packed suitcases with them.

Everyone except for the children looked distraught and confused. I thought of the thousands upon thousands of people who lived and worked in the area and felt truly terrible for them. The power was out, and all arrows were pointing to it staying out for a long, long time.

This really was a disaster, I thought, not for the first time that day. Like a flood or a hurricane, it was affecting multiple thousands of random innocent people. It was what insurance companies used to call an act of God. I wondered if that was what this was. Someone who believed he was God.

I was snapped out of my wonderings by a wiry middle-aged woman in a ratty green bathrobe who began arguing loudly with the Filipino superintendent by the front door.

"What do you mean you *can't?*" the woman cried. "Why do you think we bought the damn thing after Hurricane Sandy? As vice president of the board, I demand that you get that portable generator on now. My medication is going bad as we speak!"

"But I keep explaining. It's broken, Mrs. Schaeffer," the young, stocky super said soothingly. "Everything is broken. No one's phones work, right? See, it's not just the electricity. There must have been some kind of crazy surge or something. I talked to every super up and down the street. This isn't a normal blackout."

"But my medication!" Mrs. Schaeffer insisted.

"Your medication is toast, ma'am, unless you get out of here with it as soon as possible," Dr. Aynard interrupted in a bored voice. "In fact, unless everyone here is interested in what it's like to live in the Dark Ages, I recommend you pack up your valuables, pick a direction, and start walking until you find yourself in an area where there's electricity."

He cleared his throat.

"Ding-dong! It's fact-facing time, people," he said. "The power isn't coming back on today, tomorrow, or probably for some six months at least, and sitting around here isn't going to change it."

"Way to sugarcoat things, Dr. Bedside Manner," Brooklyn Kale mumbled behind me as we stepped up to the super.

# Chapter 34

THE SUPERINTENDENT'S NAME was Lionel Cruz, and after we told him why we were there, he led us across the lobby and up six flights of stairs in a darkened stairwell and out in the rain onto the roof.

The device was in the southeast corner of the roof, on the other side of a dark, looming water tower. A strange, narrow, chest-height aluminum box about three feet wide. I thought it looked almost like a filing cabinet. One whose sides had been ripped open from a small bomb or explosive device that had gone off inside it.

"How did it get up here?" I said to Lionel.

"That's just the thing," the super said, shaking his head repeatedly. "I like to think I run a pretty tight ship here, but I have absolutely no idea. I'd check one of the security cameras at the front door or in the garage, but they're both not working with the power loss. I'd call my staff about it, except the phones are down. I only came up to look around when Mrs. Willett, who lives on the top floor beneath here, said she thought she heard some kind of explosion."

"Does this look like the device?" Emily said to Agent Clark, who was down on one knee on the tar paper, peering with a flashlight into the strange metal box's blown-open gap.

"It has to be," said Dr. Aynard, who was looking over the kneeling tech's shoulder. "The remains of that metal cylinder there is the armature, and that segment of coiled copper is obviously the stator wiring."

"And I'd say what's left of the gas engine in there was the power source," Agent Clark finished grimly. "This is a textbook flux compression generator bomb."

"Brilliant, really," said Aynard as he knocked on the metal housing with a knuckle. "Simple, efficient, not expensive, and highly effective."

"Oh, it's brilliant, all right," said Arturo sarcastically. "Quick! Someone call the Nobel Prize people and nominate the terrorists for efficiently erasing civilization for a hundred square blocks."

"So you're saying this small box did the entire neighborhood?" Doyle said.

Aynard winced as he thought about it. He looked in again at the box's burned remains.

"Maybe not," he finally said. "Though this device definitely packed quite an electromagnetic punch, it does seem a little small. I'd say there's probably at least one more somewhere, maybe even two."

I thought about that. How a box as small as the one before us could do such unbelievable, unheard-of damage. I also thought about how there could be dozens more ready to go off at any moment.

I lifted my radio and called Miriam Schwartz, who was coordinating from the law enforcement staging area by the bridge.

"Miriam, we found the NNEMP," I said. "But it's small, and the experts on scene say there are probably more. We're going to need search teams. Boots on the ground inspecting rooftops."

"Search teams? For where? The affected area?" she radioed back.

I stared out at the wilderness of buildings in every direction.

"No—for everywhere," I said. "There could be more of these things all over the city. I think it's time to assume that there are."

# Chapter 35

THE 59TH STREET BRIDGE staging area had turned into a full-fledged carnival of trailers and tents by the time we got back to it an hour or so later. To the constant hammering of temporary generators, twenty or thirty FBI agents and double that number of NYPD officers were busy setting up a crisis command post.

We had a meeting under a rain-soaked tent, where we got some of the brass up to speed. As per my recommendation, it was needle-in-the-haystack time all over the city. Cops and firemen everywhere were now in the process of searching rooftops.

At the end of the meeting, Chief Fabretti and Bob Madsen, the New York office's assistant special agent in charge, who were now jointly running the show, named Emily and me the case's investigative coordinators.

I was definitely pleased to be getting the case lead but even more psyched about officially working with Emily again. We worked well together. We'd stopped a psychopath who was kidnapping and killing rich kids a few years before, and more recently we helped take down a Mexican drug cartel head. Not only was she particularly adept at appeasing the government pen pushers, she also probably had better back-channel contacts in the Bureau's various investigative support units than the director. She was all about results.

Emily grabbed us a couple of coffees from another tent after the meeting.

"C'mon, Mike. The rain's falling off a bit. I want to stretch my legs."

Emily said this casually, but I noticed her expression was pensive, a little standoffish. Her mental gears were spinning up to speed, I knew. Her investigative approach was like mine, one of ebb and flow. The idea was to gather as much info as possible and then back off of it in order to let things sink in. Give one's initial and intuitive impressions a little time to set, so that after a while, a telltale pattern could be detected. You couldn't talk things to death. Especially in the beginning.

I followed her out onto 60th Street alongside the base of the bridge. We walked west, staring out at the Upper East Side. An evacuation had been declared a little after noon, and it was quite a spooky scene, with all the stopped cars in the empty streets. It was so silent you could actually hear the dead traffic lights creaking in the breeze at the intersections and the needles of rain drumming on the pavement.

Up on Second Avenue, we stopped and watched as a National Guard unit wrestled a length of chain-link out of the back of an olive-drab army truck. We stood there and watched as the soldiers unwrapped the fencing and held it upright while strapping it to lampposts on opposite sides of the avenue. When they were done, it looked as if everything north of 60th Street had been turned into a prison.

"What the hell?" Emily said in horror. "That looks so wrong."

"It's to prevent looting, I guess," I said, shaking my head.

The last time I saw something like this was on Canal Street after 9/11. Definitely not a memory lane I liked to stroll down.

We turned right and walked north up deserted Second Avenue.

"How's the kids, Mike?" Emily said out of the blue. "And Seamus? And Mary Catherine, of course."

I gave her a brief family update as we walked up the desolate avenue. I left out the part about Seamus's recent memory troubles. I looked around. Life seemed depressing enough.

"That stinks about Mary Catherine stuck in Ireland," Emily said. "What are you doing about the kids?"

"Seamus finagled a temporary nanny," I said. "Some nice Irish college kid named Martin. He actually just started today. How about you? Have you been keeping yourself busy?"

"Well," Emily said, a little less pensive, "I've actually been seeing somebody. For about three months now. I guess you could say it's pretty serious. At least I think it is." I was shocked to suddenly feel a little crushed when I heard this. It was probably because Emily and I had almost gotten together a few times during previous cases. There was definitely some attraction there between us, a mostly unspoken chemistry. She was a smart, energetic, good-looking woman. And a heck of a hard-hitting investigator. What wasn't there to be attracted to? But I really shouldn't have been jealous, especially since Mary Catherine and I were serious now and getting more serious by the moment.

Emily has a right to be happy, too, right? I thought. Sort-of-ish.

"Hey, that's great, Emily," I finally said. "Who is he? A cop or a real person?"

Emily laughed.

"He's a real person, as a matter of fact. He's a line cook at Montmartre in DC. He's also a veteran of Afghanistan—a Special Forces medic. His name is Sean Buckhardt. He's this tall, serious, tough, hardworking man, but underneath, he really cares, you know? About the world, about being alive. And he's great with Olivia. He's smart and sarcastic and funny, like you. I really think you'd like him."

Wanna bet? I thought, glancing into her bright-blue eyes.

"A line cook? That's a score. Tell me he cooks for you," I said instead.

"All the time. Does it show?" she said, smiling. "It shows, right? All the butter sauce. I'll come home from a case, and it's Provence in my kitchen, with all the courses and the wine pairings. He makes this lemon-chicken thing. I swear it should be on the narcotics list. I must have put on ten pounds."

That's a lie, I thought as I watched her do some kind of re-knotting thing with her shoulder-length hair. Out of the corner of my eye, I watched as she walked ahead of me a little. Whatever she was doing, it was working out. Quite well.

But I kept that to myself. Instead, I quickly took out my phone to see if there were any new messages from Mary Catherine.

Bad corner of my eye, I thought.

# Chapter 36

THE HOTEL DINING room was all but empty as the last couple huddled together at the best table, right by the low turf fire in the massive river-rock fireplace. The candlelight was soft and low, as was the cozy romantic music playing.

"Ga! Will they never leave?" said Mary Catherine's cousin Donnell as they hung back by the kitchen door, allowing the American couple celebrating their fiftieth anniversary to enjoy a moment.

"Have a heart. It's romantic," Mary Catherine said.

"They've enjoyed about a trillion and a half moments already, by my calculation," complained Donnell. "The sun'll be coming up soon."

"Go in and help Pete, ya stone-hearted cynic,"

Mary Catherine said. "I'll get them for you and maybe even pass along the tip if you're lucky."

"Thank you so much," the silver-haired American CEO type said after he finally handed over his Amex. He patted his ample midsection. "The lamb, the wine reduction sauce, all of it was—"

"Just perfect. Really," insisted his pretty brunette wife. "Especially the dessert you sent over. Who would have thought? Real New York cheesecake in Ireland? Where do you get it?"

"I have my sources," Mary Catherine said with a smile.

Donnell was nowhere to be found when she returned to the kitchen.

"Where is he?" she asked her other cousin Pete, the chef, who tossed a thumb toward the back door.

"Romance in front and now in the back of the house, too, I see," Mary Catherine cried in mock shock as she busted Donnell canoodling his girlfriend against the side of her car. "Back to work. You can snog on your own time."

"Are all you Yanks such slave drivers?" Donnell said as he walked past.

"No, you lazy Paddy. Just me," Mary Catherine said, whipping him in the butt with a towel.

She grabbed a rack of hot glasses from the machine in the corner of the kitchen and brought them in through the swinging door into the hotel bar.

There were a lot of large and loud red-faced men at the bar and even more in the adjoining banquet space. A three-piece rock band was playing in the party room, and everyone was singing the old Squeeze hit "Tempted" at the top of their lungs and drinking Guinness and Harp Lager as fast as she and the bartender, Kevin, could change taps on the basement kegs.

An Australian-rules football club, mostly firemen and cops from Sydney, was in town to play the local Limerick club at various forms of football, and the place was packed. She smiled at the young and happy drunk men who'd been there for the last three days. She really liked the mostly good-natured Ozzies, but if she heard another one ask her what a nice girl like her was doing in a place like this, she was going to start screaming.

The best news of all was that the hotel's potential buyer, Mr. Fuhrman, a tall, dour German, had come by in the midst of all the merriment about an hour before. He had suddenly seemed pretty merry himself when he saw the place packed to capacity and all the money flying into the till.

"I'm going to make a phone call to the broker on Monday," Mr. Fuhrman had assured her before he left. "And I think you're going to like what you hear."

"Hey, Mary Catherine. Did you see this?" said Kevin, suddenly pointing up at the TV.

She looked up. The BBC was on. Behind a sleek glass anchor desk sat a sharp-faced blonde wearing a deadly serious expression.

Then Mary read the graphic on the screen beneath the anchorwoman, and the glasses in the racks rattled loudly as she set them down heavily on the bar.

NEW YORK ATTACKED! it said.

"Turn it up, Kevin," she said as the image on the TV changed to a shot of the stranded Roosevelt Island tram.

"FBI sources have confirmed that this is yet another attack seemingly carried out by terrorists," said the British anchor.

*Another* attack! What?

She flew behind the bar and grabbed her bag and dug out her cell phone. It almost slipped out of her hand, and she had to take a deep breath before she managed to focus enough to find the speed dial for the apartment. She bit her lower lip as she waited, listening to silence.

"C'mon," she said, waiting on the connection. "Pick up, Michael. C'mon, pick up!"

# Chapter 37

THAT NIGHT AT a quarter after seven, cranky, definitely drained, and yet at the same time extremely grateful just to be here, I stepped off my elevator and finally made glorious contact with the loose brass knob of my apartment's front door.

Sometimes bad days at work depressed me and stayed with me, but this was one of the days that made me happy just for the fact that it was over and I'd gotten through it in one piece.

I was locking the apartment door behind me when a horrendous crunching sound ripped out from the vicinity of the kitchen.

I peeked inside and saw Martin, with his back to me, throwing a bunch of carrots into a blender. He seems to be in one piece, I thought. The same busy, assured, positive, energetic person who'd come to work this morning. First days were tough. Especially ones that involved taking care of double-digit kids. But it was looking like it had gone well enough. Excellent, I thought. So far, so good.

Instead of interrupting him, I peeked into the living room.

Uh-oh. Maybe not so good, I thought when I saw the kids.

All the boys were there except Brian. They were lying all over the place. Eddie was passed out on the ottoman. Ricky was on the carpet, red-faced and staring, dazed, up at the ceiling. Trent, huffing and puffing, was sprawled facedown on the couch.

Seamus, who was on the end of the couch, thumbing through the *Irish Voice* newspaper, rolled his eyes at me.

"What's wrong with them, Father?" I said.

"I don't know. I just got in myself, and they won't say," said Seamus. "They keep sighing and moaning, though. I believe they've come down with some sickness perhaps mental in nature."

"Help, Dad. Just help," said Eddie as he looked up weakly from the ottoman.

"He makes us run, Dad," said Trent, pointing toward the crunching sound in the kitchen. "We were doing drills. Soccer drills."

"You made Mary Catherine disappear and replaced her with a drill sergeant," Ricky said. "We're not that bad, are we? Well, I mean, we're sort of bad, but this bad? Honestly, what did we do?"

The blender stopped, then whirred again.

"And he says he's making us smoothies," said Eddie. "But I saw vegetables, Dad. He bought vegetables from the corner market! I definitely saw carrots and even some green stuff. That's not a smoothie, Dad. That's V8 juice!"

"Give it up, fellas," I said with a smile. "You couch-potato Nintendo athletes could use some running around. Not to mention some vegetables. Mary Catherine would be pleased."

# Chapter 38

I WAS TURNING into the hallway near the back bedrooms when I ran into the female Bennett contingent near the rumbling washer and dryer. They glared at me in unison. Another group of unhappy campers, apparently.

"First the boys, now you," I said. "What's wrong? What are you guys up to?"

"Doing our laundry, thank you very much, Father," said Juliana.

"But Martin can handle that," I said.

Six sets of female eyes glared back at me in unholy unison.

"Are you nuts, Dad?" said Jane. "Do you know how embarrassing that would be? Martin is not— and I mean never—doing my laundry. Or I'll . . . run away!"

"We all will if that man in there even glances at the laundry of any female member of this family," chimed in Fiona.

"Forever!" said Chrissy.

"Forever? Wow, okay, ladies. I'll work on it. Sheesh," I said, slowly backing away.

"Hey there, Martin. How'd the first day go?" I said back in the kitchen.

"Ah, they're great, so they are," said Martin. "They complained a bit about the running around, what with the rain and all, but that's natural. Listen, I think that little one there—Trent, is it?—has some real potential as a footballer, especially for a three-footed Yank, but what are we talkin' about my day at work for? I heard it on the radio. They hit us again, have they?"

I nodded.

"Is it bad?"

"It's pretty bad, Martin," I said.

"And I thought the troubles in Northern Ireland were bad. Who's doing it? Is it those al Qaeda nut jobs again, do ya think?"

I shrugged.

"We don't know yet."

"Well, I thought it best to keep the TV off on account of the youngest ones," Martin said. "I thought you'd handle the situation best."

"Good call, Martin," I said.

And now for another, I thought, taking out my phone and hitting a speed-dial number.

"Hey, Tony," I said. "I'd like to get four large pies, one plain, two sausage, and one with pepperoni."

"Mike, whatcha doin'? Don't bother with that. I got dinner covered. I'm making them some smoothies with Caesar salad."

"Hey, that's perfect, Martin," I said. "We'll have everything with the pizza."

# Chapter 39

"MMM, THIS PIZZA sure is good," I said in the dead silence to break the ice.

It certainly needed some breaking. I looked around the table at the kids with their faces downturned at their food. It was suddenly Buckingham Palace formal and pin-drop silent with Martin having joined us for dinner.

"Fine. I'll say it if no one else will, Dad. Are we all going to die or what?" said Brian around a mouthful of pepperoni.

"What?" I said, glaring at him.

"What's wrong?" asked Bridget.

"Oh, it's nothing really, little sis. We're just under attack by a bunch of insane terrorists again," Brian said, staring at me like it was my fault. "Not for nothing, Dad, but if we have to move again somewhere, you can count me out. I'm going to lie about my age and join the marines or something."

"Relax," I said, looking around the table. "There was a blackout on the East Side. They think somebody did it deliberately. That's all. We don't know who's doing it, okay? It's a mess, and we need to pray for a lot of poor people who are affected, but it's okay. Honestly."

"Okay?" said Juliana. "First they blow up a train tunnel, then they kill the mayor, and now—"

"You're going to pass the garlic salt, young lady, and we're all going to have some nice dinner-table conversation," I insisted loudly.

I guess I was a little louder than I intended to be, because everyone stared at me like I was nuts. Except for Martin, who, I could see, was trying hard not to laugh at me and the rest of us Bennett lunatics from behind his napkin.

In the awkward silence, I suddenly tossed out an even more awkward conversation starter.

"Hey, how about those Yanks, Eddie, huh? Pettitte's looking sharp, isn't he?"

Eddie stared at me quizzically, as though I had just grown another head.

"Well?" I said again, louder.

Eddie put his slice down on his paper plate carefully.

"I don't know, Dad," he said slowly. "He's retired."

That's when Martin couldn't hold it in anymore and burst out laughing. Seamus joined him. Then everybody else.

"Go ahead. Yuck it up, everybody. See this, Martin? It's laugh-at-Daddy time here at the Bennett abode. It's a common dinnertime stress reliever," I said, sticking out my tongue at them before I started laughing at myself. "Works every time."

I leaped up immediately three minutes later when the phone rang. It was Mary Catherine, I saw on the caller ID in the living room. Finally! I was so eager to talk to her that I managed to hang up instead of pick up, and I was placing the handset back down when she called back.

"Finally, Mike! Oh, you had me so worried!" Mary Catherine said. "I had the damnedest time getting through. I just saw the news. What's going on? Tell me everybody is okay."

"We're all fine, Mary Catherine. Everybody is as healthy and sarcastic as ever," I said.

"But what is this EMP bomb? What about the nuclear stuff they were saying on the news?"

Even after I explained it to her as best I could, she—like everyone else—didn't seem very reassured.

"How's things on your end?" I said, changing the subject.

"The new buyer is looking very serious. I'll know on Monday," she said.

I could hear the smile in her voice.

"I'll keep my fingers crossed," I said, hearing music in the background. "Are you celebrating already?"

"Oh, no. That's just some Australians reliving the eighties."

"Any room for an American?" I said. "I could be there in six hours. I do a killer Depeche Mode."

Mary Catherine laughed.

"Wow, how I wish I were there with you, Michael. I can't tell you how much I miss those kids, too. All of them."

"All of them?"

"Oh, Michael, you'll never know. Every little stinker in the bunch. It's killing me not being there. What did that oil-spill CEO guy say? 'I want my life back.'"

"I want our life back," I said.

There was a pause.

"I have to go," said Mary Catherine.

"So do I," I said.

There was a pause.

"Why haven't you hung up yet?" I said.

"I was just about to ask you the same thing."

We laughed. There was another pause.

Then it happened.

"I love you," I said.

I heard a gasp and then a loud earful of dial tone a second later.

What the hell are you doing? I thought, smiling at my reflection in the TV screen.

I'm reliving the eighties, all right, I thought as I realized that I had butterflies in my stomach. I felt like I was about sixteen. I liked it.

"Detective Bennett, what have you finally gone and done?" I mumbled as I stood.

# Chapter 40

MY CELL PHONE rang a little after three o'clock that morning. Like most calls that come at ungodly hours, it was not good. It was from Neil Fabretti, the chief of detectives himself.

"Mike, sorry to bother you. I just got off the phone with the new mayor's people. The gist of it is they're beyond pissed at the pace of the investigation and want whoever's on it off it and someone new put on pronto."

Though I was a little stunned to actually hear it, part of me had been waiting for this call. I'd been on high-profile cases before, and I knew that now with several people dead, including the mayor, tens of thousands of people displaced, and millions more on edge, the •pressure to do something, even unfairly sacrificing a convenient scapegoat like me, was immense.

Good investigations were about being patient and meticulous, but that wasn't exactly a popular sentiment, I knew from reading yesterday's *New York Post* headline, WHAT THE #$%@ IS BEING DONE?

When you lost the usually NYPD-friendly *Post*, you knew you were in deep trouble.

"Is that right?" I finally said.

"Yeah, well, I told them to pound sand," Fabretti continued, surprising me. "I said that we couldn't just go shuffling investigators around because of the pressure of the twenty-four/seven news cycle. I told them you were the best we had and that I was behind you one hundred percent, yada, yada, yada.

"But there's a big meeting scheduled for one o'clock this afternoon at the commissioner's office, and you need to be there for the investigation's update with bells on, if you know what I'm saying. Nothing personal, but the reality is, if you want to keep being the lead on this, Mike, you got about ten hours to make something drop."

"I'll be there. Thanks for the 'look out' and the heads-up, Chief," I said before I hung up.

Wide awake now, I knew it was time to make

my own 3:00 a.m. calls to see if there had been any developments. Doyle and Arturo didn't pick up, but I caught Brooklyn Kale burning the midnight oil at the NYPD intelligence desk we'd been assigned.

"Mike, thank goodness. I was just going to call you," she said.

"What have you got, Brooklyn?"

"Something good for a change. We got video of the guys—two guys—bringing the EMP device into East Eighty-First Street."

"Video?" I said. "But I thought the super said that the on-site computer where they store the feed was fried with the EMP."

"It was, but we canvassed at the high-rise across the street, and it turns out their video is run by a national firm that backs up everything off-site. The security firm sent the film over about an hour ago. It's beautiful. You can see the guys bringing in the box, Mike . . . the plates on the van they were driving—the whole shebang. Check your e-mail. I just sent a clip of it to you."

I opened the video.

It was incredible.

I thought it was going to be the two men from the video of the train tunnel bombing, but it wasn't. I watched in color as two young guys in a white

179

van, college kids, maybe, pulled into the garage next to the building and unloaded the metal device onto a hand truck.

"The plates on the van look funny to you?" I said to Brooklyn as I hit Pause. "They're New York State, but what are they? Commercial?"

"Yep. Already ran them. The van is from a Hertz location downtown—or at least its plates are," Brooklyn said. "Doyle's on the phone with the manager, who's on his way in. The manager said you can't rent without a credit card and a driver's license, so we're looking good on a potential lead there. I'll hit you with it the second Doyle calls me back and I hear anything."

"Great job, Brooklyn," I said.

"One more thing, Mike, that just came up. May or may not be related," she said. "Two young men were just found shot dead at a construction site on Roosevelt Island. I called the desk sergeant at the public safety department on the island, and he told me they don't have ID on them, but the general description seems about the same as these two guys on the video. You want me to head out there or stay here coordinating?"

A lead was a lead, I knew from experience. Even if the suspects were no longer in a position to talk to us, they could still provide us with valuable information.

"No, you stay there," I said. "I'll grab Agent Parker and check it out."

# Chapter 41

TWENTY-SIX MINUTES after I hung up the phone, I sat in my unmarked on Seventh Avenue and 50th Street, staring at the garish neon lights as they geysered and flashed silently on the beautiful people-filled billboards above the worn and empty concrete canyons of Times Square.

As the song says, New York City never sleeps, but between 4:15 and 4:30 a.m., it sometimes takes a quick catnap. Even so, it was weird seeing Times Square devoid of people. Not to mention quite off-putting under the horrible circumstances.

I saw that Emily's hair was still wet from her shower when she finally appeared at a run from her glass-fronted hotel. I smiled to myself as she pulled the car door open. The sight of her was anything but lonely.

"Let me bring you up to speed on some economic forensics I did on the mayor's shooter, Alex Mirzoyan," Emily said, thumbing her smartphone as we headed east for Roosevelt Island.

"First, the good news. That robotic gun-aiming device used in the mayor's assassination is highly specialized, and we were able to track down the manufacturer. The company is giving us some pushback after we asked for their customer list, but we have the US attorney drawing up a warrant, and I think we'll be making progress there."

"What about the ownership of the apartment the shooter was in?" I said.

Emily scrolled through screens on her phone.

"No dice there, unfortunately. Apparently, the owner is a Columbia University international law professor who's in Brussels for a semester's sabbatical. It doesn't seem like he's involved. He rented it out anonymously for a thousand dollars a week through one of those Internet house-swapping services to a fake e-mail address that Mirzoyan must have set up called woopwoop-two-two-six at AOL dot com."

"Well, it eliminates me as a suspect, at least," I said, shaking my head. "My fake e-mail address is woopwoop-two-two-six at *Yahoo* dot com."

"Very funny," Emily said, tapping her smart-phone screen again. "But what's more promising is some weird stuff we found with Mirzoyan's finances. Last week he opened a PayPal account that had three thousand dollars wired into it, which he immediately withdrew from a bank in South Miami."

I glanced over at her.

"Expense money?" I said. "So he could come up to New York?"

"Could be. Like we're doing with the rifle company, we're in the process of having the attorney's office try to persuade PayPal to tell us who the mysterious someone who wired the money is."

# Chapter 42

WE WERE IN Queens twenty minutes later. I got turned around after I got off the first exit of the Midtown Tunnel and wandered around the industrial maze of Long Island City for a bit.

"How are we lost, Mike?" said Emily, yawning. "I thought you were Mr. Native New Yorker."

"I am, Emily, but this isn't New York, it's Queens," I said, making a U-turn. "I mean, we just passed Forty-First Avenue and Twenty-First Street—or was it Twenty-First Avenue and Forty-First Street? Cops from other boroughs usually have to leave a trail of doughnut crumbs behind them in order to find their way back out."

"What is this crazy place, Mike? Roosevelt Island, I mean," Emily said as we rolled south under several varieties of train and car underpasses and finally swung onto the small, two-lane Roosevelt Island Bridge.

"Oh, just another one of the bizarre real estate situations you find in this crazy city," I said. "I think it used to be the site of a mental asylum in the early 1900s, and then they put up some kind of rent-subsidized housing complex. I guess its claim to fame is that it has its very own ski chalet–like cable car you can take to get into Manhattan."

"A Euro ski tram in New York City?" said Emily, her midwestern face scrunching. "Is it a heavily Swiss immigrant neighborhood or something?"

"Like I said, this is Queens, Emily." I nodded out at the water. "What happens in Queens stays in Queens."

The crime scene was at the base of the 59th Street Bridge, toward the south end of the small, narrow island.

I could see that the contingent of cops already waiting for us was definitely much larger than what you'd see at a regular homicide scene. In addition to at least four blue-and-whites from the island's public safety people, there was a wagon circle of various unmarked detective cars, FDNY ambulances, the medical examiner's mobile command center, and even an NYPD Emergency Services Unit truck.

Walking through the flashing blue and red lights toward the tape, I spotted Lieutenant Bryce Miller standing with his ESU intelligence commando cowboys. Even before the crack of dawn, the tall and polished pretty boy, looking like a soap opera actor, was in his power suit, ready for his close-up.

"Hey, Bennett. Glad you could make it," Bryce said sarcastically as we went past him.

He must be a pretty good intel guy after all, I thought, nodding at him. It seemed that he, too, had heard the rumors about my upcoming demise as case lead.

I was coming around the back of the buslike medical examiner's mobile command center when I saw the ME himself, Tom Durham, helping one of his assistants slide the first of the two stretchers with the already body-bagged suspects on them up a ramp to the vehicle's back door.

"Hold it there, Tom," I said to the NBA-tall medical examiner, whom I'd worked with a few times about a decade earlier, when I was in Homicide.

"Mike Bennett," Durham said, peeling off his rubber glove to shake my hand over the corpse. "Well, well, out of the mists of time. You've put on weight."

"Ah, c'mon, Tom," I said. "You know how these blue and red lights always put on ten pounds. This is my partner, Emily. Any chance you find any ID on these two?"

"Nope. Not a thing. We already printed them, too, for that guy in the suit over there. No help there, either, apparently."

"You mind if we take a quick peek at them?" I said.

"Nope," Tom said, grabbing the body-bag zipper. "And neither will they, I imagine."

I placed the video still of the darker kid next to the kid on the gurney. The kid's head was grotesquely deformed from several gunshot wounds, but I thought the picture looked like him.

"What do you think?" I said to Emily.

"I think it's him," she said.

Tom looked over her shoulder.

"Me, too," the ME said with a nod.

We quickly ID'd the other suspect as the second guy who dropped off the EMP device. We needed names, though. Somehow. There was no way I was going to allow this to be yet another dead end.

I thanked Tom, but instead of heading back to the car, I pocketed my phone and walked with

Emily away from the police lights to the rocky edge of the island's dark shore.

"Wait a second," I said after a minute of looking out over the water. "Look."

Across the quick current of choppy water, not too far away at the Manhattan base of the bridge, were the lights of our crisis post for the Yorkville disaster.

"The bastards were right here watching us yesterday, weren't they?" Emily said in shock. "Watching us scramble. The panic. All those poor souls having to be evacuated from the hospitals. They just stood here happily watching the results of what they'd done."

"And by leaving the bodies right here, I guess they want us to know it," I said.

"I'm really starting to not like these fellas, Mike," Emily said as she kicked a broken kayak handle into the water. "I mean, not even a little bit."

# Chapter 43

SEVERAL HECTIC HOURS later that day, at ten to one, Emily and I waited in a narrow, crowded hallway before a set of double doors on the eighth floor of One Police Plaza.

On the other side of the doors, we could hear a voice droning on as we hastily went over the final details of the report we were about to give to the police commissioner and acting mayor and various and sundry other officials.

The door of the thunderdome opened after a minute, and Chief Fabretti was there.

"Mike, you ready?" he said.

The coliseum-like, bowl-shaped CompStat conference room behind him was a pen pusher's paradise, I knew. It was a place where innovative computer-model formats were used to illuminate detailed processes that were compared for effectiveness of indices of performance before implementations of flexible tactics to achieve the development of comprehensive solutions were discussed in a team-building environment.

In plain English, it was a bureaucratic version of hell on earth.

But before I could answer the chief's question, Emily and I were inside, front and center.

There were about twenty or thirty people up on the amphitheater-style seats surrounding us, a lot of tense-looking NYPD and FBI brass, and the acting mayor. Also some suits from the White House, we'd been told.

If I needed any further indication of what was at stake, I saw it on the whiteboard that the last speaker had been using. Two words had been written with a Sharpie in large black letters.

EVACUATION PLAN

"Who the hell is this again?" said the acting mayor over the rim of her eyeglasses.

The tall, long-necked, white-haired woman's name was Priscilla Atkinson, and I almost felt like asking the Park Avenue–raised grande dame the same question, as her only experience before being named deputy mayor was running public events for the Central Park Conservancy.

Instead I began.

"Hi. I'm Detective Bennett. This is Special Agent Parker, and we'd like to bring everybody up to date on what we have so far."

An aide whispered in the acting mayor's ear.

"One question," Atkinson said, interrupting me. "What's going on, Detective Bennett? Who's doing this to us, and why the hell haven't you found them yet?"

Instead of pointing out that she'd just asked, in fact, three questions, I continued.

"I'm here to answer everybody's questions, Ms. Mayor, okay? I've been informed that everybody has already been briefed about the EMP device we discovered. What you may not be aware of is that last night, we were able to obtain video footage of men—two men—placing the object on the East Side building's roof."

"Are they the same two men seen on the video at the train bombing?" said the commissioner from the row beneath the mayor.

"No, they're not, Mr. Commissioner," said Emily. "They were different men."

"Have you ID'd them? Who the hell are they?" demanded the mayor.

"We've located them, ma'am," I said, "and we've actually just ID'd them as two recent NYU grads."

"Why'd they do it?"

"We don't know. We found them this morning in a Dumpster at a construction site on Roosevelt Island, both shot multiple times in the head."

That got the murmuring going.

"The men ran a marketing firm. They're local kids with no terrorist ties," Emily said before the mayor could jump in with another stupid obvious question. "We think they were hired by the people behind this."

"So we're still in the dark?" said Ms. Atkinson.

"Not entirely," I said. "We scoured their Internet and phone records and discovered that both were paid large sums of money over the Internet through what seems to be the same PayPal account. With the help of federal authorities, we are in the process of tracking down the owner of the account."

"Get to it, Bennett," the commissioner said after a beat. "Keep us apprised."

I nodded at him and at Lieutenant Bryce Miller sitting below the commissioner like the good little doggie he was.

Guess I'm still on the case after all, Brycey, I mentally texted him.

As Fabretti showed us the door, I saw one of the White House suits start BlackBerrying like crazy; I hoped they were putting some pressure on PayPal to cough up a name. The mayor nodded at us before she took off her glasses and rubbed her eyes. Seeing the obvious great concern and worry in her suddenly old-seeming face, I felt bad for her. She was just as strained and concerned and tired as the rest of us. And that was saying a lot.

# Chapter 44

THAT NIGHT AT around 9:30, approximately fifty-five miles due north of New York City, Emily turned off her phone as I pulled my unmarked off a backcountry road into a remote campground at Clarence Fahnestock Memorial State Park, on the border between Putnam and Dutchess Counties.

Unfortunately, we weren't at the state park for a midnight weenie roast. There were at least a dozen New York state trooper vehicles already in the large parking lot, along with the same number of unmarked FBI Crown Victorias. Beyond a trooper command bus were two matte-black BearCat troop trucks, and at the end of the lot, in a muddy clearing, sat a bulky olive-drab Black Hawk helicopter with military markings.

We were finally on the hunt now. At around five

that afternoon, PayPal had revealed the name of the person who had sent funds to both the mayor's shooter and the dead EMP guys, and it was a doozy.

The name on the PayPal transfer was Jamil al Gharsi. Al Gharsi was a Yemeni-born Muslim cleric who was already on the FBI's terrorist watchlist, suspected of running a militant and potentially violent Islamic group on a grubby cattle farm five miles due east of Fahnestock State Park.

Al Gharsi's two dozen–strong group had a website that billed them as a kind of Muslim Cub Scouts, though they were anything but. The FBI had been following them closely since their inception six months ago, and they had been observed training with weapons.

The group also had ties to al Qaeda in Yemen, which boggled my mind. Why hadn't they been shut down already? No one knew, or at least no one would say. If al Gharsi's group turned out to be responsible for the bombings and for the assassination in New York, I was truly going to kick somebody's ass. If Homeland Security had let yet another Islamic terrorist attack occur, I was going to be the first to propose its disbanding.

Emily and I passed a bunch of troopers wearing their Smokey the Bear hats and climbed onto the crowded bus, where the FBI's Hostage Rescue Team had already started its briefing.

A flat screen behind the driver's seat showed a series of photographs from reconnaissance that had already been done.

The pictures featured a cluster of buildings in the center of a large hilly field near the bottom of a ridge. There was an old farmhouse—a low concrete building that almost looked like a school—and a large dilapidated barn that was listing so far to the left it looked as if some magic spell had frozen it in the midst of collapse.

"This is al Gharsi," the HRT leader, Terry Musa, said as he handed out a printout showing a mean-looking bald guy with a beard that would make any of the Boston Red Sox's starting lineup green with envy.

"He is six foot three," Musa said as he tightened a strap on his helmet. "He is also a mixed martial artist and one tough bastard, apparently. We don't know what kind of weapons or explosives we're going to encounter. I wouldn't even recommend going in on the bird with this EMP shit, but there's no other way. So bottom line, be very, very fucking careful, okay, folks? Paying these assholes back won't be any fun if you're dead."

# Chapter 45

AT THE END of the briefing, Emily and I, along with two trooper teams, were assigned to watch a back road up on the ridge behind the farm.

Fifteen minutes later, with our headlights off, we coasted to a stop on a tree-lined gravel road beside a barred cattle gate. Beyond the gate was another gravel road that curved down to the left, out of sight through some trees. Down below the trees were the fields and farm.

When the other two teams radioed that they were in position a hundred feet back down the road behind us, I turned off the car and rolled down the window.

I looked down at the farm's rugged, unkempt fields. It was some desolate-looking country, all right. An almost constant wind whistled in the creaking roadside pines and white birches around us, like something out of *The Blair Witch Project*. Like most born-and-bred New York cops, the country at night always scared the hell out of me.

"Did you know they say Rip Van Winkle fell asleep around these parts?" I said after a minute to fill the creepy silence.

"I thought that was the Catskills," Emily said.

"You're right. Maybe I'm thinking of the Headless Horseman," I said as I heard a low thumping.

I looked up as the FBI's Black Hawk swung over the ridge above the car.

"Here we go," I said, turning up the radio.

The world went green as I peered through the night-vision telescope we'd been supplied with. As I got the farmhouse below in focus, I could see the chopper hovering over its roof and the FBI commandos already fast-roping into the front yard. Blasts of green-tinged light blazed at the house's front windows as the FBI guys tossed flashbangs.

That's when I heard a sound up on the wooded hill beside the car. I heard it again. Something crackling, something moving through the trees and underbrush to our left.

"A deer?" Emily whispered beside me as I swung the night-vision scope.

She was wrong.

At the top of a small hill through the trees, I could see three men coming directly at us. I made out that they were large and in camo and had long beards before I tossed the night scope and swung around for the backseat.

"Shit! It's them! Get behind the car!" I hissed at Emily as I turned and grabbed my M4 off the backseat.

I double-clicked it from safe to full auto and flung the door open. Wet mud sucked at my knees as I rolled beside the car into a prone shooting position.

The men, who must have finally seen the car, stopped suddenly halfway down the hill.

My heart bashing a hole in my chest, I managed to sight on the first man as I yelled, "Police! Down! All of you! Now!"

They looked at each other, then started whispering as they stayed on their feet. One of them was taller than the other two, I saw. Was it al Gharsi? Damn it, what were they doing? Did they have guns? Suicide vests? I wondered.

They definitely weren't listening. I decided I needed to change that.

# Alert

The silence of the night shattered into a million pieces as I went ahead and squeezed off a long burst of about a dozen or so .223 rounds up the hill. Wood splinters and leaves flew as I raked lead all over the trees and forest floor in front of them.

"We give up! Please don't shoot!" one of them said as all three of them dropped into the fetal position.

I stood with the gun to my shoulder and my finger still on the trigger as I heard the sweet sound of the first trooper car screaming up the gravel road.

# Chapter 46

"THIS IS TOTAL bullshit! This is racism! I know my rights. How dare you shoot at me on my own property?" said the large and broad-shouldered al Gharsi as he glared hatefully at me in the back of his crumbling farmhouse a tense twenty minutes later.

"Hey, I'm not the daring one, Al," I said, kicking a cardboard box of double-aught shotgun shells across his dirty, scuffed floor. "Running a jihadist camp in New York State sixty miles from Ground Zero? Talk about chutzpah."

And talk about living off the grid, I thought, shaking my head at the surroundings. The house was barely habitable. There was no phone, and what little electricity there was, was provided by a small propane generator. I couldn't decide which part of the decor was more charming—the little room off the kitchen, where a roughly butchered deer lay on a homemade plywood table, or the upstairs bedrooms, where Arabic graffiti covered the walls above sleeping bags.

Handcuffed behind his back, al Gharsi shifted uncomfortably on a ratty, faded orange couch, where he sat bookended by two standing FBI commandos. The only other furniture was a massive green metal gun locker in a far corner and twelve pale immaculate prayer mats set in a disturbingly precise four-by-three rectangle in the center of the room.

The locker had kicked out some good news for a change. Several of the semiautomatic AK-47s inside had been illegally converted to fully automatic. A felony federal weapons violation would be a good start at gaining some leverage to find out just what in the hell was going on.

"This is not a jihadist camp," al Gharsi said through yellow gritted teeth. "We are woodsmen, hunters."

"Woodsmen," I said with a laugh. "I guess that Arabic on the walls up there says, 'Give a hoot, don't pollute.' You're not woodsmen, but I'll concede that you are hunters. It's *what* you're hunting that's the problem."

I walked behind al Gharsi and took the photographs Emily was holding. The black-and-white blown-up stills showed the two men from the subway tunnel bombing.

"Who are they?" I said, flapping the photographs in front of al Gharsi's face.

He shrugged as he studiously refused to look at them.

"Who are they?" I said again, patiently.

"Wait. I know them. Yes," he said, nodding, as he finally glanced at the pictures. "The one on the left, his name is . . . let's see . . . Fuck. That's it. His name is Fuck, and the one on the right is . . . um . . . You, I believe. There they are together, Fuck and You, my dear old friends."

"That's pretty good, Al. Your delivery needs a little work, but it's almost happily surprising to see that you have any sense of humor at all."

That's when I walked behind him again and took a document and another picture from Emily. I showed him the PayPal stuff along with a photo of him sending funds from the nearby library.

"Last Thursday at three o'clock, you sent money to these two different accounts. I want to know why."

"What?" he said, peering at the photo.

"You sent money. Why?"

There was a glimmer of something in his face then. Recognition, definitely. Then a little confusion. Then his mask of impertinence was back. After a moment, he gave me a cold yellow smile.

"I want my lawyer," he said.

I smiled back.

"Don't worry, Al. A lawyer will be provided for you. That's what makes our country so great, you see. Free lawyers, stuff like that. Maybe one day you might want to ask yourself why you want to wreck it so badly."

He started laughing then.

"More amusement, Al?" I said. "I got you all wrong. You're just a big teddy bear, aren't you?"

"You're here about the attacks," he said. "The mayor, the bombing, the EMP."

"Why, yes," I said. "Have you heard anything about these things, by chance?"

"No," al Gharsi said calmly. "But I must admit, I am quite a fan of whoever is so brilliantly attacking New York City and bringing this corrupt-to-the-core Great Satan to its knees."

Al started chuckling again.

"You think I have something to do with it. Me! You come up here with your helicopters and men kicking in the door. But you are clueless. You are losing. You are flailing. You don't even know which direction to duck. Allah willing, you are about to be defeated, I think."

A minute later, I left the living room and followed Emily out of the house and onto the back porch.

In the farmyard's sole electric light, thirty yards to the south, some shoeless middle-school-age kids, al Gharsi's, probably, were kicking a basketball around as troopers interviewed black-clad, burka-wearing aunts and mothers. I wished suddenly that I were home with my own kids.

"What do you think?" I said to Emily.

"I think what you think," Emily said. "I think we just dug ourselves another dry hole."

# Chapter 47

SIXTY-FIVE MILES due south, between the Brooklyn neighborhoods of Fort Greene and Bedford-Stuyvesant, three glowing windows stood out sharply on the top floor of the Pratt Institute's otherwise dark North Hall building.

On the other side of the translucent window shades was a large, white-walled lab space that was the showpiece of Pratt's brand-new robotics facility. At its center, a young man and two young women sat at the largest of the stainless steel lab tables, side by side, working busily.

They had an assembly line going. Aaron started off with the brushless motor controller and flywheel and the flywheel's braking mechanism. Gia, who had a light touch with the soldering iron, fit in the tiny electronics board and the radio receiver, while

Shui popped in rolling-pin-like magnets and put additional magnets onto the face of the small, square white plastic panels.

The finished product was a white-and-silver cube about the size of a quarter. It looked innocuous enough, like a tiny futuristic children's block.

But these definitely were not Junior's LEGOs, Shui thought as she clicked on the mini robot's test software on the iPad.

Immediately there was a whirring sound as the computer-initiated radio signal activated the bot's interior flywheel. When the computer-dictated amount of RPMs were reached, the flywheel halted suddenly, catapulting the bot across the table. Another whir and flip, and the bot snapped into position onto the end of a line of six minibots that were already arranged in a straight row.

Then, with another click on the iPad, the magic really began as the tiny minibots started leap-frogging each other, moving steadily across the table just as a half-track would roll over a tank. Shui knew she was supposed to place the bots carefully into a foam-lined box at the end of the counter, but the boss wasn't around, was he? One by one, she made the minibots whir and flip into the box.

"Ah, my aching wrists!" said Gia, a 4.0 junior, as she removed her magnifying goggles. "There has to be a labor law against this. How long have we been at it? Ten hours now? I feel like one of those kids in India forced to hand-roll cigarettes. I mean, I really think I'm getting carpal tunnel syndrome."

"Now, now. Time is money. We're not getting paid by the hour but by the minibot, remember? Keep rowing the slave boat so Aaron the Baron here can score himself some nice front-row seats at Coachella," Aaron said, snapping components together and flicking them toward Gia as though they were lunch-table footballs.

"No one is going to get paid a dime if these bots are damaged, damn it," said Dr. Seth Keshet as he stormed in.

Fresh from running the world-renowned PhD program at Carnegie Mellon's Robotics Institute, tall, dark, and cocky Keshet was one of the top three people in the world in digital topology. But with his meticulously tailored casual suits and visible chest hair, he acted more like a scuzzy Eurotrash club lizard than a famous scientist.

"How many?" he wanted to know.

"A hundred and eleven," said Aaron.

"I need another hundred."

"Another hundred? We've been hitting it since three this afternoon. By when?"

"Six a.m."

"Six? You're effing kidding me. We've been going ten hours now."

"Stop whining. We're on a deadline," the doctor said, checking his Patek Philippe. "That's why I pay you the big bucks."

Aaron pondered this for a moment with a thoroughly depressed look on his face. Then he finally stood.

"I'm sorry, Professor, but I'm done," he said. "You keep your fifty a bot. I can't take it anymore. I'm done. Total toast. I'm going to drop right here."

"Exactly, Seth," said Shui, with an uncharacteristic defiance in her voice. "We're not bots, we're humans. You seem to have lost sight of that."

"Okay, okay," the professor said, changing his tune instantly from demanding to charming. "Sorry for being such an ass. I'm under a lot of pressure. I'll double your pay for tonight. A hundred a bot, but only if you finish."

Aaron looked at him and blew out a breath.

"Fine," he said. "But we're going to need more pizza."

"And Red Bull," said Gia.

"As you wish, my children. Daddy will go get the refreshments," said Keshet as he left the lab.

His iPhone jingled as he hit the school building's concrete stairwell.

How are we looking? the client had texted.

We're on target, Mr. Joyce. No worries. Everything will be ready by six as you said, Keshet texted back.

# Chapter 48

THE SUN BROKE over the top of the trees on the High Line in Chelsea as a dingy white van with the words HARRISON BROS PLUMBING on its side pulled to a stop on West 27th Street between Eleventh and Twelfth Avenues.

As the van idled, a waiflike man-child in a designer business suit biked past over the side street's half-lit, worn pavement. Then a whistling homeless man followed, towing a dirty white leather PING golf bag piled with jingling empties.

Once the men had passed, Mr. Beckett opened the rear door of the van and stepped out onto the street dressed like a plumber.

With the minibots secured, he was there to retrieve the last item on their shopping list. And it was, as the Americans said, quite a doozy.

The plumber's getup was probably a little overkill, he thought. But his image had to be in the hands of the authorities by now, so every caution was most prudent, he knew, as he hit the buzzer of a familiar faded brick tenement building on the street's north side.

Upstairs, Senturk, the bodyguard, was already standing in the open doorway at the end of the second-floor corridor. He wore gray slacks and nice Italian shoes and a white silk dress shirt that was just a little too tight for his soda machine of a torso.

Mr. Beckett felt a rare bead of sweat roll down his back as the green-eyed, muscular Turk wanded him with the metal detector. He knew the man had been in the Milli Istihbarat Teskilati back when the Turkish version of the CIA had been run by the brutal military. Since then, he had been a bodyguard for Middle Eastern billionaire businessmen and sultans and was a hard man of legendary reputation.

Senturk led him in through a door into the back. The rest of the building was a rotten, dusty dump, but back here, it had been transformed into a posh loft. It was the size of an indoor basketball court, with fabric wallpaper and million-dollar lighting and massive modern paintings on the walls.

Ahmed Dzurdzuk, the young man Mr. Beckett had come to see, was sitting behind an impressive, shining chrome desk that looked like it had been made out of a World War II airplane wing. Dzurdzuk didn't bother looking up from whatever he was doing on his iMac as Mr. Beckett sat in the midcentury modern chair in front of the desk.

Mr. Beckett sighed silently at this disrespect. These kids today. He'd been doing business with the psychopathic Chechen crook for the last year. The least he could do was acknowledge Mr. Beckett's existence, but alas, no.

Many people were afraid of the twenty-five-year-old, but Mr. Beckett—not only an experienced connoisseur of dangerous people but also a dangerous person himself—did not fall into that category.

Senturk was a problem, without question, but Ahmed was sloppy, often high, and always distracted.

He could, to borrow an expression from an American book he had once read, swallow the slight, girlish fop with a glass of water.

"Ahmed? Yoo-hoo," Mr. Beckett finally said after a long two minutes.

"Well, my friend, what brings you by for a

face-to-face? You miss me? Ha-ha . . . of course you do. We still have some of that beautiful new Ecstasy from Denmark. Plenty of it. All you want," Ahmed said.

Mr. Beckett glanced to his left at Senturk standing back by the inside of the interior door, just out of earshot. Good. He slowly crossed a leg as he leaned back in his chair.

"The Ecstasy was excellent, but I don't need that. I need what we spoke of on the phone, Ahmed. Remember that item I ordered about three months ago?"

"Come, now," Ahmed said, frowning. "Please, I told you that that fell through, remember?"

"I remember, Ahmed. I don't mind if you want to negotiate, but I'm in a hurry, so you win. I'll double your fee."

"You don't understand. It was seized," Ahmed said as he took a rolled joint out of a cigarette box on his table and lit it with a match.

He tossed the burned match into a filthy crystal ashtray and shrugged.

"That's the risk," he said, blowing ganja smoke up at the twenty-foot-high ceiling.

"I know all about risk," Mr. Beckett said. "I also know that one of your cousins who does your smuggling for you came in on a Nigerian freighter out of the Canary Islands last week. He had a large bag with him when he jumped ship off the coast of Coney Island. It was filled with twenty-seven pounds of C-four plastic explosive. You have it here. Now trot it out, and let's do business."

"How do you know this?" Ahmed said in surprise, putting the joint down. "Scratch that. I don't care. That wasn't your shipment. That was for another client. I can't help you. Honestly. You need to be going now. I have some girls coming over."

"You don't seem to understand," said Mr. Beckett calmly as he reached over and took a long puff on Ahmed's joint. "Here's what you're going to do now. You're going to tell your other client that his shipment was seized, and then you're going to sell his product to me. Simple, okay? Now get off your ass and go get me what I want like a good little boy."

# Chapter 49

AHMED SAT UP in his chair, a dark look on his face, a deeper darkness in his eyes.

"Senturk, can you believe the balls on this fat bastard? No one talks to me like that. Throw this asshole down the stairs. Hard."

"My apologies," said Mr. Beckett in fluent Chechen, smiling. "We've gotten off on the wrong foot. I know the friends you ordered the plastic for. We have the same friends. We are all on the same side here, Ahmed. Don't you see? I'm the one who bombed the subway and killed the mayor and set off the EMP. That was me."

The young punk's jaw dropped.

"You?" said Ahmed in dismay.

Mr. Beckett nodded.

"Yours truly," he said. "And the plastic is needed

to continue our campaign. We are on the same righteous path."

The kid thought about it. You had to give him that. He sat nodding to himself. He wasn't that dumb. Then he shook his head.

Mr. Beckett was up and rolling over the desk faster than the kid could kick out from behind it. They went to the floor in a heap. When they stood, Mr. Beckett had the punk by his curly hair and the ceramic knife he'd hidden in his belt to the kid's throat.

"I'll cut him!" Mr. Beckett exploded at the bodyguard, who had his gun out and trained. "I'll open his carotid artery and write my name on this wall in his spraying blood! Get me my explosives now!"

"You've made a mistake," the evil little Chechen hissed. "Cut my throat and Senturk will blow your fat head off and cut off your balls. You don't know who you're fucking with."

"That makes two of us, I guess," Mr. Beckett said as he finally saw what he'd been waiting for.

It was a refreshing sight, all right.

Mr. Joyce, having picked the locks of the building and apartment doors, stood silently behind Senturk with a suppressed Mossberg 500 in his hand.

Mr. Beckett dove to the floor behind the desk with Ahmed again as the shooting started. The report of the suppressed shotgun was almost musical, like a cymbal shaken in a blanket. Mr. Beckett stuck his head back up after four clangs and smiled.

Senturk, the giant, now looked like a pile of bloody laundry dumped on the floor.

"Where is it? You have it here. We know you never leave here. Where the fuck is it, you little twerp?" said Mr. Joyce, putting the hot metal barrel of the shotgun to Ahmed's forehead.

"Screw you maniacs. I am willing to be martyred!" said Ahmed as he tried lamely to push off Mr. Beckett's iron grip.

"I thought you might say something like that," said Mr. Joyce as he shrugged off the backpack he was wearing. He took something bulky out of it and clunked it onto the desk.

"Let us test your faith, shall we?" Mr. Joyce said as he plugged in the home-kitchen meat-slicing machine they'd just bought from Bed Bath & Beyond.

Ahmed pissed himself as Mr. Beckett chocked his hand into the meat holder, inches from the spinning, shining stainless steel circular blade.

219

"It's in the bedroom closet!" said Ahmed, weeping. "Please! In the upstairs closet—I swear!"

"What a pigsty, Ahmed. Didn't your mommy ever teach you how to make your bed?" Mr. Joyce said after he came down from the bedroom with the duffel bag full of explosives a minute later.

"Please, I can help. I have money. Millions in cash. You know that. I want to help you!" Ahmed said as he dropped out of Mr. Beckett's grip onto his knees.

"You want to help?" Mr. Joyce said.

"Yes, of course. Please," Ahmed said, still weeping.

"Then don't move an inch," Mr. Joyce said, and he raised the shotgun one-handed and shot Ahmed point-blank in the face.

# Chapter 50

UNDER NORMAL CIRCUMSTANCES, Peter Luger Steak House, an old redbrick Brooklyn landmark, would have been a sight for sore eyes.

But nothing is even close to normal, I thought as I pulled into the parking lot across from its famous brown awning.

Emily and I weren't there to chow down on some USDA Prime but to meet up with Chief Fabretti. They'd put the mayor in the ground at Queens's Calvary Cemetery this morning, and a lot of brass and pols had gathered with the mayor's family at his favorite restaurant after the service.

Still too busy scouring through everything we'd found at al Gharsi's to attend the service, Emily and I had watched snatches of it broadcast live on TV.

Several thousand people had attended, including the vice president.

Watching Mayor Doucette's bright American flag–draped coffin being brought through the cemetery gates on a horse-drawn carriage, I couldn't stop shaking my head.

I also couldn't stop thinking about the rousing speech he'd given right before he'd been shot and how he'd bravely insisted on holding the speech outside to help the city heal. Though the sun was shining, it was one very dark day for the city.

I spotted Fabretti straight off inside the door at the end of the three-deep bar talking to a white-shirted female cop who split as we stepped up.

"Mike, Emily—thanks for meeting here on short notice. Drink?" Fabretti said over the crowd hum.

Fabretti tipped his glass at us ceremoniously after the bartender brought us a couple of ice-cold Stellas.

"First, I want to congratulate you guys on a job well done. I knew you wouldn't disappoint me, Mike."

Emily and I looked at each other.

"I can't tell you what a relief it's been to tell those press jackals that we finally have someone in custody," Fabretti continued as he patted me on the shoulder.

"Whoa, boss," I said, shaking my head. "I don't know who you've been talking to, but this thing ain't over."

"What do you mean? You bagged al Gharsi last night, right? He hasn't escaped, has he?"

"No. Al Gharsi is involved. He obviously knows something about the PayPal thing, but he's not behind it," said Emily.

"This guy isn't it?" Fabretti said. "He runs a frickin' terrorist training camp! This guy's affiliated with al Qaeda."

"All that is true, but the level of sophistication of the attacks implies a lot of money and massive technical expertise. A deep thinker with deep pockets. That doesn't exactly describe al Gharsi."

"Emily's right," I said, "especially about the deep pockets. I'd say al Gharsi was on a shoestring budget, except his kids didn't even seem to have any shoes."

"Precisely. The whole place stinks of poverty and desperation," Emily said. "I think al Gharsi was used. Like the NYU students. He was a patsy, a cutout."

"What about his pocket litter? You know, his

computers and cell-phone records. What have you found?" said Fabretti hopefully.

"Nothing conclusive and nothing new," Emily said. "We're not back to square one, but we're close to it."

"Shit," he said, staring a glum hole through the bottles at the back of the bar.

Of course he was upset. Careers had been smashed to pieces over far lesser cases than this. But it wasn't just that, I thought as I remembered Fabretti with his dog in his house—a meeting that felt like it took place a billion years ago. He lived here, too. This was killing him. Killing all of us. The city hadn't been this psychologically screwed up since 9/11.

"We need to find these people," Fabretti said.

I nodded as I stared over the crowded bar into the restaurant. The Tudor beams and dark paneling. The busy waiters in their old-fashioned white shirts and aprons and black bow ties. Looking at them, I thought of all the millions of busy people in the city trying to keep the wheels on, trying to do right, to support and protect their families.

But nothing was safe. Not anymore.

## Part Three

# ALL WORK AND NO PLAY

# Chapter 51

THE NEXT DAWN'S early light found Emily and me on Nineteenth Avenue in East Elmhurst, Queens.

Near the on-ramp of the bridge to the Rikers Island jail, we had the unmarked tucked behind an abandoned truck trailer. To our right was an old chain-link fence with empty gin bottles and scraggly trees behind it. To our left was a four-square-block industrial zone of manufacturing firms and warehouses.

I glanced at my phone as the metal howl of an unseen airliner from nearby LaGuardia Airport ripped through the gray sky overhead.

"What time you got?" I said.

"Another five minutes," Emily said, much more calmly than I felt.

I tucked my phone back into a pouch of my heavy Kevlar vest and blotted sweat off my face with a Dunkin' Donuts napkin.

I'm sweating, all right, I thought as I blinked at the black barrel of the automatic M4 rifle propped upright on the dash beside my knee.

Sweating bullets.

We were about to hit one of the industrial buildings on our second antiterrorist raid in forty-eight hours. This newest lead had come in last night around midnight. It had been sifted out of the electronics that we had collected from al Gharsi's dump upstate. It had been pulled from his kids' Xbox, of all things. The Wi-Fi–linked gaming networks that allowed players to communicate with each other were being used by al Gharsi to make contact with the group of Queens-based terrorists to whom we were about to pay what we hoped was an unexpected morning visit.

This group of nefarious and dangerous American-hating losers was a new one for me. They were Nigerians, and it was speculated that they were members of an offshoot of al Qaeda based in Nigeria called Boko Haram. A hasty surveillance operation on the locale had spotted at least six to eight Nigerian men working, and apparently living, inside a massive carpet- and rug-importing warehouse.

Two of the Nigerians had been identified from photographs as being on student visas. What had really set off alarm bells were the cell-phone records of one of the two students, who had apparently been in contact with a man overseas named Abubar Kwaja. Kwaja was a wanted Nigerian-based wealthy arms dealer who supplied Boko Haram with weapons.

That a half dozen likely heavily armed jihadist jackwads were in such close proximity to LaGuardia Airport was blood-chilling. That's why the brass had let the leash off on a tactical raid immediately. We needed to go on this and go on this now.

Although the new lead was a godsend after such a lack of progress, it was actually a rough setup in terms of takedown. Our target, two blocks away, was an old one-story brick industrial building that covered the whole block from 47th to 46th Streets. The fortresslike building had closed steel shutters over both its doorway and driveway and rusted wire mesh over its windows. It was also somewhat isolated, sandwiched between two storage yards, which put a damper on any kind of flank stealth approach.

There were more than a hundred cops and agents about to swoop in, but I still had a bad feeling. You wanted to model and game a raid for a bit before going into such a heavily fortified target; have backup plans for backup plans; be as prepared as possible. But we didn't have time for all that. Getting in there was not going to be quick or easy by any stretch.

"If there's anything good to say about things," I mumbled to Emily, "at least there aren't a lot of people around."

"Besides me." Emily nodded with her eyes closed and her hands clasped as she said the Lord's Prayer under her breath.

I decided to join her when her phone suddenly pinged with a text.

"Hit it, Mike," she said. "It's a green light. All units converge."

She didn't have to tell me twice. I pinned it, peeling out behind a half dozen other units waiting up and down the desolate block.

Two BearCat armored personnel carriers filled with FBI hostage rescue agents and NYPD ESU cops were already on target by the time I made the corner of 46th. Over the convoy of cop cars, I watched the two formidable black commando trucks swerve into the brick building's driveway, the chug of their big turbo-diesel engines roaring. Two jarheaded commandos in olive-drab Kevlar popped out of the left side door of the lead truck and quickly attached the cable of the truck's winch to the gated doorway. A moment later, there was a high-pitched whine followed by an enormous ripping sound.

"Now, that's what I call a no-knock warrant," I cheered as the entire housing of the target building's rolling gate was torn from the facade.

But I'd spoken too soon. Way too soon.

The wrecked gate had just clattered onto the driveway when the heavy drumroll bang of automatic gunfire erupted from the now gaping hole in the building. The agents on the sidewalk dove behind cars and the balaclava-clad agent in the BearCat's rotating roof turret turtled down as a swarm of bullets and tracers exited the building and raked the truck's thick metal plate.

Then a moment later, I watched in jaw-dropped awe as a series of whooshing, smoking orange flares streaked out from the black, cavelike gap in the building. Smoking contrails accompanied the light streaks as they skimmed inches from the sides of the now rapidly reversing BearCats. Then a string of thunderous explosions ripped chunks off the brick warehouse across the street from the target.

Glass and bricks rained on cop cars as a huge cloud of pale dust billowed, instantly obscuring and darkening the entire narrow street.

"Shit! Back it up! Back it up! We have rockets! RPGs! RPGs!" screamed a voice through the crackling radio.

My mind wobbled as the pale fog billowed over the windshield of my unmarked, leaving behind a pink-sugar dusting of pulverized brick on the hood.

This can't be happening, I thought. *It's impossible*. Am I dreaming? Am I still home in bed?

But I wasn't home in bed. No matter how much I wanted that to be true.

War had come to Queens.

# Chapter 52

I SNAPPED OUT of it as a bullet hit the asphalt just to the right of the car. I bailed left, keeping low, as I put a parked car between me and the gunfire ripping out of the rug warehouse. When there was a pause in the shooting, I bolted out from behind the parked car and across the sidewalk, pressing myself against the building's brick.

I'd just made it when our side recovered and began returning fire. I'd never heard anything like our return fire before in my life. It seemed like a single sound—one ragged, deafening, smashing death wall of gunfire as fifty or sixty agents and cops went full auto at the building at the same time.

I was hunkered down against the brick, thinking that maybe I should head back to my car before I was hit with friendly fire, when someone blew past me in the brick-dust fog. The tall, dark figure flashed past me so fast that I was just able to recognize that instead of a raid jacket he was wearing a light-brown sweat suit with the hoodie pulled up.

And carrying a small AK-47.

Had he come out of a window? Hadn't anyone else seen him? How had he avoided getting shot in the barrage? I wondered as I gaped at his fleeing back.

As if it mattered. I leaped up and bolted after the figure.

It was only as the speeding suspect turned the near corner that my adrenaline kicked down enough for me to realize that I'd left my radio and long gun back in the car. No time to go back now, I thought as I turned the corner, pumping my drawn Glock handgun like it was a relay baton.

I knew per the raid plan that the surrounding blocks were supposed to be in lockdown, patrolled by the local precinct, but someone must have lost the script, because the running Nigerian and I were all by our lonesomes.

When the lean, sprinting Nigerian shifted out into the street, I could see he was almost three-quarters of a block away and getting more distant by the moment. I tried valiantly to keep up, but being past forty and non-Kenyan and wearing Kevlar, I had my work cut out for me.

I cursed when I got to the corner of the next block and saw that the industrial area had become a residential one. As small houses blurred past, I pictured buses and kids going to school.

"Get down! Stay where you are!" I screamed at a woman coming out of her house with a baby in a stroller. How could this thing have gone wrong so quickly?

I'd just made the next corner when I saw the Nigerian start firing at a tow truck passing through the intersection. The driver didn't have a chance as his side window blew in. The truck jumped the curb and smashed into the side of a C-Town supermarket.

The Nigerian wasn't trying to get away, I realized as he ran into the supermarket. He was on a suicide mission, out to kill as many people as possible.

I'd just made the corner past the honking crashed tow truck when automatic gunfire boomed from inside the supermarket and the glass on the market's sliding doors shattered into a million pieces. I dove headfirst beside the truck as screams came from inside, followed by more gunfire.

Wait or go? I thought. Then I climbed back up on my feet, keeping low as I crunched over the broken glass into the store. I swung my Glock over the open produce section on the left. Nothing. No one. I peeked into the first aisle. Again nothing— just cereal boxes.

I broke into another run when I heard screams and then gunfire at the back of the store, in the far right-hand corner. When I got there, I saw the Nigerian raking gunfire over the butcher and fish counters.

I fired my Glock—emptied it at the figure so fast I thought maybe I'd forgotten to fully load the fifteen-round magazine. I reloaded and trained it on the Nigerian as I walked over.

He was down on his back wheezing as he lay in the refrigerated meat case. The hoodie had come down now, and I could see for the first time that it was a woman.

I couldn't believe it.

A tall, regal black woman. Smooth, dark skin shining with sweat and blood from the bullet wound in her jaw. She was still alive. She looked at me, dazed. Then she seemed to notice that the small AK-47 was still in her lap.

"Don't do it!" I said. "Don't!"

But she wouldn't listen.

She went for the gun, and I shot her twice more as the gun in her hand fell over the rim of the meat case and clattered to the worn linoleum.

"Mike! Mike!" said Emily at my back when I knelt in front of the woman a minute or so later. "Mike, are you okay? Are you hit?"

"No," I said. "What happened out there? Did we get them?"

"We got them, all right. Our intel was FUBAR. There were twenty of them, Mike. They all fought to the death. They're all dead."

"Did we lose anyone?"

"No, thank God. An agent was shot in the calf, but he's going to be fine. Are you sure you're okay?"

I nodded, sweat pouring off my chin and cheeks. I shook my head at the Nigerian woman's brains on the glass of the meat case, her blood on the plastic-wrapped packages of sausages and drumsticks.

I stood there searching her face, her expression, her eyes for something—anything—that might explain any of this.

But even after another minute, I didn't see a damn thing.

# Chapter 53

APPREHENSIVE, ANGRY, AND still very much stunned numb, I peeled myself away from the incredible Queens crime scene at a little past one in the afternoon. I looked out at the rubble and the pockmarked, bullet-scarred brick walls as I put the unmarked into drive.

"Welcome to Beirut, Queens," I said to myself as I peeled out around a just-arriving news van.

I decided to head home.

First I showered, then I threw my clothes into the wash, since they were making the apartment smell like a firing range. As the machine filled with water, I poured myself a stiff measure of Wild Turkey and cracked open a bottle of Bud and sat on the couch in the blessedly silent apartment.

Probably not what four out of five doctors

would recommend at quarter to two in the afternoon, but it actually did the trick. My hands stopped shaking, and I was momentarily able to get the image of the dead Nigerian woman's brains out of my mind.

I was well into my next round of Irish therapy when the phone rang. It was Chief Fabretti. I sipped bourbon and listened idly as he chewed my ass about the raid. I wasn't completely sober, but somewhere in there I caught the implication that he thought I might have been responsible for all the deaths.

I decided to hang up on him and shut off my phone.

"There. Much better," I said as I poured another drink.

I was busy making dinner when Seamus came in around two thirty. Corned beef was on the menu tonight. Being an Irishman from New York, I of course did it the Jewish way, deep-sixing the cabbage and replacing it with rye bread—heavy on the caraway seeds—and mustard to make huge Carnegie Deli–style sandwiches.

I wasn't really in the mood for eating, but it was Chrissy's favorite dinner. After what I'd seen today, I wanted to make my baby happy for some strange reason.

"Corned beef? Is it Saint Paddy's Day again?" Seamus said when he peeked into the pot.

"'Tis," I answered as I poured a measure of Wild Turkey into a tumbler for him. "And lucky you: you're just in time for the parade."

He took a sip and smiled and rolled his eyes. He looked good. Still kicking, which was good, because I loved the old man.

"Ye can stop with the eagle-eye treatment, ya know."

"What do you mean?" I said.

"I see you watching me like I'm going to fall over and die. That little incident was a one-off. I'm fine."

"I wasn't worried about you, Father, so much as the glass you're holding," I said as I patted him on his white-haired head. "That Waterford crystal is a family heirloom."

"Little early for the bar to be open, eh?" Seamus said. "Was it that thing in Queens?"

Boy, was the old codger still on the ball.

He hugged me then. Wrapped me in his frail arms like I was five years old again, though I was twice his size. As he did it, I could see the woman lying there in her meat-case coffin. I tried not to cry about it, but I failed.

"God bless you, Mike. It wasn't your fault," Seamus said.

"God bless us all," I whispered through my falling tears.

# Chapter 54

AT FOUR MINUTES past 3:00 a.m., the image appeared on the tablet's touch screen with the light press of a finger.

It was a live video feed, a grainy picture of a dimly lit downtown alley. With a flick of the touch-screen controls, the camera moved forward, zooming in on the dark face of one of the alley's shabby apartment buildings. Then, with another flick, the image teetered suddenly as apartment building windows began to scroll vertically, as if the camera were attached to a crane and someone were raising the boom.

The screen showed a window with a yellowed lace curtain, then, on the floor above it, a window covered by some old broken blinds. The next floor's window was shadeless and showed a bedroom in which a lean Asian woman was in the process of unbuttoning her blouse in a lit bathroom doorway.

The camera went up to the next dark window for a moment before it reversed itself to the disrobing woman.

"Mr. Beckett, please," Mr. Joyce whispered harshly. "We have a schedule, you know. If you can't resist distractions, then promptly hand over the controls."

"Fine," said Mr. Beckett, smiling sheepishly as the camera-equipped drone returned to its ascent.

They were wearing EMT uniforms now and were standing in the back of an idling ambulance parked in a little alley off Worth Street in the heart of downtown Manhattan. They needed to be in the area overnight, and, after some research, they realized that no vehicle was less suspicious or more ubiquitous than an ambulance waiting for a call.

Mr. Joyce nervously wrung his hands as Mr. Beckett piloted the large quadcopter drone over two blocks of buildings and lights. Down at the far end of the alley, across Worth, was some kind of underground dance club. It must have been '70s night or something, because there was a constant muffled thrum of disco music.

He massaged his temples as the drone

approached the imposing, almost industrial-looking square office building that was their target. All they would need was some fool spilling out of the club to take a piss and see the drone.

He knew their attack plan was unprecedented and therefore almost impossible for the enemy to guard against. He'd thought of it himself after much deliberation—had gamed it twenty times, looking for every possible glitch. He knew in his well-informed gut that it would work. But still. Any damn thing could happen in this city. There was knowing it, and then there was actually doing it.

With the drone finally alongside the target, Mr. Beckett swung it right until it was around three feet away from the building's northeast corner, the best route for avoiding detection from the windows. It continued to ascend. Five more floors scrolled past, then ten, and then a few more, and they were finally there. They were finally up on the roof!

"There it is," said Mr. Joyce, pointing at the top left corner of the screen.

"All over it," said Mr. Beckett as he piloted the drone over to the teal-colored metal box that housed the air-conditioning unit.

He pressed a button, and the image on the screen shifted to the camera at the bottom of the drone, beside the power screwdriver they'd installed.

Mr. Joyce held his breath as Mr. Beckett took the drone down slowly toward the edge of the grate covering the AC unit's fans. He maneuvered it carefully, hovering over the first of the Phillips-head screws holding the grate in place. Closer and closer, and then . . . yes! He was there. The tip of the drone's magnetic screwdriver was snug in the groove of the first screw.

"The Eagle has landed," Mr. Beckett said happily as he hit another button.

Forty minutes of meticulous maneuvering later, seven of the eight screws were off, and Mr. Beckett engaged the drone's small grabber, hooked it on the grate, and began shifting the grate little by little. Five minutes after tugging it millimeters at a time, he disengaged the grabber and hovered the drone up to take a look.

Mr. Joyce smiled through the streaks of sweat dripping off his face.

About a third of the AC unit's intake opening had been exposed.

They were in. The door was open. They now had access to the entire iconic building through the HVAC ducts. Every floor and every room!

Mr. Joyce looked away from the screen at the other four large quadcopter drones on the floor of the fake ambulance. Attached to each one of them were the four corners of a dark plastic tarp. Inside the bulging tarp were hundreds and hundreds of cubelike mobile minibots.

Each one of the bots had been filled to capacity with several ounces of the precious plastic explosives, along with a radio-controlled detonator. Once the bots were poured into the AC ducts, they would distribute and maneuver the eighty pounds of explosives to appropriate areas of the building's most vulnerable struts and trusses.

Then, tomorrow morning, just as the enemy sat down at their cubicles with their no-whip nonfat cappuccinos, the two men were going to press a button and blow it up. They were going to blow up the building with everyone in it in the most spectacular way possible.

Mr. Joyce opened the rear doors of the ambulance, then powered up the four big drones using another tablet. He and Mr. Beckett took a step back as the swarm of drones began spinning their quietly whirring blades. It took another thirty seconds, then slowly, with incredible coordination and precision, they began lifting the payload out of the back of the ambulance and upward into the air.

His sweat cooling in the rotor wash, Mr. Joyce giggled as he realized that he actually recognized one of the disco songs that was playing from the other end of the alley.

"I love the nightlife," he sang, bopping his head.

Then he and Mr. Beckett were both laughing as the drones ascended through the dark alley toward the night sky.

# Chapter 55

UP AND AT 'EM at 7:00 a.m., I saw from my e-mail that another massive VIP emergency meeting had been called, this time at One Police Plaza.

Though I had snagged an invite, I hadn't been asked to speak at the meeting for some strange reason. Actually, I knew the reason all too well. My boss, Miriam, had called at dawn and told me that I'd been taken off as lead in the case and would now be taking orders from and reporting to Lieutenant Bryce Miller.

I arrived early enough to score a precious visitor parking spot at One Police Plaza, which was no small feat, considering how many people worked in the neighborhood's courthouses and government buildings. On the crowded eighth floor of the brown brick monolith, I spotted Chief Fabretti in the hallway. Instead of giving me his usual hail-fellow-well-met routine, he blew past me with his iPhone glued to his ear and an evil look glued to his face, like I was empty air.

I actually didn't really care or really even blame him. The situation and the stress level everyone was under had reached the impossible zone. I knew we all wanted the same thing—for the killing to stop and for this horror to be over.

I had a little time before the meeting, so I hit the break room, where I managed to score the last three survivors in a box of cinnamon Munchkins. There was no more coffee, so I had to settle for green tea that I made semitolerable once I poured in a lot of half-and-half and sugar.

I took my grub over to a corner window over-looking the Foley Square courthouses to the northwest and gave Emily a call.

"Hey, Agent. There you are," I said when she answered. "I tried to call you earlier, but you must have been in the shower or something. I'm down here at One PP at the latest big emergency meeting. Are you heading over or what?"

"Not this time," Emily said. "Like dogs and people without shirts, feds aren't allowed, apparently. The press is asking questions about what they're calling 'shortsighted and brutal' tactics at the Queens raid yesterday, and now everybody involved is working overtime to throw anyone they can grab under the bus. So much for our happy task force. Looks like the feds and the department are so pissed at one another this morning they're no longer talking."

I laughed grimly.

"Great. Dissension and infighting are just what we need while the city is being dismantled brick by brick. So what are you doing?"

"I'm at *our* VIP emergency meeting, of course. Just a couple of blocks from you at Twenty-Six Fed."

"So close and yet so far," I said, looking at the federal building two blocks away, above the courthouses. "Hey, after our respective ass-covering sessions, how about Chinese for lunch? Wo Hop. My treat."

"Wo Hop?" Emily said. "How could I turn that down?"

# Chapter 56

*So . . . how's your morning going?*

Gary Friedman smiled as he dropped his mop in the corner of the stairwell landing. He sat down, light-headed, as he looked at the text that had just come in on his phone from Gina.

He couldn't stop smiling. Or reading the text.

"Thank you, Lord," he said, kissing his Galaxy.

He really wasn't one for screwing off and getting lost in his phone like a lot of the other guys on the maintenance crew. Especially after his rat bastard of a boss, Freddie, busted him playing Angry Birds two weeks back and chewed him out in front of everybody. Just because they worked in a law enforcement building, Freddie thought he was *in* law enforcement, the stupid jackwad.

But after last night, after *the* best night of his

life, Gary didn't care, he thought as he reread Gina's text. Things were changing in the life of Gary Irving Friedman—for the better, finally.

Like a lot of his classmates at Brandeis, he'd moved to Brooklyn from Boston straight after graduation. With his cinematography degree and his award-winning short film under his belt, he'd thought it'd be just a matter of hooking up with other young artists in the borough's vibrant arts scene, then it would be Hollywood, here I come.

But he soon woke up and smelled the fair trade coffee, because practically everybody he knew in Williamsburg had a cinematography degree and a short-film award or was in a band or had a writing MFA. What none of them had were connections. Or jobs in their respective winner-take-all fields.

Six months in, when his summer job money ran out and the janitor job came up through a friend of a friend, he was dumbfounded. A fucking janitor? It was a government job, with job security and benefits and all that, and it actually paid pretty well, but his father was an eye doctor, for the love of Pete, and he was going to be scrubbing urinals?!

But in the end, he took it. Swallowed his pride. Because it was either start mopping or go home to Dr. Friedman's musty beige basement in Brockton.

He'd decided to stick it out and mop it up.

And the whole time he'd been trying to meet girls, but it had been one depressing strikeout after another. Until last night. There he was, wallowing in the misery of his Xbox as usual, when the doorbell rang and the black-haired Katy Perry look-alike from downstairs was standing there, drunk. She'd broken her key in her door, and could he help her? Why, yes, as a matter of fact he could! Five minutes later, he was knight-in-shining-armoring it down the fire escape into her apartment window.

In thanks, she poured him a Grey Goose, and they started talking, and the rest of the night was a blur of vodka shots and telling her his life story and showing her his short and her going gaga over it and then they were making out on her bed. They didn't go all the way but damn close. Damn, damn close.

And now she was texting him!

Gary stared at the screen again, still not completely convinced it wasn't a mirage. There was probably some advice about what to do next, play hard to get or something, but he didn't give a shit. She was hot and she liked him. Told him he was talented and funny, and it was like his Brooklyn dream was finally coming true and—

That's when Gary heard it. It was a weird sound. It seemed to be coming from above him, on the ceiling of the stairwell. It was a little whirring sound followed by a couple of metallic clicks.

He looked up as he heard it again. It seemed like it was coming from inside the rectangular AC duct above him. Then there were more of the sounds. A lot more. "What the hell?" Gary said, standing. It sounded like someone had dumped a box of Chiclets into the aluminum duct, only weirder.

"Freddie?" Gary said, keying his radio.

"What now?" said his perpetually surly bastard of a boss, who was outside hosing the sidewalk.

"I don't know. There's something weird up here. I'm on the sixth floor in stairwell C."

"Weird how?"

"I don't know, but you should come up."

"This better be good," Freddie replied.

# Chapter 57

THE AMBULANCE WAS on Park Row beside a coffee cart when the sun came up. They'd had to move twice during the night to avoid suspicion. It didn't matter where they were as long as they were within the two thousand feet of the bots' radio receiver.

"Hey, what the hell is that?" said Mr. Beckett around a crumbling apple turnover as he suddenly saw something on the screen.

The tablet screen was divided into a grid of hundreds of little boxes now, a view from the camera on each individual bot. Mr. Beckett didn't know how Mr. Joyce was keeping track of them all. It looked like a lot of gobbledygook to him, but then again, he wasn't a mathematical genius with an IQ of 170, like Mr. Joyce.

"Which? Where? What?" said Mr. Joyce, who was as frazzled as Mr. Beckett had ever seen him. The guy had been a ball of sweat and nerves all night as he clicked at the keyboard, moving all the bots around. It was a miracle he didn't have carpal tunnel syndrome.

"It's a face, I think. In this one. Can you make it larger?" Mr. Beckett said.

Mr. Joyce hit a button and, lo and behold, a confused-looking Hispanic guy wearing a maintenance uniform appeared on the screen, as if he'd just snapped a puzzled selfie.

"Maintenance!" Mr. Beckett cried. "They must have heard the bots in the duct. Shit! Detonate now! It's our only chance!"

"No," Mr. Joyce said, clicking the man off the screen and going back to his typing.

"What are you talking about?"

"I need more time," he said calmly. "It's not ready yet."

"Time just ran out," Mr. Beckett cried as he shook Mr. Joyce's shoulder. "We're discovered. We need to go with what we got now!"

"No," said Mr. Joyce more firmly. He flipped a page in the pile of the building's schematics on the workbench beside the tablet and began typing even faster.

"I need ten minutes," he said. "We're that close. My calculations do not lie. We can still get it done. Think about it. They don't know what the bots even are. It will take time for them to call the bomb squad and piece it together and sound the alarm. By then I'll be ready. I promise."

"Well, hurry up already, would you please?" Mr. Beckett said, going to the aluminum blinds on the ambulance window that faced the target.

# Chapter 58

I IMMEDIATELY SPOTTED the commissioner and the acting mayor, Priscilla Atkinson, in attendance when I entered the huge, crowded conference room. As I glanced up to the nose-bleed section of the amphitheater seating, I was happy to see Brooklyn Kale and Arturo and Doyle and climbed up and sat down next to them.

Down on the floor in the center of the room, I could see my new fair-haired leader, Lieutenant Bryce Miller, going over his notes. I was almost glad I'd been taken off as case lead. It was high time to allow another Christian to be fed to the lions.

Someone dimmed the lighting, and a satellite image of the Queens warehouse from yesterday's raid appeared. Bryce had just stepped to the podium and was still adjusting the microphone when the conference room doors burst open and two uniformed cops rushed in.

One of them made a beeline for the commissioner and whispered in his ear. I sat up straight when the puzzled, annoyed look on the commissioner's face became one of intense concern.

"Ms. Mayor, everyone, excuse me," the commissioner said, standing as the lights came back on.

Brooklyn and Arturo and Doyle and I all looked at each other with the same wide-eyed expression.

"Good grief. What the hell now?" Brooklyn said.

"Something has come up," the commissioner said. "I'll explain in a minute, but right now I'm going to need everyone to please stand and calmly head for the stairwells and proceed outside."

He cleared his throat as everyone started freaking out.

"Quiet, now, everybody, okay? Head for the exit immediately. We have a problem. A red terrorist alert has been issued. We need to evacuate the building."

# Chapter 59

"I TOLD YOU, you stupid bastard," Mr. Beckett said from the window, where he looked at the building through binoculars. "They're coming out now! They're evacuating! Blow it now!"

"One more minute," said Mr. Joyce.

"No! Now!" Mr. Beckett cried. He watched as a truck pulled up in front of the building and a guy leaped out with a black Lab in tow.

"It's the bomb squad! Do it now!"

"One second," said Mr. Joyce, clicking away at the keyboard like a jazz piano soloist. "Just a couple more adjustments."

Mr. Beckett tore a schematic in half and kicked the cooler. "You've adjusted it enough! It's now or never!"

Mr. Joyce ignored him, eyes on the screen, clicking buttons like mad.

Mr. Beckett looked through the binocs again, then started banging his head against the ambulance's metal wall.

"Blow it," he whimpered. "Blow it."

"How many times do I have to tell you?" Mr. Joyce said. "It's all about the placement, otherwise it'll do cosmetic damage at best."

"I don't give a shit! Blow the damn thing now!"

"Fine," said Mr. Joyce. "You win. Just so you know, it's not ready."

"Blow it!"

"First say that it's your call," said Mr. Joyce. "I don't want you blaming this on me later."

"It's my call! It's my call!" Mr. Beckett cried.

Mr. Joyce set off the detonators on the eighty pounds of plastic explosives with a soft press of his thumb.

# Chapter 60

WE WERE IN the stairwell, nervous, feeling as powerless as schoolchildren in a teacher-led fire drill. It wasn't the weird sound we suddenly heard that was that concerning. It was the hard shudder that a moment later came up through the ground and wrenched through the stairs and walls into the marrow of our bones.

Everyone stopped dead on the stairs with a collective gasp as the concrete drunkenly swayed back and forth under our feet. I looked up immediately at the ceiling, along with everyone else, suddenly feeling the hard beating of my heart as I wondered if it was about to drop down on top of us.

"Oh, my God, Mike! Look!" said Brooklyn, elbowing me in the neck as she pointed up at the stairwell window.

I looked.

Behind the courthouses, up on Broadway, about two long blocks away, I saw 26 Federal Plaza, the huge, monolithic FBI headquarters building. Something was wrong. Smoke was rising in the air above it. The smoke seemed to be coming from many of its seemingly blown-open windows.

*Emily!*

I watched helplessly as more of its windows blew out simultaneously, almost in a left-to-right diagonal line, flashing with a blinding white light.

I looked silently at what happened next.

The top floors of 26 Fed seemed to tremble and waft back and forth. There was a thunderclap crack of concrete and a horrid creak and groan of shearing steel. Then the top stories of the building freed themselves from their blown moorings and slowly slid away into empty air.

"Dear holy God," I said. The building around us rocked again as most of 26 Fed's million-pound avalanche of glass and stone crashed down onto the streets below.

When I peeled my eyes away from the mushrooming dust cloud out the window, I could hear somebody crying. It was the mayor, two steps above me. She was bawling her eyes out.

"They're dead," she kept saying as she crumpled to the floor. "They're dead. They're all dead."

Every cop there turned and looked at each other as the dust plume rose into the sky. Doyle and Arturo and Brooklyn and Chief Fabretti. The shock was fine. What wasn't so fine was the fear. The pale and shivering crazed looks of fear.

"Déjà vu all over again," said Doyle, licking his lips. He had his gun in his hand. I gently helped him put it away.

"This is crazy. This is crazy. This is crazy," said Arturo hysterically.

I put my arm on Arturo's shoulder. I opened my mouth, but I was speechless. He was in shock, the same as me. He was also right.

Then I was running down the stairs two by two, speed-dialing Emily as I began to pray that she miraculously might still be alive.

# Chapter 61

I HIT THE street and ran as fast as I could up narrow Saint Andrew's Plaza toward the destruction.

I couldn't tear my eyes away from the sky above the buildings. A misty cloud of gray dust was above it. It kept billowing wider and wider. Within the expanding gray cloud was a confetti-like, glittering mass of debris that I realized after a moment was paper.

I kept trying to call Emily as I ran, but her phone kept kicking into voice mail.

Maybe she's just on the phone, I thought with desperate hope. Or her phone needs charging. Or the cell sites are down.

As I neared Foley Square, the Irish prayer to Saint Michael, the patron saint of cops, which Seamus had made me memorize when I graduated from the academy, suddenly popped into my head.

*Blessed Michael, archangel, defend us in this hour of conflict. Be our safeguard against the wickedness and . . .* something, something *. . . thrust Satan down to hell and with him those other wicked spirits who wander through the world for the ruin of souls.*

"And please let Emily be okay, God," I whispered. "Let me have this one. You have to let me have just this one, please. Amen."

Fire-truck horns blatted and blasted in the distance as I finally sprinted past the row of Corinthian columns fronting the Thurgood Marshall courthouse into Foley Square. I was going at a pretty good clip, but when I glanced up and got my first good look at 26 Fed, I immediately slowed, then abruptly stopped in my tracks and just stood there in the street staring up, completely overwhelmed by what I was seeing.

Twenty-Six Federal Plaza's normally perfectly sleek rectilinear forty-one-story glass-and-stone slab now looked like a giant cereal box that had been chewed up by a rabid pit bull. I grimaced at the grid of exposed offices in the horrifically wrecked upper half of the skyscraper. Everything was completely pulverized. Every ruined nook and cranny was filled with smoking wreckage.

An even harder pulse of dread shuddered through me as I suddenly noticed that what remained of the structure was still visibly swaying back and forth. I gripped down hard on my cell phone, wondering if I was about to watch the rest of it go, about to see it start pancaking down like the Twin Towers on 9/11.

When it didn't happen immediately, I started racking my brain, trying to remember the one or two times I had been in the FBI building. I tried to think what floor Emily's office or morning meeting room might have been on, but for the life of me, I couldn't remember. All I could do was stand there feeling numb as I stared up at the torn-apart office tower.

I wasn't the only one. All over Foley Square, I saw people standing silently out on the steps of the courthouses and on the sidewalks in front of the government buildings. The ones who weren't filming with their smartphones were like me—just standing there frozen, a regiment of jaw-dropped statues staring up.

Somehow, after a minute or two, I shook myself out of my stupor and continued haltingly up

Lafayette Street. When I got to the next corner, at Worth Street, I looked to the left—west, toward Broadway.

When I saw the devastation up close for the first time, I shook my head. I couldn't believe it.

*How could anyone?*

It looked like the entire top half of 26 Federal Plaza had fallen into Worth Street, filling it up like dirt in a trench. Through the concrete dust, I could make out a dark, immense, almost three-story mound of debris that completely blocked the street and both sidewalks.

At its top, a half dozen steel girders stuck up crookedly like a stand of burned, branchless trees. Around the girders, huge folded sections of the office building's distinctive facade were slumped over on themselves like unspooled bolts of cloth. In the warm breeze that hit my sweating face, I smelled the acrid, industrial stink of burned metal and plastic.

A falling, flapping sheet of paper suddenly hit me in the temple like a tap, and I began shuffling forward at the terrible mound through the haze.

# Chapter 62

THERE WAS A soft flapping sound as a steady rain of printer-paper sheets fell down around me. The dust above must have been doing something to the light, because everything was tinted with a strange, unreal bluish tinge.

I walked up the wide sidewalk around a haphazard maze of splintered desks, smashed office chairs, and cracked computer screens. I blinked down at an intact framed bachelor's degree from Tulane University propped up against the gutter as if someone had placed it there.

As I continued my approach, a tall, skinny black bike messenger with a scratched face silently staggered past in the street, covered in a pale-gray coating of dust.

Then I came closer and saw something really amazing.

People were already up on the mound of debris, a dozen or so people. There were a few uniformed cops, but mostly they were civilians—office workers, a guy in a white doctor's coat, a loose line of people silently passing down debris and rubble.

I climbed up over some chunks of concrete, immediately joining them. As the dry, stale taste of concrete and drywall dust filled my nostrils and mouth, I accepted a huge hunk of concrete from a short, Italian-looking guy in a ruined pinstriped suit above me. As I turned to heave it, I saw that a burly uniformed security guard had arrived behind me, waiting to accept it.

"What happened?" the guard said to me as I passed him the concrete.

I squinted at him. He was a really distinctive-looking guy. He had longish brown hair under his navy ball cap and bright, light-blue eyes. He must have played football in college or something, because he was jacked.

"Someone said it was a plane," he said as I continued to stare at him stupidly. "Was it a plane?"

After he handed the concrete to the next person down the line, I shook my head and carefully passed him the two-yard length of fractured rebar I'd just been handed.

"It was explosives," I finally said. "I saw it. They blew it. Someone took it down with high explosives or something. Demo'd it, like. I didn't see a plane."

That's when my cell phone went off in my pocket. I crouched down in the wreckage, frenziedly wiping the dust-covered screen to see who was calling.

I closed my eyes with relief as my heart somersaulted in my chest.

All was not lost. There was still hope. A tiny drop.

"Emily?!" I yelled as I put the phone to my ear.

"Mike! Are you okay?" she said. "We got hit. I just made it out of the building. Someone said you guys were hit as well. Are you okay?"

Thank you, God. You came through. Thank you. And Saint Michael. You guys came through. I owe you.

I clenched back my tears of relief. Then I couldn't anymore.

"Yes," I said, wiping dust and tears off my face. "I'm fine. Perfect now. Where are you?"

"On the west side of Broadway near Worth."

"Okay, stay where you are. I'm coming to you."

When I stood and turned around again to ask the muscular security guard to take my place in line, I stopped and just stood there blinking.

Because all of a sudden the guy, whoever he had been, *whatever* he had been, was gone.

# Chapter 63

THE NEXT THREE days were some of the most tumultuous in New York City's history.

Twenty-two people had died in the blast. Eleven special agents (one of them the direct assistant to the head of the New York office), three civilian clerks, and eight maintenance and security people. More than a hundred were still in the hospital, many with internal injuries from being crushed under heavy debris when the building collapsed. Many people were missing fingers, arms, eyes, feet. The fact that half of Manhattan's hospitals were still out of commission after the EMP blast in Yorkville did not help the situation at all.

The initial investigation into the bombing showed that it had been as ingenious as it had been devastating. Incredibly, robots had been used.

Investigators had found three unexploded robots in the pile. They looked like miniature children's blocks, but inside they had intricate flywheels and radio receivers and electronics that allowed them to be moved around remotely, like a swarm of insects. In addition to the electronics, the bots had been laden with explosives and had been inserted probably through the AC unit on the roof into the air ducts.

Experts were speculating that whoever had radio-controlled the bots into position must have been an engineer or a demolitions expert, because each unit had been precisely placed alongside the building's support struts for maximum destruction.

As in the aftermath of 9/11, the governor of New York had issued a citywide state of emergency, and the National Guard was called in. Soldiers armed with rifles stood at multiple checkpoints throughout the city, with countersniper teams on various rooftops. There were even rumors that there was a CIA surveillance drone high in the air above New York City 24-7. It was truly unreal.

But instead of committing the mentally unhealthy act of dwelling on things, Emily and I and my Ombudsman Outreach squaddies busied ourselves by doubling down, trying to shake out everything we could on the investigation. It was all dead ends so far, but something would break. It had to. Or at least we couldn't stop believing that it would.

"If they're terrorists, Mike, then why won't they contact us, claim credit?" said Noah Robertson, starting up our Friday morning team meeting at the Intelligence Division building in Brooklyn.

We were all camped around my desk—Emily and Arturo in commandeered office chairs, which were in high demand since about a hundred cops had been reassigned to the case. Doyle and Brooklyn and Noah were actually sitting on the floor against the partition wall among the stacks of paper and coffee cups and pizza boxes that were strewn around the once-fancy office space.

Everyone was in jeans and hoodies and T-shirts—even Emily, who was usually in her FBI-mandated fancy office clothes. Non-stop sixteen-hour days tend to make everyone a little less formal.

"Because that would be the conventional thing," Emily said, picking one of the little bots they'd found in the rubble off my desk.

"These guys don't do conventional," she said, tossing the bot into the air and catching it.

"They figure it's even more terrifying to not claim credit, to continue to stay in the shadows being a faceless menace," I said.

"I think they might be right," said Arturo around the straw of his blue Coolatta.

"But they are terrorists, right? I mean, they have to be, considering how well financed they are," Brooklyn said. "Only a team of computer experts could have come up with that robot swarm bomb, or whatever the hell you want to call it."

"Or built those EMP devices," said Doyle, yawning. "Hell, we've all heard the rumors. It's most likely being sponsored by a foreign government."

"No," I said as I stared up at the ceiling.

"Earth to Mike," Doyle said after a beat of silence.

"It's not a government or even a team of terrorists. It's too . . . elegant," I said, snatching the bot Emily was tossing out of the air.

"For all its destruction, this is handcrafted," I said. "It's one or two people. This is being done to precision. The attacks. The head fakes. And if you want something done this right, you have to do it yourself."

# Chapter 64

"ONE OR TWO people are systematically leveling New York City?" said Arturo as he made an annoying squeaking sound with his drink straw. "How? It's impossible."

"In 2000, there was a famous article in *Wired* magazine," I said. "Some computer genius sat down and mapped out how all these new computer-assisted breakthroughs in technology will pan out. The potential pitfalls of things like artificial intelligence and nanotech and robotics and biotech."

"I think I read it," Noah said. "It was written by the guy who cofounded Sun Microsystems and created Java, right?"

"That's the guy," I said. "One of the theories in the article is that as computer tech gets more powerful for regular folks and makes their lives easier, this more powerful tech could also put power into the hands of disgruntled individuals."

I rolled the bot in my palm like it was a die.

"That's what I think is happening here," I said. "We're seeing the pivot where cutting-edge technology, being very well utilized by two or even just one motivated nut job, can kill a massive amount of people."

"One guy is doing all this?" Arturo snorted. "C'mon."

"You don't believe me?" I said. "Then what about the Unabomber?"

"Who?"

"Ted Kaczynski. For twenty years, this guy went on a nationwide bombing campaign from a cabin in Montana that didn't have electricity or running water. What he had instead was an extremely keen intelligence that he used to make incredibly intricate letter bombs. And that was in the seventies and eighties. Imagine what he could do today if he was free.

"What I think we have here is a Kaczynski-level intelligence running amok."

"I can't believe you just said that," Emily said, suddenly frantically thumbing her phone.

"What?" I said.

"Ted Kaczynski. Two days ago, I got an e-mail from the Washington office," she said, tapping her cell screen. "Here it is. The Bureau of Prisons sent a request from Kaczynski to the FBI. He said he saw the news of the bombing and put in a request through his lawyer to help us.

"Which I and everybody at the Bureau dismissed as crazy. Until now. I think you're right, Mike. About the intelligence involved here. It's very similar to Kaczynski's. Maybe we should interview him."

"Interview the Unabomber?"

"Yes," Emily said. "Why not? He's completely brilliant and crazy. Just like the person we're trying to catch. Maybe he can give us some insight."

"How is the Unabomber still alive?" said Brooklyn. "Didn't the feds execute him?"

"You're thinking of Timothy McVeigh, the Oklahoma City bomber," said Doyle.

"Doyle's right. Kaczynski is alive," Emily said. "He's in his seventies now and housed at the fed supermax in Florence, Colorado. So what do you say, Mike? My bosses couldn't be more ready to do something. This is the worst loss of life in the Bureau's history. Let's go talk to him."

"When?" I said.

"Ain't no time like the present," she said. "There's a Bureau plane at Teterboro that flew in the director for all the funerals. I'll get us on it. What do you say?"

I rolled the strangely heavy little bot across the blotter of my cluttered desk and peered at it.

"I say let's go to Colorado."

# Chapter 65

IT WAS EVENING when the FBI Gulfstream V bounced down hard onto the tarmac of the Fremont County Airport in Colorado.

Two young male agents were standing beside a black Ford Explorer outside the aircraft's dropped door. They speedily helped move us and our files and bags into the backseat before spinning the roof lights as they floored it out of the rural airport and onto the service road.

As we got onto a highway, outside my window in the distance, I could see the blood-orange glow of the sun that must have just settled behind the dark, serrated peaks of the Rocky Mountains.

"Well, what do you know?" I said to Emily through a yawn as we looked over the piles of Unabomber case files. "Those mountains actually do look like the ones on the beer cans, huh? Speaking of which, where is the Coors brewery? Close by? Do they give tours? With tastings?"

"Unfortunately, that'll have to be the next trip, Mike. The warden is waiting on us," Emily said as she opened a laptop. "But believe me, when this is over, the first six-pack of Silver Bullets will be on me."

Known sometimes as the Alcatraz of the Rockies, ADX Florence is a 490-bed concrete-and-steel hotel that the feds reserve for its system's most notorious and most extremely violent prisoners. In addition to Kaczynski, it houses convicted foreign and domestic terrorists, spies like the ex–FBI agent scum Robert Hanssen, and leaders of the Aryan Brotherhood and the Gangster Disciples.

"So, Mike, what do you think? You've read the files. You ready to talk to Ted?" said Emily as our SUV went up the long driveway and was buzzed in at the gate, flanked by towers manned with armed guards.

"I don't know," I said as we rolled in past the twelve-foot-high fencing, topped with razor wire. "The guy isn't your regular perp, is he? I never interviewed a killer who went to Harvard at sixteen or was a Berkeley math professor at twenty-five.

Why do you think he wants to talk to us now? He's never offered his help before."

Emily shrugged.

"I guess we're about to find out."

The assistant warden was a tough, matronly Native American woman named Marjorie Greene. She met us at the administration building's sally port and helped us get through processing, where we handed over our service weapons.

The inside of the prison was like no facility I'd ever been to. Everything was made of smooth poured concrete—the floors, the walls, the ceiling. There wasn't a window in sight. Prisons are usually loud, with slamming gates and people yelling, but here it was quiet and almost bizarrely serene.

"Like walking into a spaceship or something, isn't it?" Marjorie Greene said as she led us with four guards down a meandering corridor to the interview room. "They designed it that way on purpose, so the prisoners don't know where they are in relation to the outside. I don't even know myself half the time, and I've been here seven years."

"Seems like overkill, no?" said Emily. "Aren't they locked down in their cells twenty-three hours a day at a supermax?"

"Well, it's not so much that the inmates will escape from in here per se," Marjorie explained as we walked. "It's that some of these guys are heads of the kinds of organizations that actually might try to break them out from the outside."

"What's Kaczynski like as a prisoner?" I said.

"Tidy cell. Nice rapport with staff. Reads a lot. Figures, his being a genius and all. Never caused any kind of trouble. Quiet as a church mouse, really. He's . . . different. You'll see."

We came down some steps into another concrete corridor with a lower ceiling and a frosted, probably bulletproof, Plexiglas door at the far end. One of the four guards slipped a long tubelike key into a metal box beside the door as Marjorie Greene spoke into her radio. A moment later, there was an electric buzz and the crack of a lock snapping open.

I took a deep breath as the guard opened the door.

And then I was standing there looking at the Unabomber in the flesh.

He didn't look like the famous crazy-mountain-man picture of him taken when he was arrested. He was clean-shaven and just looked sort of oldish, with age spots on his forehead and skin drooping off the sharp bones of his face. You wouldn't know who he was—just some sickly-looking man in a baggy orange jumpsuit.

It was actually bordering on ridiculous that this scarecrow of a man, who looked as threatening as a kitten, was cuffed to a concrete desk behind a set of thick steel bars that divided the room.

"Thank you for coming," he said, smiling weakly, as one of the guards slammed the door closed and locked us in. "I didn't think you'd take me up on my offer. I'm surprised, not to mention hopeful."

# Chapter 66

"I'M AGENT PARKER. This is Detective Bennett. We don't have a lot of time here, so why don't we get to it?" Emily said, clicking her phone to record the conversation as we sat in the two folding chairs in front of the bars. "Why did you want to talk to us today, Mr. Kaczynski?"

He looked at us with his lips pursed for a second, like he was mulling something over.

"They're going to destroy New York City—you know that, right?" he finally said. "That's going to be next. The next step. The entire city will be destroyed."

Emily and I exchanged a glance.

"Um, how do you know that?" I said. "Do you know the people who are doing this?"

"It isn't people," Kaczynski said. "There is one

person behind this. One genius, and he's good. And he's toying with you. Punishing you. Unless you get a bead on this person in the next few days, I would recommend evacuating New York City. Because the loss of life will be like nothing ever seen."

We stared at him. What was disturbing was the dead certainty in his tone. He seemed incredibly sure of what he was saying.

"You didn't answer our question. Do you know these people?" Emily repeated.

"No. I don't know them personally, of course," Kaczynski said, "but I know what they're like. I used to be this person. Technically gifted, highly intelligent, dedicated, and very, very angry. You should be looking for someone like me. Someone who knows advanced math and computer science, maybe a chess master or a think-tank guy. Whoever it is, he is highly analytical and lives alone, most likely in a messy place. Look for a hoarder, probably someone on the autistic spectrum, a man who lives exclusively inside the expansive confines of his own head."

"What do you think will happen to the city?"

"Something huge and unexpected—something biological, perhaps. Or who knows? Even something to do with nanotechnology. Schopenhauer said that a smart man can hit a target that others can't reach, but a genius can hit a target that others can't see.

"I think you're up against a genius here, unfortunately. God help all of us if this guy knows nanotech. He could come up with an artificial virus that destroys the world's vegetation or oxygen or water supply. You really have to catch this guy!"

# Chapter 67

"WHY DO YOU think total destruction will be next?" I asked.

"Because it's the next logical step," Kaczynski continued. "The last and final upping of the ante. The perpetrator hasn't asked for money, has he? He hasn't claimed credit for some cause. That's because the man behind this doesn't have any ulterior motive. He just wants to destroy New York City— or who knows? All of humanity, maybe."

"Why do you care about all this, Mr. Kaczynski?" I said. "I mean, three people were killed and many others maimed, and the entire country was terrorized by your campaign. You even tried to blow up an airliner. I'd think if anything you'd be rooting for the destruction of New York City."

He took a deep breath and looked down at the

floor. His bony fingers began to drum loudly on the concrete desk.

"How many times do I have to explain this? In the beginning, all I wanted to do was to live freely by myself in Montana. I didn't want a damn thing from anyone. Just to be left alone. But one day I went for a hike, and I saw that industrial society would never leave me alone. I'll admit I was angry and motivated by revenge against the system. But quite quickly, I began to see my bombing campaign as a way to wake people up to the existential threat posed by technology, which I detailed in my *Times* article.

"The fact that someone is now blowing up New York with advanced technology is the very outcome I was trying to warn everyone about. Your bomber wants to destroy New York City and maybe the world. I never wanted that! Don't you see? I wanted to stop humanity from killing itself. I wanted to stop things so a guy like the one you're dealing with here would never have the power to do what he's doing. My campaign was to see the world saved."

He was referring to his antitechnology manifesto, which the *New York Times* and *Washington Post* had agreed to publish in 1995 in order to stop him from sending mail bombs. I'd read it on the plane, and though it was definitely bonkers in parts, I found it surprisingly well written.

"So you still think technology is going to destroy the world?" Emily said.

"Going to?" he said, wide-eyed. "It's happening right before our very eyes! How much time do you spend with your smartphone? A lot, I bet. More than you spend with your spouse. Than with your children. Even the guards here. I see them. They're good men set to keep watch and protect the world from some of the worst criminals on earth, and here they are sneaking little peeks at the screen. It's here. We're already dependent on the machines."

He winced as he rubbed a hand through his hair nervously.

"It's simple, really. The more we ask technology to do for us, the more power we have to give it. Right now, the world's most brilliant minds are designing artificial intelligence and robots that they think will solve all our problems but will only spell doom for the entire human race! Human beings can't handle this kind of power. Who could? Once AI and robots are in place, they will either destroy humanity outright or give one person—the head of Google, say—a measure of godlike power that Caligula never dreamed was possible.

"Right now, who is really more powerful? Google or the NSA? How about tomorrow? I tried to stop all this from happening. I saw what was coming. Now, if you actually solve this case and prevent this nut from wiping everyone out, I think you have another chance to finally make the threat visible to the world. You have to open people's eyes!"

"But I don't understand. How does what you've said relate to the bombings in New York?" Emily said.

"Can't you see what you've got here?" Kaczynski said, starting to rock back and forth in his chair. "This case is an opportunity for you guys in the political system and law enforcement to do your jobs and protect the public. You need to highlight the dire danger that computer technology is posing.

"You need to use this as a lever to urge politicians to pass cautionary laws to put a stop to drones and especially robotics and artificial intelligence. People urge gun control after a school shooting, right? Well, we won't have to worry about a school shooter in the near future because he'll be cooking up a genetically engineered supervirus in his basement, and everyone on earth will be dead. You need to ensure that these technologies are treated like radioactive nuclear material, because that's how dangerous this is, and—"

"Thanks for the advice, Mr. Kaczynski, but unfortunately, we didn't come out here to sit and talk the politics of technology. Do you have any more specific information on our case?"

"Well, no," he said, gaping at Emily.

"Okay, this interview is over, then. Thanks for your help, Mr. Kaczynski," I said, standing with a sigh.

Tears sprang into his eyes as we knocked on the door to summon the guard. Kaczynski rapidly tapped at the concrete desk with a gaunt finger.

"We're at the precipice, don't you see?" he said. "The precipice! Only you guys can slam on the brakes here! You have to! This is bigger than New York City! It may be our last chance."

# Chapter 68

"SORRY, MIKE. THAT was pretty fruitless," Emily said as we were driving back into Manhattan from Teterboro Airport after our return flight the following evening.

"What do you mean?" I said as I tapped impatiently on the steering wheel. We sat at a dead stop after going through the George Washington Bridge tolls. Up ahead on the span, blue and red emergency lights flashed around a broken-down charter bus they were trying to tow away.

"I should have anticipated that Kaczynski would only use this as an opportunity to spew his warped ideology. We probably would have done better if we'd hit the Coors tour, like you said."

"Chin up, Parker," I said. "We took a stab. Besides, I think he gave us some insight into our perpetrator or at least confirmed what we were already thinking. And oddly enough, some of the stuff he said about technology I think is actually true. These military robots they're starting to build really are scary.

"And this self-driving smartcar idea? Maybe it'll make some things cheaper, but won't it also put every truck driver and cabbie and FedEx and UPS worker in the world out of work? For what? So college kids can drink and drive safely? That you can do something amazing is amazing, but when is it too much?"

"You got me," she said. "Come to think of it, his comments about the perpetrator's anger and intro-version are actually pretty interesting. Kaczynski left the world to live in his cabin until the world intruded upon him in a way that truly pissed him off. Maybe that's what happened with our guy. He's sitting there hoarding and counting buses or what have you, and suddenly the world—or, more specifically, New York City—hurts him in a deep, fundamental way. Name some ways the city can hurt you."

"Gee, that'll be hard," I said, gesturing at the unbelievable traffic. "Let me count the ways. Taxes, tickets, traffic, red tape, fines, towed cars, broken buses, broken trains, stuck elevators, jury duty, getting mugged, no place to park, homeless people urinating on your doorstep. How am I doing so far?"

"You're on a roll," she said. "Maybe this guy is an ex–city employee who got fired without justification. Or he lost a lawsuit. Got screwed on a business deal by a city councilman. Maybe he was hurt on the subway, considering the first blast."

My cell rang. I glanced at the screen.

"Open the window. Maybe I'll start my Luddite conversion after all by chucking my phone into the Hudson. It's my angry boss, Fabretti."

Instead, she lifted my phone and hit the Accept Call button and handed it to me.

"Hey, Chief. Just got off the plane," I said.

"Good. Get over to City Hall as fast as you can. They just called."

"Who just called?" I said.

"The bombers. They just called the acting mayor. We have first contact. Get over here now."

# Chapter 69

I TOOK THE West Side Highway and drove all the way south, until it turned into West Street.

Half a block east of our exit, we had to stop abruptly at a checkpoint where a massive Bradley Fighting Vehicle was parked sideways in the intersection. After we showed our ID, a young bespectacled National Guardsman in khaki camo mirror-checked the underside of my cop car for a bomb.

We'd heard that there were similar National Guard units at Times Square and in Rockefeller Center. The whole borough of Manhattan was suddenly in lockdown, apparently.

Coming up onto Broadway, we saw heavy dump trucks and front-end loaders were still sweeping up what was left of 26 Federal Plaza. There was even more security around City Hall's little fenced-in park off Broadway. I counted at least twenty cops and National Guard guys as we slowed alongside the bomb-shield concrete planters by the gate.

As we were ID'd again and finally let in through the wrought iron, I remembered the last time I was here. It was in 2009, and I was with the kids at the ticker-tape parade along the Canyon of Heroes, where the Yankees were being honored by the mayor. It had been a great day: Chrissy was up on my shoulders, laughing and swatting at the shredded business-paper confetti as the Yankees went by on a flatbed truck.

Way back in the days when ticker tape wasn't paper raining down from blown-up buildings.

FBI technical analyst Ashley Brook Clark and Dr. Michael Aynard, the NYU physics professor, who'd both helped us on the EMP portion of this case, were already inside City Hall's grand foyer.

"You can cool your heels, guys," the ever-acerbic Aynard said with an epic eye roll as he looked up from his iPad mini. "They said we'd be granted an audience with Her Honor in ten minutes—oh, I'd say almost half an hour ago. I'm so glad I'm volunteering my time here. It's not like I have a life or anything."

Instead of responding, I decided to take a peek around. Through a threshold, I could see a massive life-size oil portrait of George Washington on the wall of a darkened room. A brass plaque on the wall said that the museumlike building was the oldest city hall in the country that's still being used as a city hall.

"Hey, Mike, you want to check out the upstairs?" Emily said, reading another plaque. "It says Lincoln lay in state up there after his assassination."

"Nah, I'm good," I said, glancing at the unlit landing beneath the rotunda. "I find history much less interesting when it starts to repeat itself before my very eyes."

Chief Fabretti appeared about ten minutes later and led us through a wood-paneled space that once might have been a chapel. The pews had been replaced with a warren of cubicles and desks, and at them, half a dozen wiped-out-looking mayor's deputies and staff were mumbling among themselves, trying to stay awake.

Three more staffers were conferring quietly by a corner desk when we finally made it to the mayor's office. Acting mayor Priscilla Atkinson, in yoga clothes and with her sneakers off, sat in a club chair beside a huge stone fireplace talking on her cell phone. Though she was dressed casually, the heavy concern on her tired face was anything but.

"Would you like anything? We don't have coffee, but there's green tea," said one of her slim majordomos as he came over.

The mayor got off her cell and stood before we could answer.

"Thank you for coming, everyone," she said, padding over to her desk in her No-See-Um socks.

"This came in about a half an hour ago," she said, opening an audio file on a laptop.

"We are the ones who bombed the subway and killed the mayor," said an electronically disguised voice. "We are the ones who set off the EMPs and blew up Twenty-Six Federal Plaza. Do we have your attention? On the northwest corner of Thirty-First Street and Dyer Avenue is a mailbox. Inside the mailbox, you will find a FedEx envelope that will prove we are who we say. We will call back tomorrow with what you are to do next."

"We grabbed the package half an hour ago," said Fabretti as he handed out a short stack of papers. "There were no prints on the package or the papers. This is a copy of what was in it."

"What's the drop site looking like?" I said.

"We're canvassing, but it's just old office

buildings and warehouses around the drop."

I shuffled through the stack of papers. There were blueprints, technical schematics on the cube robots, some computer programming stuff, and a diagram that looked like one of the EMPs next to a series of mathematical equations.

I couldn't make heads or tails of it, really. Neither, apparently, could anyone else, as all eyes were on Dr. Aynard. He licked his thumb and flipped quickly through the papers, mumbling from time to time. We all stood and stared and waited as he rattled through page after page.

"This is fascinating," he whispered to himself.

"Screw fascinating," said Fabretti sharply. "Is it real? Are these the people?"

The NYU professor looked up and nodded vigorously at Fabretti, his eyes very wide.

"Without a shadow of a doubt," Aynard said.

# Chapter 70

AS WE LEFT the mayor's office, I didn't know what to think about the contact the attackers had made. By that point, I was too tired to even try. Luckily, Robertson and Arturo were pulling the night shift at the intel division, so I sent an e-mail of the schematics over to them to see what they could make of it.

I dropped off Emily at her hotel and headed home. I gauged that I was about 10 percent awake when I stumbled in through the front door of the Bennett Estate half an hour later. Make that 5 percent, I thought as I almost tripped ass over teakettle on a *Frozen* princesses lunch box in the hall.

I wasn't the only sleepy one, apparently. I found Martin on a stool in the kitchen with all the lights on. He was facedown, snoring lightly between some engineering textbooks open on the counter. He woke up as I crouched down and lifted a worn paperback of the science fiction classic *Ender's Game* that had fallen on the floor beside his stool.

"Mr. Bennett!" he said, sitting up suddenly, stifling a yawn. "There you are. You're back from your travels, I see. What time is it?"

"Eleven thirty."

"Eleven thirty so soon?" Martin said, checking his phone. "Well, let's see. The kids are all fed, teeth brushed, and sacked out, et cetera. I got the boys' laundry done. The girls didn't have any. They never do. Funny. I had the boys running sprints down in the park. While I had Trent doing calisthenics, Eddie lost the soccer ball. We looked and looked but couldn't for the life of us figure out where it had gone to. The Hudson River? But I told Eddie not to worry. I have plenty of practice ones I can bring from my dorm tomorrow.

"I wanted to do vegetarian for the crew, but Seamus came by and insisted on making turkey clubs. He's quite a heavy on the mayo and bacon, if you want my opinion. Especially for a man of the cloth. That's about it. So if there isn't anything more, I'll be on me way."

"Nice try, Martin," I said, my head still spinning

from his dispatch. "Only place you're going, kid, is the couch," I said, pointing toward the living room. "There's blankets and a pillow on the top shelf of the hall closet."

"I couldn't impose," said Martin, yawning again. "Besides, I have an eight o'clock exam."

"Don't worry. I'll wake you up and drive you to campus."

"In your cop car?" said Martin, excited. "Get out! Never been in a fuzzmobile. That'll be a gas, so it will. Will you hit the siren and lights?"

"If you're good, Martin. Now, good night."

I smiled as he left. There was at least a little silver lining in all the current chaos. Seamus had hit one out of the park by finding Martin.

He really was a great kid. It was especially funny how he was running the couch potato out of the boys. They griped, but if Ricky's request for a FIFA Soccer PlayStation game for his birthday was any indication, Martin was starting to grow on them as well.

I made the mistake then of glancing at the mail table.

There was a letter on top addressed to me, and I stood there staring at Mary Catherine's familiar perfect handwriting.

One part of me wanted to tear it open imme-diately and devour it, but something else told me, "Not so fast." Maybe it was just my exhaustion, but I suddenly felt like there was something ominous about it, as if the news in it actually might not be so good.

Mary Catherine and I had become so close recently. Closer than ever. And yet here we were, still with an ocean between us. Her last call especially spooked me, how comfortable she seemed running her mom's hotel. I couldn't stop thinking that somehow we were drifting farther and farther apart.

Bottom line was I couldn't deal with bad news. Definitely not now.

I left Mary Catherine's letter on the mail table untouched and quietly turned off the light in the hall as I headed to bed.

# Chapter 71

AS IT TURNED out, I actually ended up using my lights and siren to deposit Martin back at Manhattan College after all.

We didn't have time to stop for coffee as I slalomed the Chevy at speed through the West Side Highway traffic, but I could see by the size of the whites of Martin's eyes when I screeched to a stop under the elevated subway tracks on Broadway and 240th Street, near the Leo Engineering Building, that he was pretty wide awake.

There was actually a method to my mad dash to Riverdale. There'd been a breakthrough on the case. Robertson had done it. He had found a plate on a surveillance camera near the drop.

Thirty-First Street and Dyer Avenue was a boxed-in intersection; 31st Street, like most of the odd-numbered cross streets in the Manhattan grid, runs one-way to the west. If a car had come to drop off the package, it had three options when leaving: west, north, or south.

As it turned out, two of the exit routes—the ones to the west and to the north—actually had surveillance cameras pointed at the street. The camera aimed at the western route was highly visible on the corner. The camera to the north was much less visible, so that's where Robertson had concentrated his search.

The last pickup on the box had been at 5:00 p.m., so Robertson had recorded the plate of every car that had stopped at the intersection since then. More than two hundred plates. From the DMV database, he got a list of names, then cross-referenced them with everything we had on all three outstanding cases, every lead and tip. Finally, at six fifteen this morning, something popped. A name.

A *Russian* name.

Dmitri Yevdokimov was a Russian immigrant with no priors. His name had been on the list of the more than nine hundred anonymous tips that had come in after the publication of the subway bomber stills.

The anonymous caller had said that Yevdokimov resembled the younger of the two subway bombers from the paper and that he was a chess genius with such a negative, unpleasant, antisocial personality that the Russian-accented caller said he "wouldn't put it past the bastard to blow up the city."

The note on the follow-up report by the FBI agent who'd worked the lead stated that Yevdokimov had been interviewed and had provided a solid alibi for the morning of the subway bombing.

But now that his car had been found a block from the drop site, it was time for a follow-up interview, I thought as I ate a light on Bailey Avenue and roared east.

Arturo and Robertson were already on scene with an ESU breach team at Yevdokimov's last known address, in the East Bronx. The entire block and most of the neighborhood were slowly and meticulously being surrounded by half the department. Since the bloody fiasco in Queens, we were expecting the unexpected, and no one was taking any chances.

I'd gotten as far as East Tremont Avenue when my cell rang with Arturo's number.

"What?!" I yelled.

"We bagged him, Mike! We were just setting up

when a car turned the corner, and Doyle verified the plates. We swooped in as he was getting out of his car. Not a shot fired. ESU has him on the ground, and Mike, listen. There was another guy with him. It could be Tweedledum and Tweedledee. We may have just ended this!"

"Great job, Arturo. I hope you're right. I'm about five minutes out. Where are you taking him? The Four-Five?"

"Yep. The Four-Five. We'll meet you there," said Arturo.

Could it be that we actually caught this guy? I wondered as I tossed my phone into the passenger seat. I screeched around a double-parked fish truck and turned on the jets, the siren screaming.

"Let it be. Let it be. This must be the answer. Let it be," I sang hopefully as I pinned it up East Tremont.

# Chapter 72

THE FORTY-FIFTH Precinct station house, near City Island, was on Barkley and Revere Avenues. I parked and flew up the stairs to the DT department on two and found Arturo and Robertson outside the detective CO's crowded office. I happily greeted them as well as Brooklyn and Doyle, who were just inside with an ESU sergeant and the precinct captain.

"It looks like them, Mike," was the first thing out of Arturo's mouth. "No facial hair, but they look like the suspects from the subway bombing."

"Anything on the other guy yet?" I said. "Tell me there's a Facebook selfie of him holding a bunch of plastic explosives."

"His name is Anatoly Gavrilov," said Brooklyn. "Like Dmitri, he's claiming he doesn't know what the hell is going on—that they're just cousins who work together as computer programmers and were coming back from a night on the town. They claim they've worked for plenty of Wall Street firms, which, from our preliminary look into it, might actually be true. Odd, though, since I wouldn't exactly peg these two on first glance as Goldman Sachs consultants."

"You had to see the guy's house, Mike," said Arturo. "Hoarders, except organized. Stacks upon stacks of labeled plastic containers of comic books, chess magazines, newspapers—mostly *Daily News* dating back to the fifties."

"Exactly," said Doyle. "Real strange shit."

I remembered what Kaczynski had said about the bomber being a hoarder. And that he might play chess. *Had we actually caught these guys?*

I looked at the two men on the interview-room monitor on the lieutenant's desk. The resemblance was there. They easily could have shaved their goatees because of the manhunt.

"It's them. Has to be, right?" said Arturo.

"Nothing has to be, Lopez," I said. "But so far, not bad."

# Chapter 73

I SPOKE TO Yevdokimov first.

"What the fuck is this? Russia?" were the first words out of the Russian's mouth as I opened the door.

He was not a handsome man, but his casual clothes were expensive—a fastidious sandwashed silk T-shirt; tailored jeans.

"Why'd you do it?" I said.

"Blow up the subway?" he said, staring at me with bulging eyes. "Oh, I don't know. I was bored. No, wait. I thought I'd start the Fourth of July off early this year, that's it. Plus of course my mother didn't *really* love me."

His chair creaked as he attempted to shift his weight with his hands cuffed behind him.

"How many times do I have to say it?!" he cried

as he began rocking back and forth. "It wasn't me. I have a lot of enemies, okay? That happens when you're a genius. Most people are stupid, and when they come into contact with a towering intellect, they become fearful and jealous. I was at work when that bomb went off. I have twenty witnesses who will testify to it."

"Where were you last night around six fifteen?"

He stared at me as he rocked.

"I was at Orchard Beach in the Bronx. I walk my dog there. Why?"

"Bullshit. You were at the corner of Thirty-First and Dyer Avenue in Manhattan, Dmitri. Your genius must be slipping a bit, because you didn't think about that second camera on the corner past the box."

He laughed as he rocked, shaking his head.

"The box? What box? The jack-in-the-box? You're unbelievably wrong," he said as he started squeaking around again in his cheap hard plastic chair like the world's largest hyperactive four-year-old.

"That's the spirit, Dmitri," I said. "Rock that boat, but remember, just don't tip the boat over. Get real comfy, because we're going to be here for a long, long time."

He whimpered.

"This is unreal," he said. "Let me guess. You guys are out of ideas, and since you have no clue who's doing this and never will, the plan now is to find a scapegoat."

"Your car was there, Dmitri," I said. "A gray Civic. Your car, your plates. You were there."

"No, I wasn't," he said sadly as he finally stopped squiggling around. He shook his head and looked down at the floor.

"Someone is framing me."

"Oh, a frame job," I said. "I haven't heard of one of those since television came in black-and-white. Tell me more."

He lifted his head.

"Do you play chess?" he said.

"No. I put murderers on death row."

"Ah, very funny," he said with a pained grin. "New York City is one of the most competitive chess arenas in the world, especially for big-money underground games. I haven't lost a game in six years—six years—and I play every day. They set them up, and I knock them down. Some people are gracious winners. I'm not one of those people.

"I crow. Sometimes I laugh. It's emasculating to get owned. At least I suppose so, because I wouldn't know. And now I guess one of those very bright people I beat has had enough. This is their moment to make their mark or whatever. Why not get me back, right? School the master. Revenge! Now, please take off these cuffs. I want my lawyer. Let me out of here. I have to feed my dog."

# Chapter 74

I THOUGHT ABOUT what Dmitri had said as I came out of the interview room into the bull pen. Some of it actually made sense. Anyone who blew up 26 Fed with robots and all the rest of it could easily have framed this guy. A thought that was pissing me off. Were we being played again? Was this loser actually being framed?

I turned to see Emily Parker coming up the precinct-house stairs.

"I just heard, Mike. You have these guys in custody? Do you think it's them?"

"Maybe, Emily," I said as Brooklyn and Doyle came out from questioning Anatoly Gavrilov.

"He's not talking, Mike," Brooklyn said. "At least not in English, except when he demands a lawyer."

"What about your guy, Mike?" Doyle said.

"Same," I said.

"What now?" Doyle said.

"There's no way we're letting them go anywhere until we can confirm their whereabouts in the last few weeks. And months and years," I said. "We need a full background on these guys. Immigration records, educational background, political affiliations, finances, any recent upheavals in their life that might have set them off."

That's when my cell phone rang.

"Mike, what the hell is going on? I thought your team grabbed these guys," Fabretti said when I picked up.

"So did I. What's up?"

"The bastards just made contact again five minutes ago."

I closed my eyes. Shit. Not again.

So the Russians we had weren't involved? *What the hell was this?*

"They've listed their demands, Bennett. I can't talk about it over the phone. You need to get back to City Hall now."

# Chapter 75

WE WERE COMING over the Macombs Dam Bridge near Yankee Stadium when a lot of frenzied chatter started up on the NYPD-band radio.

I turned it up. They were shifting roadblocks, apparently, and rerouting traffic in midtown. Traffic crews were being mobilized in various precincts and, for some unknown reason, they seemed to be shifting all traffic flow to the north.

"I just got a text from my brother-in-law, who works at Midtown South," said Doyle from the backseat. "You gotta be kidding me! They're calling in everyone. And I mean everyone. Every Tom, Dick, and Sally in the NYPD is being told to get their ass in to work!"

I looked at Emily anxiously. The only time I'd ever heard of that happening before was on 9/11.

The first thing the Unabomber had said to us rang in my head.

*They're going to destroy New York City—you know that, right?*

"Something must be up," said Arturo, shaking his head in the seat next to Doyle.

"Ya think, Lopez?" Doyle said, rolling his eyes.

We were thrown another curve as we were coming up on City Hall on lower Broadway twenty minutes later. Fabretti called and told us that they'd moved the mayor six blocks northwest, to the Office of Emergency Management's new crisis center, at the western end of Chambers Street.

It was a crisis, all right. By the time we got to the new twelve-story glass building on the shore of the Hudson, they'd cordoned off the entire block. Past the roadblock, there was pandemonium on the street outside the building, where cops and National Guardsmen and techs were moving boxes and equipment in and out of trucks.

When it was finally our turn at the checkpoint, the tall, middle-aged female sergeant told me in no uncertain terms to turn around, as no one was being allowed in. I actually had to call Fabretti three times before he radioed the gate and told the hard-ass lady cop it was okay.

There was a city park beside the facility filled with dozens of cop and fed cars and SUVs parked haphazardly up on the grass. We left the car in front of an idling Office of Emergency Management bus, and as we got out we looked up and watched as an NYPD Bell helicopter landed on a helipad beside the building.

The chopper dumped out a half dozen people who looked like feds and civilian professor types. Beside the helipad, at a dock, an NYPD Harbor Unit boat was unloading more smart-looking folks. One of them had on a blue Windbreaker with yellow letters on the back.

"NHC?" I said to Emily. "What the heck is the NHC?"

"National Hurricane Center?" she said, staring at me wide-eyed.

"What? We're going to have a hurricane now? These guys can make it rain, too? That can't be!" Doyle said.

"All hands on deck and batten down the friggin' hatches," Arturo said as the Harbor Unit boat sped past in the water with a roar.

# Chapter 76

INSIDE THE SLEEK, low-ceilinged lobby of the building, it was even worse.

Every political staffer and cop we saw rushing to and fro was looking completely freaked. I stepped aside when a tall balding guy grunted, "Out of the way!" as he hustled past with a stack of printouts. I even tried to wave down Lieutenant Bryce Miller, who appeared at the end of the lobby, but he blew right past me with his phone glued to his ear and a bewildered look on his face.

"Well, at least everybody is keeping it together," Doyle cracked.

As Bryce Miller left, Fabretti popped out of a stairwell door and rushed over to us.

"Bennett, tell me you got something—any-thing—on these Russians that you just picked up."

"Not exactly," I said. "They're claiming that they were framed. I'm not sure if I believe them, but their alibis look pretty solid so far. But even if they were framed, we're definitely getting closer now, Chief. Because the real bombers—whoever they are—had to know the Russians in order to frame them. We just have to find the link. What the heck is going on here? Why is all hell breaking loose?"

"Because it is. C'mon," he said, leading us down the crowded hallway. "These bastards FedExed a video this time. They're showing it in the press room."

"A video?" said Arturo.

"Don't get your hopes up, buddy. I doubt it's from Netflix," Doyle said.

The video was rolling on a screen set up on the stage as we came into the crowded press room.

It showed what looked like stock news footage—people running on a beach as waves crashed at their backs.

As the terrified people ran for their lives, the same strange electronic voice from the first phone call started up like a documentary voice-over.

"During the 2004 tsunami in the Indian Ocean, two hundred thirty thousand people died within minutes as a thirty-foot-high wave struck coastal areas of Indonesia, Sri Lanka, India, Thailand, Somalia, and the Maldives. It was caused by a massive undersea megathrust earthquake. But that isn't the only way tsunamis are created.

"Welcome to an undisclosed location," said the voice as the image on the screen shifted.

Up-to-date digital film was showing what looked like some type of cave or mine corridor. A beam of light moved along a rough, brownish-grayish rock wall in a descending, low-ceilinged shaft. When the light and camera panned left, a thin braided-steel cable hanging from rock bolts embedded in the wall came into view. Running alongside it was a red plastic-coated cable of some kind—electrical, maybe.

The camera stopped as the red cable suddenly led into a large rectangle of strange white blocks. It looked like explosives—a charge the size of a kitchen cabinet stuck to the rock wall. The camera shifted to the center of the shaft, where the length of cables running down the seemingly endless corridor revealed charge after charge after charge stuck to the wall.

"This is Semtex," the voice said as a hand clad in a black work glove patted the explosives. "The red cable is detcord, and the steel cable beside it is for spreading the force of the blast nice and even, to maximize shear. It's not the most elaborate bomb I have ever made, but it is certainly the biggest. After all, there is an elegance in simplicity sometimes.

"As I have possibly convinced you with the subway bombing and the razing of 26 Federal Plaza, I am actually pretty good at blowing shit up, no? I like to think that no one has ever been as good at it as I am, but that is for history to decide, I guess."

As the cameraman turned all the way back around, in the distance, up the shaft, we could see a bright opening in the tunnel, thin clouds in a pale-blue sky.

The camera guy started walking up toward the opening, and then as he reached it, everybody in the room gasped.

Through the cave mouth or mine shaft or whatever it was, the camera showed a bunch of dark, jagged volcanic peaks and a sheer drop-off down an immense cliff into a crashing ocean. The cave mouth was insanely high up—a hundred stories, maybe two hundred. Far below, down the dizzyingly immense slope of the mountain, there were dozens of little moving dots—seabirds flying above the spraying surf.

"Here's what you need to know now," said the voice. "If my calculations are right, and I believe they are, when I carefully detonate my network of explosives, I will peel off this entire peak and send a landmass roughly the size of Manhattan Island into the Atlantic Ocean at more than a hundred miles an hour.

"According to my computer models, this slide will create a tsunami a little more than twice as powerful as the 2004 Indian Ocean tsunami and send it directly into the Eastern Seaboard of the United States. Six hours from the time I detonate, Manhattan Island will be inundated with an unstoppable seventy-five-foot wave."

"No," said Arturo, beside me, in a whisper to the screen. "Just no."

"New York City will be destroyed. As will Miami and Baltimore and Boston."

There was a pause in the narration.

"I have one simple demand. Within twenty-four hours, I want three billion US dollars deposited into a list of numbered accounts that I have already sent to the mayor's office by e-mail. That this amount is roughly the equivalent of the mayor's personal fortune is not accidental. She can divert her money easily in the time allotted. The question is, will she? Your city's fate lies solely in her hands.

"There will be no negotiation. The money will either appear in the accounts in the time allotted, and tomorrow will be just another day. Or it will not appear, and I will wipe New York City, along with the rest of the eastern United States, off the map."

There was a second pause.

"Please know that, of course, any attempt to find and approach the place where the bombs are now located will result in immediate detonation. I will not contact you again. That is all."

# Chapter 77

HALF AN HOUR later, we were in the insanely crowded OEM's seventh-floor war room. The packed, open room had monitors everywhere. Monitors on desks, monitors built into a long cherrywood conference table in the center of the room, and a movie screen–like monitor that took up an entire wall.

The wall screen was actually composed of a grid of smaller screens that showed different parts of the city—Times Square, Grand Central Terminal, the street out in front of the UN. As I watched, the screen changed into a still of the cave or mine housing the explosives.

At the head of the U-shaped conference table packed with scientists and government officials, the acting mayor looked pale. It was impossible to know what she was feeling, but it couldn't have been good. It was incredible that all this—the bombings and assassination—was about cleaning her out financially.

Or at least that was what was being said now. I wasn't entirely convinced that this was the case.

"Please, someone, anyone, tell me what the hell is going on here," the mayor said.

The scientists at the table stared at each other until a tan, lean, white-haired man who reminded me a lot of the famous college basketball coach Bobby Knight stood up, along with a pretty woman with chin-length chestnut hair.

"Everyone, my name is Larry Duke, and this is Dr. Suzan Bower, and we're the coheads of the American Geophysical Union," he said.

"Tell me this is a joke, Mr. Duke," said the mayor. "It's a bluff, right? Dr. Evil, James Bond bullshit? It's too implausible. There are no islands near New York City in the Atlantic. How is this even a threat?"

"Actually, ma'am," Larry said, "off the west coast of Africa, there are dozens and dozens of volcanic islands."

"Africa! That's what? Three or four thousand miles away!" she screamed.

Dr. Bower smiled calmly as she raised her palm.

"Allow me to explain," she said politely. "The potential destructive force of a truly massive landslide into a seabed is almost impossible to comprehend. In Lituya Bay in Alaska in the fifties, after an earthquake, a one-mile-by-half-mile chunk of rock slid off a coastal mountain into the water, causing a wave the size of a one-hundred-and-seventy-story building.

"Think about that. If a similar incident happened in the Atlantic basin, even from as far away as Africa, a tidal wave the size of the Indian Ocean tsunami would hit the Eastern Seaboard six hours later, just as the man on the tape said."

"And nothing could stop it?" said the OEM head.

Larry shook his head sadly.

"Nothing," he said. "For years, Suzan and I have been advising the government of exactly the problem here—that some of the West African islands are potential tsunami dangers from eruption-caused landslides."

"But you said the landslide in Alaska was caused by an earthquake, an incredible geologic event," said the mayor. "You can't cause an earthquake or erupt a volcano with explosives, can you?"

"No, you can't. But you can cause a landslide with explosives, especially if an area is already unstable, like many of the areas on some of these islands," said Dr. Bower.

"Bullshit," somebody said.

"I wish it was," Larry said. "In 1903, there was a disaster called the Frank Slide in Canada. A segment of mountain about the same size as the one in the Lituya Bay incident fell and flattened a mining town. How did it happen? By miners blasting in one of the mines."

"Exactly," said Dr. Bower. "Today, demolition experts are so good with explosives, they can blow things up so buildings fall wherever they want. For example, demo guys took down a half-mile-long section of nine bridges in Ohio with only one hundred and thirty-eight pounds of plastic explosives. You get a geologist together with a demo expert and place the pow in the right place, and you just might be able to do it. You simply need to give it a push, and millions and millions of pounds of rock and gravity do the rest."

"Shit," I said to Emily. "Just like Twenty-Six Fed. A little bit of explosives placed perfectly took that building down pretty as you please. They know how to do it."

"So you think it's possible for these terrorists to actually use explosives to cause a landslide to create a tsunami?" said the mayor.

"I'm sorry, ma'am," Larry said with a sad smile. "But the answer is yes."

# Part Four

## PLEASE STAND BY

# Chapter 78

TWO HOURS LATER, we were sprawled out in a corner of the OEM building's third-floor cafeteria. We sat at a new folding table—which still had a sticker with the Walmart bar code on it—washing down vending-machine candy with coffee. I had my feet on a chair by the window and was sharing glum looks with Doyle and Arturo and Emily.

"Gosh, it's tiring to beat your head against the wall," said Arturo. He was right. We'd just gotten off the phone with Robertson and Brooklyn. They'd called to let us know that Dmitri Yevdokimov and Anatoly Gavrilov had lawyered up.

Not just with any lawyers, either. Two seven-hundred-dollar-an-hour mouthpieces from a white-shoe Wall Street firm had actually shown up at the precinct house raising hell until the precinct captain relented. The fact was we didn't have enough on them to charge them with anything. Not yet, anyway. Like it or not, they'd been released, and our best leads just walked out the door.

To add insult to injury, we'd put surveillance on them, but they seemed to have shaken it. We'd also just received a forensics report from the FBI on the Russians' credit cards and cell phones and Internet searches. There was nothing. They had no electronic trail of any kind. The two computer experts were Luddites, apparently.

I groaned as I looked out the window at the Hudson and Jersey on the other side. Then I looked south at the Statue of Liberty in the harbor and imagined a wave coming over her.

In the silence, Arturo got up and made himself another coffee.

"Look on the bright side, guys. They've got free K-Cups up here. Yummy. I love K-Cups," he said sarcastically.

"Yeah. Nothing like a smooth, soothing K-Cup to while away the afternoon before the destruction of your city," said Doyle, flicking a coffee stirrer at him.

I stared out the window down to the courtyard, where soldiers were setting up cots.

Were the cots for the soldiers? Were they expecting refugees? What the hell were cots going to do when the water came? Become flotation devices?

I only knew that we had to keep our heads about us in this whirling dervish of a mess. I sat up.

"Okay, let's do this again. Theories," I said to Emily.

"I almost can't believe it's a ransom," she said as she swirled her coffee. "I was really leaning toward a Unabomber-style suspect. One man on a mad mission, like you said. This now? Three billion? This is a real curveball."

"It's the Russkies. Has to be," said Doyle as he rolled out of his chair onto the floor and started doing push-ups. "Think about it. The fed forensic report shows they have no credit cards or computer records, yet they're computer experts? They have stuff. They just know how to hide it. They're in on this."

Then the real chaos began.

Chief Fabretti came into the cafeteria talking on his phone.

"You're kidding. Jeez. Wow, just like that. Okay, thanks."

"What's up, Chief?" said Doyle as he hopped to his feet.

"Turn on the TV," Fabretti said, pointing to the set in the cafeteria's corner. "This is unbelievable."

Doyle ran over and clicked on the set. I stood up as I saw something there I hadn't seen since I was a kid.

There was a blue screen with two words in yellow.

STAND BY.

Doyle changed the channel. It was on every one. A long and bright beep sounded out, followed by a squawk of radio feedback. Then it did it again.

"This is not a test," said a calm, feminine voice. "I repeat, this is not a test of the Emergency Alert System. Please stand by. Please stand by."

"What is this?"

"The mayor just came out of another meeting with the scientists. She's doing it. She's pulling the trigger."

I listened to the beep repeat.

"This is not a test," said the voice. "I repeat, this is not a test of the Emergency Alert System."

"Pulling what trigger?" said Lopez. "You mean she's going to give them the money?"

"No. She's going to evacuate, right?" I said as I stared at the STAND BY on the screen.

Fabretti nodded.

338

"That's right. God help us all," said Fabretti. "The mayor is going to call for the complete evacuation of New York City."

# Chapter 79

CHIEF FABRETTI RECEIVED a text from the deputy mayor, and we followed him up the four flights of too-warm stairs and then through a corridor crowded with cops and suits into the main war room again.

In a fishbowl office in the corner, beyond a row of printers, stood the mayor, along with the glaring lights of the small camera crew that was filming her live for the emergency broadcast.

I watched as the blue screen on the wall was replaced by an image of the mayor.

"Fellow New Yorkers, hello. I am sorry to tell you this, but we have received word that an undersea earthquake in the Atlantic may be imminent within the next six to eight hours. It is believed by experts that this quake may cause an

Atlantic Ocean tsunami large enough to be a serious threat to people throughout the city. We are not one hundred percent sure that this is the case, but for the sake of caution and the preservation of life, I have signed an order to evacuate the entire city."

"Why is she lying and talking about an earthquake?" said Arturo. "Like people have been sleeping through the bombings and assassination?"

"Who knows?" Doyle said. "Maybe she—"

"Shut the fuck up, both of you!" said Fabretti, standing behind them.

"This evacuation is a legal order not a recommendation. All the people of the city—in Manhattan and Brooklyn and Queens and Staten Island and the Bronx—must leave their homes as soon as possible and head inland. If you have a car parked in Manhattan, we are asking you to leave it where it is, as roads will soon become impassable with traffic. Please use public transport.

"The MTA and Port Authority have already been ordered to mobilize the mass transit system. All buses, trains, subways, and ferries will be open to the public at no charge in order to move people inland. Shelters in New Jersey and northern Westchester have already been set up, and we are working on opening more shelters farther north and inland as the number of people increases.

"We urge any and all of you to stay with family, but remember to stay away from all coastal areas within thirty miles of the shore. Please do not panic. We need to have as orderly an evacuation as possible. You have time to pack, and everyone will be given transportation and shelter. Stay tuned to local media. If you have not done so already, prepare a go bag."

The mayor was saying that the fire department had been mobilized to help the hospitals when I stepped over into a corner and called Martin.

"Mike, how goes it?"

"I guess you're not watching TV."

"No. What is it?"

"Listen to me carefully, Martin. This isn't a joke. They think an Atlantic Ocean tsunami is coming, so they're evacuating the city. Do you have a driver's license?"

"Not a New York one," he said. "I can drive, though."

You had to hand it to the kid. I thought he sounded alert yet calm. I just told him the world was ending, and he was immediately ready to deal.

"Good," I said. "In the front hall closet is our

seventy-two-hour kit—a big knapsack containing food and water, first aid, maps, flashlights, glow sticks, a crank radio, and five hundred bucks in cash. There's also an extra set of van keys in it. The van's in the lot at Ninety-Eighth, just off West End. I want you to go get it and pick up the kids and Seamus at Holy Name.

"When you get everybody, don't get on the highway. Go north up Broadway and over the Broadway Bridge into the Bronx. Keep going north until Broadway becomes Route 9A up in Westchester. Just keep going then, okay? Call me when you have the kids."

"How far do you want me to go?" said Martin.

I thought about what the geophysical experts had said about the 170-story wave.

"I have a cousin in the Catskills. You should head there."

"The Catskills! That's, like, a hundred miles. What the hell is coming? A meteor? Is Ireland going to be hit, too?"

"Don't panic, Martin. It may be nothing, honestly, but better safe than sorry. Now hop to it. Grab the kids and call me back."

# Chapter 80

HALF AN HOUR later, I sat at a desk in the OEM war room quietly watching the big screen. It was divided up into a grid of nine screens, just like it was at the beginning of *The Brady Bunch,* but instead of seeing Carol and Mike and the gang smiling, various parts of the city were visible. The center was losing hold, and things were falling apart.

What looked like war footage was being beamed in from the traffic-light cameras. In SoHo, Times Square, Central Park, Harlem, and everywhere else, the streets were packed with cars and the sidewalks were filled with people carrying things. Knapsacks, rolling suitcases, paintings, dogs. On the screen that showed Broadway and 72nd Street, I watched as a short black guy in a gray business suit pushed a shopping cart up the middle of Broadway with an old black woman, probably his mother, lying in it.

I'd never seen so many people in Grand Central Terminal. They were packed in like sardines, a lot of them pushing and shoving. As I watched, a tall, curly-haired old lady by the information booth went to the floor as her cane was kicked out from under her by a group of stupid kids pushing past her. She was trampled by three or four other thoughtless jerks before some nice Asian teen boy stepped in. I was almost heartened as he dragged her back to her feet, but then as I watched, blood began gushing from her nose.

Then there was the eighteen-wheeler on fire in the middle of the Verrazano Bridge. The whole thing—the cab and the trailer—just blazing along. It would continue to do so, I knew, until it burned out, because a fire truck had as much chance of getting through the stalled traffic as I had of becoming the starting power forward for the Knicks this season.

No one was listening about not panicking, and who could blame them? It was every man for himself now, as hard as that was to believe.

From time to time, I looked away from the sickening screens to just stare at the items on the desk I was sitting at. I blinked at a bottle of hand sanitizer, a *LEGO Movie* mouse pad, a tube of ChapStick. All of it was going to be underwater in a few hours?

Beside the computer was a framed picture I couldn't stop staring at. Two coltish girls and a tall blond mom smiling as they waded among the rocks of a river.

It looked like it was taken in New England somewhere, with autumn-yellow leaves on the trees. The girls were adorable, with braces, and the smile on the mom's face was room-brightening. It looked like an old Coca-Cola ad or something. Americans being happy. It was time to say *sayonara* to that now?

Squinting angrily at the photo, I suddenly didn't want to just catch the sons of bitches responsible anymore. I wanted to hunt them down and kill them with my bare hands.

When I called Martin for the twentieth time in the last twenty minutes, it kicked into voice mail. Martin was on the road now. Everyone was with him except Brian. They were in northern Manhattan, trying to get across the Harlem River to meet up with Brian at Fordham Prep. The problem was that Brian wasn't picking up his phone, which meant he had forgotten to charge it. But Martin had called the school and left word to have Brian stay there for pickup, so maybe all was still good.

I balled my hands into fists as they started to shake.

Who was I kidding? I felt completely helpless.

I looked up as Emily came in.

"Did you get your kids out?" she said.

"Almost. How about you? Are you near the coast in Virginia?"

"No, thank God. My brother got Olivia out of school, and they're at Costco stocking up," she said glumly.

Emily's face lit up suddenly as she got a text.

"Mike, get up! C'mon!" she said, grabbing my hand.

"What?"

"Arturo and Doyle are at the scientist meeting on six. They say they might have something."

# Chapter 81

"THEY KNOW WHERE the bombs are!" said a wide-eyed Arturo, grabbing my shoulders as I stepped into the doorway of the sixth-floor conference room.

"Where?" I said.

"Árvore Preta," said Doyle, looking every bit as pumped as Arturo. "It's Portuguese for 'black tree.' It's a volcanic island just south of the Cape Verde archipelican."

"Archipelago, you mean, moron," said Arturo.

We all backed out into the hallway.

"Slow down, fellas," said Emily. "Where is this island?"

"The Cape Verde island chain is off the coast of Africa," said Doyle. "They said it's roughly three hundred and fifty miles to the west."

"Why do they think this particular island is where the bombs are?" I said. "Didn't they say there's a bunch of different island chains in the area?"

"Well, these two rock scientists were in there arguing endlessly," said Arturo. "They kept looking at the video, and this guy from UC Berkeley—"

"Cut to the chase, Arturo," I said, trying to be patient.

"All of a sudden, this little guy, a Brit, in the corner of the room stands up and points at the screen and says, 'Excuse me, but are those petrels?'"

"Petrels?" I said.

"They're freaking birds!" said Doyle. "Those little birds you see in the video when the guy pans the camera down the cliff. They're an endangered seabird that nests on this Cape Verde island, Árvore Preta."

"That's when Larry Duke and Dr. Bower went bonkers," said Arturo. "Árvore Preta has an active volcano that last erupted in 1963. They actually knew all about it. They'd listed Árvore Preta in a paper they did in the late eighties about potentially unstable volcanoes."

"Bottom line is they think this is it, Mike," said Doyle. "We know where the bombs are."

# Chapter 82

FOUR HOURS LATER, at a little after 11:00 p.m., Emily and I came out the OEM building's side entrance alongside the dark Hudson River with Larry Duke and Dr. Bower. A moment later, a loud roaring sound drew our eyes upward, and we watched as a huge helicopter appeared over the lip of the building.

"Oh, my! It's like from that movie. What's it called? *Black Hawk Down*?" said Dr. Bower as we ducked back from the whining turbo-rotor wash.

"Yeah, well, let's hope this one stays up," I said as it touched down on the concrete pad twenty feet in front of us.

The imposing military chopper, bearing an emblem of a rearing winged white centaur, was from the army's elite 160th Special Operations

Aviation Regiment, known as the Night Stalkers. The 160th worked hand in glove with the Navy SEALs and had actually been on the mission that had killed Osama bin Laden.

All stops were now officially pulled out. After a tense closed-door teleconference with the US president himself, the mayor had pulled the trigger. We had only one option left on the table, and the mayor was taking it.

The Night Stalkers were here to give us a ride to the airport. We were heading to Cape Verde, off the west coast of Africa, with the military to find the explosives.

Though it was probably a buzzer-beating long shot that we would find them before the terrorists' deadline, it was definitely the right move, I felt.

Because what if the three billion dollars were paid? What was to stop them from blowing up the cliff anyway? Or charging another three billion next week?

Though it wasn't announced, the mayor had also decided that, deadline or no deadline, she wasn't going to give them a single penny of her or the city's money. Which, again, was exactly right, in my humble opinion. Terrorists needed to be dealt with head-on. Whoever was doing this to us needed to be found and stopped, not negotiated with.

After a quick strap-in by the Black Hawk's crew chief, the chopper took off and stayed low as we headed north up the Hudson. Through cold air blasting in my face from a half-open window, I stared out at the glittering strings of Manhattan's lights on my right.

The glittering, *unmoving* strings of Manhattan's lights.

Despite the mayor's directive not to drive, it was obvious that the streets were completely impassable because of traffic.

Staring at the sea of dead-stopped cars, I thought about Martin and the kids. The last message I had received from them, about an hour and a half ago, was that they were all together and crossing into Westchester.

Were they far enough away? I wondered, looking north up the lightless river. They had to be, right? Or at least they would be far enough away by the deadline tomorrow.

At least that's what I was going to keep telling myself, I decided, as I took out my phone again.

"Mike? Hello? Are you there?" said Seamus as my call, surprisingly, went through.

"Yes, Seamus. It's me," I said straining to hear over the engine whine. "Where are you? Did you get out? Where are you?"

"We're—"

Then the signal went screwy.

I ripped the phone off my ear and stared at the screen. It was still connected.

"Seamus?" I said. "Seamus?"

Then I looked at the screen again and cursed.

The line was dead.

# Chapter 83

"MIKE? ARE YOU there, Mike?" said Seamus as he lifted the phone off his ear and stared at its screen.

"It cut off," he said.

"Ah, the cell sites are just melting, Father. Must be millions trying to get through now," Martin said as he let out an extra-large breath.

Martin's glance went from the standstill traffic to the needle of the gas gauge, which was at the halfway point now, then back to the traffic again. He wiped his sweating forehead. He'd give it another minute, then turn off the engine to conserve gas, he decided.

They were on Broadway in Yonkers. It was a sketchy part of town—run-down houses and buildings and stores. They'd been stopped for almost five minutes, which meant God only knows what was happening up ahead. In the last hour, they had probably traveled less than a mile.

As Martin watched, two stocky young Hispanic kids zoomed past on a Kawasaki dirt bike. The one on the back was seated backwards, and he gave Martin and the good Father the finger as his buddy threaded between the cars.

"Did ya see that, Father?" Martin said. "That wasn't very neighborly, now, was it?"

"We're not on the old sod anymore, Martin," Seamus said, shaking his head. "It's probably best to pretend you're blind."

Martin turned to his left and looked beyond an empty parking lot as the Metro-North Hudson Line train went slowly by. It was incredibly packed with people in and even standing between the cars. On the last car, there were several people sitting on the roof!

It was like something out of news footage from the Great Depression or a science fiction film, Martin thought. This crazy country. He'd just wanted to make a little pocket money with the nanny job, and now look where he was. Wandering the set of *The War of the Worlds 2*.

When the train finally passed, he could see the Hudson River. Great, he thought, drumming his fingers on the wheel. They were right next to water, the one place Mike had specifically told them not to be.

Should they leave the van and try to get on a train? Martin thought, staring at the gas gauge again. He let out another long breath as he bit at his lower lip. It was impossible to know what to do.

"Martin?" Jane called from the back, distress in her voice.

"What is it?" Martin said, trying to keep his tone light for the children.

"Bad news, Martin," she said.

"How is that even possible?" Martin said under his breath.

"It's Jasper. I think . . . well, I think he has to tinkle."

"You want to walk the dog out there in the 'hood?" Seamus said, turning around in the passenger seat with a flabbergasted look.

"It's either out there, Gramps," said Jane, shrugging, "or right here in the van."

"Okay, okay. Brian and Eddie and Ricky and— what the heck—you, too, Trent. Look lively and get the leash. I have an important mission for you boys. You're all on Jasper tinkle patrol," Seamus said.

"Yes!" said Brian, putting the now-moaning

Jasper on the leash. "Finally something to do!"

"Buddy system, okay, boys?" Martin said. "Leave no man behind."

"Or dog!" said Chrissy frantically. "Or dog!"

"Exactly. No man or dog, okay? Now hit it!"

They burst out of the van and ran with Jasper through the traffic to a concrete wall beside a run-down tenement.

"I see them," said Bridget, cupping her hands over her eyes and looking out the window. "He's tinkling! Jasper is tinkling!"

"Yay!" said Fiona.

"That's the best news I've heard all day, isn't it, Father?" said Martin.

Seamus rolled his eyes.

The van burst into applause as the boys arrived back, breathless, with the pup. The happy, excited dog started barking like mad as Chrissy grabbed him to her chest in a bear hug while Socky, the cat, remained aloof, snuggled in one of Shawna's sweatshirts on the floor of the van.

"We're clear," said Brian, slamming the door. "Quick! Martin! Hit the gas!"

If only, Martin thought as he stared out at the sea of brake lights.

# Chapter 84

THERE HAD TO be well over a hundred military people scurrying around three large cargo planes on the tarmac of Teterboro Airport in northern New Jersey when we landed in the helicopter ten minutes later.

And it wasn't just men being moved in and out of the C-130s. As we landed, I watched a Jeep drive up a ramp into the plane's belly, followed quickly by a small tractor towing in a Black Hawk helicopter with its rotors folded back.

"The US military is truly incredible, isn't it?" I said to Emily. "I mean, the mayor made the call—what? Four hours ago? Now look at this! It's unbelievable how quickly this thing is being mobilized."

"Let's just hope it's fast enough," Emily said.

We asked around, then met up with Lieutenant Commander Nate Gardner, the leader of the SEALs team that had been assigned to head up the mission. Nate was a tall, fit, clean-cut guy around thirty, with light-blue eyes and black hair. He was sitting on a four-wheeler under the wing of one of the planes eating pizza with his team of commandos.

He and his thirty or so SEALs were sitting beside their weapons and kit bags talking quietly with one another or napping. They seemed to be the only still and calm people in the whole airport.

Make that the tristate area, I thought as we walked up.

"NYPD!" Nate said, smiling and wiping pizza grease on the thighs of his olive-drab desert-camo uniform before standing up to shake our hands. "Now we're talking. I love you guys. I'm from Rochester, but I lived in a shit hole in Alphabet City with my friends after college and saw up close how you guys operate. I was actually on the cop list before deciding to join the navy."

"Pleased to meet you, Lieutenant Commander," Emily jumped in. "But what are we supposed to do now?"

"Please, it's Nate," the soldier said, grinning. "Or Commander Nate, if you must. Basically, ma'am, we'll board after the toys are packed. You got my two teams as well as five of the army's explosive ordnance disposal teams en route."

"Right, but how are we going to play this?" she said. "What's the strategy? Just head to Árvore Preta and start looking?"

"The US ambassador to Cape Verde will meet us at the airport on the other side to smooth things out with the locals," Nate said. "They will provide us with island guides, and we'll locate these bombs. Once we find them, we let the EOD teams do their thing disarming them. My team will provide security for everybody. I recommend you guys try to get some sleep on the flight."

"That's it?" said Dr. Bower.

"That's all she wrote, ma'am," Nate said, winking one of his baby blues.

"How to save the world in three easy steps," Emily said as the tall, energetic SEAL rejoined his men. "I admire his confidence. If only I shared it."

"You and me both," I said as I took out my phone to check on my guys for the eleven billionth time.

# Chapter 85

COMING ON SIX hours later, I woke up sweating as someone two or three seats down along the vibrating metal wall of the loudly buzzing cargo plane started coughing uncontrollably.

More than seventy people were strapped into the benches along both walls of the military plane. There were SEALs, army explosives techs, a fully staffed medical unit, several plane refueling techs, and pilots and crew from the 160th.

I didn't know what the weight limit for the C-130 was, but it had to be massive, since between the rows of soldiers, tied down with heavy canvas straps in the middle of the plane, was a Black Hawk helicopter bookended by a couple of Jeeps.

It was the same deal in the two other planes flying alongside us. More than a hundred highly trained men and women along with who knows how many millions of dollars' worth of equipment.

When the US military went for it, they apparently went all the way.

I glanced over at a wired-looking Emily beside me. She was reading the Cape Verde info packet the CIA had provided for the hundredth time. She looked like she hadn't slept at all. She glanced at her watch, then back at me uneasily. I checked the time on my phone and joined her in wincing.

We had just eight hours left before the 1:00 p.m. deadline, and we hadn't even landed yet.

I checked my phone for any messages from Robertson or Brooklyn. About an hour into the flight, they had contacted me with the great idea to cross-reference our suspects with the manifests from any and all flights from the New York City area to Cape Verde over the previous six months.

It only made sense. *If* the bombs were on Cape Verde, that is.

In the front of the plane, past the nose of the Black Hawk, daylight was spilling into the cabin through the open door of the cockpit. I unclipped my belt and decided to join SEAL commander Nate, who was standing by the cockpit door.

As I got to the doorway, the plane swung left,

then down below, through the windshield, islands suddenly appeared—small oblong islands with rims of beach standing very white against the dark teal of the Atlantic.

"Fifteen minutes!" the female pilot called back.

I stared down at the bright, sandy flat strips of land. I'd already read the info packet. It said that, like a lot of the islands in the eastern Atlantic near Africa, Cape Verde had originally been settled in the 1500s by the Portuguese. Once an important hub of the African slave trade and a notorious haunt of pirates, it had gained its national independence in the early 1970s, when a Marxist revolutionary—a Fidel Castro–like figure named Amilcar Cabral—had fought for its independence.

Now, with all that in its rearview, the packet said Cape Verde was actually thriving. It was an up-and-coming, laid-back, beachy island vacation destination with microclimate vineyards and eco tours.

Too bad I didn't feel that laid-back as the plane began its descent. The video showing all those bombs in the cave wouldn't stop replaying in my head.

Maybe the pirates had come back, I thought.

We received permission to land at Amilcar

Cabral International Airport on an island called Sal ten minutes later. It certainly looked like a vacation destination, I thought as we came in low over whitewashed stucco houses and colorful fishing boats in an ultramarine bay. As we touched down, I spotted a small passenger plane on a distant runway—bright green, yellow, and red, like a parrot.

Too bad the cheery welcome-to-the-Bahamas feeling lasted about a New York minute. When we were walking down the plane's ramp into the bright glare, several vehicles shot out from around the terminal building.

There were three pickup trucks with a dozen or more armed uniformed men standing in the beds. The long stretch Mercedes limo that followed the trucks had Cape Verde flags flying from each corner.

"Is it the ambassador?" one of the SEALs said to Nate Gardner.

Nate suddenly frowned as the cars came right at us.

"Olender, get Colorado on the horn," he said. "I don't like the looks of this. These guys look pissed. Something must have gotten screwed up. Find out what."

"I am Vice President Basilio Rivera!" yelled a short and sleekly handsome brown man with a little mustache as he leaped from the Benz. "What the hell is going on here? Why are those men armed? You are US military, yes? Who gave you permission to land? I demand to know what you are doing here!"

"Mr. Vice President," Nate said, smiling warmly at the little tin-pot dictator and his soldiers. "My name is Lieutenant Commander Nate Gardner of the US Navy. There must have been a mix-up, sir. Everything is okay. We have permission to be here from your government. It was very last-minute, though, so perhaps not everyone was informed. I'm calling my people right now to get confirmation. I encourage you to do the same, sir."

The tense, silent soldiers hopped down, palming their automatic rifles. They flanked the limo as Nate and Vice President Rivera walked back toward its open door. Emily and I stood next to each other in the sweltering wind, sweating as the small man spoke in Portuguese into his phone.

"This is all we need," I said, checking my phone to see exactly zero messages from my kids. "I wasn't expecting mai tais with little umbrellas in them, but this is ridiculous."

The VP hung up, and he and Nate spoke tensely for a minute.

Then suddenly they were laughing.

"What are you waiting for?" Nate yelled to his guys as he jogged back. "Don't just stand there. Let's get these planes unpacked."

# Chapter 86

OUTSIDE THE TILTED-OPEN door of the Black Hawk, the sun glittered off the flat sapphire surface of the Atlantic, blurring by less than fifty feet below.

It had been a little more than an hour since we had landed, and we were twenty miles south of Sal, heading in two Black Hawks for Árvore Preta. The choppers were packed. The SEALs sat clipped by safety harnesses to the aircraft's deck, their feet dangling out the open door, while everyone else had to sit on one another's laps. It was dead silent but for the whirring whine of the rotor. I saw a SEAL check his watch, so I decided to check my own. We had seven hours to the deadline, I saw.

Seven hours to find the needle, I thought as I

slowly let out a breath, and we haven't even arrived at the haystack yet.

Vice President Rivera actually turned out to be extremely agreeable and helpful once he was brought up to speed on the threat. He had his men race off in one of the trucks and bring us back a man named Armenio Rezende.

Rezende, one of only two government-licensed nature guides on Árvore Preta, readily agreed to show us around the island. The happy-seeming middle-aged black man with dyed blond dreads told us he hadn't seen any suspicious activity on Árvore Preta but confirmed that there were several vent caves very high up on the ocean side of the unstable northern rim of the volcano's caldera.

I looked over at Rezende, sweating across from me in the Black Hawk's jam-packed cabin, then out at the water as a hopeless, horrible thought occurred to me.

What if we're wrong? What if this is just another head fake and the threat is coming from somewhere else altogether?

Bursts of white water exploded off jagged black rocks as we finally drew alongside Árvore Preta's desolate shore. It got a little cooler as we began to fly higher up the slope of the volcano toward the summit. Our two Black Hawks seemed tiny against the immensity of the volcanic black-rock mountain, like flies attempting the ascent of a cathedral roof.

Rezende directed the pilot over one of the jagged peaks near the summit, and we landed in a clearing of dull, light-brown dust at the bottom of a shaded gorge.

I closed my eyes against the pebbles and grit that stung my face as we piled out, and when I opened them, I just stood there gaping.

There had been some pines at the southern end of the island near the water, but up here there was nothing. In every direction was a dusky lunar landscape of black rock and black ash on which nothing moved.

"These are the four caves that I know about," Rezende said as he knelt and began drawing a crude outline of their locations in the dirt with his finger.

We decided to split up into four teams. Emily and I and Mr. Duke went with Nate's team west, up a slope of loose, black, sandlike volcanic dust. When we arrived at the top of a ridge, we climbed up an outcropping and looked down into the caldera of the volcano itself.

Mr. Duke had just pointed out what looked like

a cave opening in the dried lava bed a couple of hundred feet below when Nate's radio started popping, chattering frantically.

"Commander Nate! Nate!" came over the radio.

"What is it?"

"The island guide, Rezende. He just went nuts or something! He tried to shove Olender off a cliff, and now he's running up the hill! He's almost near the top. What do I do?"

"Drop his ass!" said Nate without hesitation. "In the legs if you can, but drop him. He could be going for the explosives!"

We heard the crackle of gunfire as we quickly headed for the eastern slope. When we got to its top, we saw a cluster of SEALs about a football field away, standing near the edge of a cliff, looking down. When I got to the edge of the cliff, I was hit with vertigo. It was insanely high up, a sheer hundred stories or so straight down to the sea.

"Mike! Look! This is it! This looks like the still from the video!" Emily said.

"What the f happened?" Nate said to his guys.

"I did like you said, Commander," one of them said. "I put two in him, one in the back of each knee, but then he crawled to the edge and just rolled off."

"He committed suicide, sir," said another SEAL. "I swear on a stack of Bibles. It was completely deliberate."

"But why?" said Mr. Duke.

"He must have been in on it is why," I said, looking around. "He was one of only two licensed guides, right? He had the run of the island basically to himself. He must have been paid to help the bombers. Damn it, I didn't even think of it."

Then I saw it. Off to the left, down the ledge of the cliff, about a hundred feet away was a fissure in the rock wall. A familiar one.

I stared at the almost circular opening in the wrinkled black rock, then way down the cliff, where petrels were flying this way and that like confetti. Emily was right. This was the place from the video. We'd actually found it.

The needle in the haystack.

# Chapter 87

THE SWIRLING LINES in the rock at the mouth of the volcanic cave reminded me of the mouth of the weird-looking guy in that famous painting *The Scream*. I felt like doing some screaming myself as we sat on our hands waiting and waiting.

We'd found the bombs.

One of the army bomb techs had done a recon, and there they were, just as the video had shown. Fifteen individual twenty-pound charges of Semtex had been found down the sloping three-hundred-yard channel of the cave. A three-football-field-long daisy chain of death and destruction connected with detcord and a shitload of wires and cables and who knew what else. Trip wires? Motion detectors?

Or maybe something new. With these bombers,

if we'd learned one thing, it was to expect the unexpected. Anything could happen now.

I stared down the cliff and imagined an explosion, the ground sliding as we rode half the mountain into the sea.

"You know, you really shouldn't be here," said Commander Nate, crouching down next to me.

"I know," I said as I stared at the silent radio in my hand. "I should be home making pancakes."

"No—I mean right here. We should get back."

"Nate, if those bombs in there go off, this whole mountain is coming down. Here is as good a place as anywhere to be blown into the bottom of the sea."

I stared at the mouth of the cave again. It was up to the army bomb squad guys now. Into that mouth thirty minutes before had gone five three-man army EOD teams with their spaceman bomb suits and remote-controlled robots known as wheelbarrows.

The wheelbarrows were armed with cameras, sensors, and microphones along with a "pigstick" device that could shoot an explosive jet of water to disable a bomb's firing-train circuitry. They'd even set up a cell-phone-jamming device connected to one of their Toughbook laptops to thwart any cell-phone triggers.

But even with all their high-tech gear, they had their work cut out for them and then some.

I stared at my radio, which had been completely silent for the last ten minutes, then I couldn't take it anymore. I stood and walked over to the cave and stuck my head in. Inside the entrance, it began to slope sharply down. It was oddly uniform. It looked almost man-made, like a subway tunnel to hell. Mr. Duke had explained that the cave, known as a lava tube, was a channel in the rock formed during a previous eruption. There was a raised stringy pattern in the floor and benchlike ledges along both walls where the explosives had been placed.

The radio I'd left behind me finally crackled for the first time, and I ran over to it.

"Render safe one. I repeat, render safe one. We got the first one," came over the radio.

"Two. Render safe charge two."

I looked up at a smiling Nate as he arrived.

"We got three. Three is down," said a voice as Nate gave me an amped-up high five.

"Mattie, this is Alpo," came an urgent voice over the radio a moment later. "We see something smoking up the cave to our left. I repeat. We see something smoking over by you along the wall."

There was a pause, then a one-word reply.

*"Down!"* screamed a voice as the rumble of an explosion went off deep inside the cave.

In super slow motion, I turned toward the mouth of the cave as I felt the shudder through the rock around me. It was the same shudder I felt when 26 Fed had come down, and I stared up at the blue of the sky waiting for the world to end.

# Chapter 88

GREAT. JUST GREAT, Martin thought, looking out the van's windshield as he woke up.

It was 6:00 a.m., and, no bones about it, his *Escape from New York* bid with the kids had failed spectacularly.

He was on I-95, but not outside the city, as per the plan. No, he was heading the wrong way—back into the city—in the East Bronx, parked off the side of the road, pointing south.

How it had happened he couldn't say. He had tried valiantly to get upstate, like Mike had told him, but everywhere they had gone the roads had been blocked by accidents or police. All night long he kept getting shunted this way and that. Bottom line, he'd been forced back in exactly the wrong direction.

It got worse. They were now on a concrete bridge above a body of water, an inlet of some sort. The last sign they had passed before he had gone to sleep said CITY ISLAND.

He didn't know too much about the Bronx, but even an Irishman knew that City Island was a place where there were seafood restaurants and fishing boats you could charter. Things really couldn't be more dire. They were now stuck in the Bronx right by the not-so-beautiful sea.

He looked in the rearview mirror at the sleeping kids. At least they had finally zonked out. They were fed and watered after a stop at a gas station around three. There was no gas at the station, of course, as all the tanks were empty, but he'd let them go to town on sweets in the store.

They'd come out with Pringles, Combos, sodas, every variety of M&M's known to man. Anything to keep them blissfully unaware of—what? Coming disaster? Apocalypse?

"Unbe-shighting-lievable," he mumbled as he stared out at the graying sky, then at the *E* on the gas gauge.

"What was that?" said Seamus, sitting up.

"Nothing, Father," said Martin. "Go back to sleep. We're good.

"Actually, Father . . . ," he added as he glanced out the window to his right.

"What is it, son?" said Seamus, yawning.

"Father, I was just thinking. We weren't able to make it upstate, right?"

"I'll say," Seamus said, looking around. "We didn't even make it out of the Boogie Down."

"Well, look over there," said Martin, pointing out the window at a stand of high-rises a couple of miles west on the horizon.

"That's Co-op City," said Seamus. "What about it?"

"Well, you know how in the tsunami videos from Indonesia a lot of people on the beach didn't do so hot? But you can see plenty of folks on the roofs of the hotels and what have you doing seemingly okay. What do you say we head over there to those buildings and see if we can't gain some higher ground?"

"But I thought you said that we still had some gas," Seamus said.

"Bless me, Father, for I have sinned. The tank is dry, I'm sorry to report. We need to get off this bridge, at any rate. For all we know the wave could be heading toward us right now."

Seamus turned to the rear of the van.

"Kids, kids! Wake up! Wake up now!"

"What now?" said Eddie with his eyes still closed. "Is the van on fire?"

"No," said Seamus. "Grab your things. We're all going for a walk."

"A walk on the highway?" said Brian.

"In the Bronx?" Juliana joined in.

"Rise and shine, Bennetts. One and all," said Seamus. "It's time to abandon ship!"

# Chapter 89

BUT THE WORLD didn't end.

The world and the mountain held. We didn't know how. All we knew was that the echoes of the blast finally dissipated and the shudder slowly subsided in the rock. Miraculously, the mountain and the molecules of our bodies all decided to stay happily together.

"We got it!" came over the radio. "Coming out!"

Twenty minutes after they had gone in, the EOD guys came out of the godforsaken cave in their green astronaut bomb suits. The last guy out was a tight-lipped bomb tech, a short and wiry Italian-looking fortysomething guy with dark, hooded eyes. His buddies helped him take off the tool smock hanging down the center of his chest and pull off his spaceman helmet. His sweat-soaked hair was plastered to his forehead as if he'd just gotten out of the shower.

He put down the red-and-black portable X-ray machine they used to check for booby traps, then rolled onto his back in his eighty-pound suit like a dusty upended turtle. One of his buddies handed him something, and he began expertly rolling a cigarette with his oversize, muscular mechanic's hands.

His name was First Sergeant Matthew Battista of the 789th Explosive Ordnance Disposal Company. He taught at the EOD school at Eglin Air Force Base, near Destin, Florida, and was said to be the best and most technically proficient and experienced bomb tech in the army and perhaps the world.

"Okay, Mattie, what's the story? If we all weren't currently having heart attacks, the suspense would be killing us," Commander Nate said, handing him a baby wipe.

Mattie wiped at his sweaty face as he lay against the rock, staring up at the cloudless sky. He smoked his cigarette in the corner of his mouth without touching it.

"The blast was from a disposal failure," he finally said. "We were pulling out pieces of detcord through the ring bolts next to cables in the walls, and something must have screwed up—probably a bad piece of deteriorated cable. It's the same really old Soviet shit we saw in Iraq. Bad cable coupled with some friction burn is my guess. Only a small piece went off, though. About four feet. Thank God we cut it up beforehand."

"So you were able to defuse everything else?" said Emily. "Did you find the detonator? Was it on a cell-phone trigger? A mechanical timer?"

"That's what I can't figure out," he said, shaking his head. "It's all wired up, ready to go. We found this."

He reached over and took two items out of his smock. He held up a small black box with some wires sticking out of it and a brown plastic device with three buttons on it.

"Is that a garage door opener?" I said, looking at it.

He nodded.

"And the black box is a garage door receiver," he said. "Seen them before. You press the opener, and it sends a signal to the receiver, just like a cell-phone trigger. The whole daisy chain in there was wired up to this receiver except for one crucial detail. The receiver also has to be wired up to a

382

battery in order for it to set off the detcord. There was no battery. Also, there was no battery for the opener, either."

"So there was no way to set it off," Emily said.

Battista shook his head.

"They left out the final piece. Makes sense in terms of safety. I wouldn't want any juice within twenty square miles of this much explosive. Much safer to bring the final pieces together right when you want to blow it."

"So what do you think, Mike? Rezende had the batteries on him?" Emily said. "Remember how he insisted on hitting his house and throwing on his hiking boots before getting on the bird? The first thing we need to do is retrieve Rezende's body and begin scouring his records. He didn't do this by himself."

"No, that's the second thing we do," I said, taking out the satellite phone. "First we call New York City and cancel the evacuation."

# Chapter 90

THIRTY-EIGHT NAUTICAL MILES due north of Árvore Preta, back at Amilcar Cabral International Airport on Sal, the first-class passengers on a flight from Munich had cleared customs and were entering the main terminal.

The terminal was very modern—clean and bright, with white walls and polished glass and floors. The in-flight magazine had said its recent remodel was evidence of Cape Verde's growing appeal to vacationing Europeans looking for an exotic tropical experience.

As he walked, Mr. Beckett remembered what the place looked like in the early '70s, when he arrived on his first field assignment during the rebellion. The Portuguese military helicopters behind sandbags out on the tarmac; the bullet holes in the barred windows; the nervous-looking troops and press. It had been an exotic experience then as well.

"Gorgeous day. Truly breathtaking," Mr. Joyce commented, staring at the shining squeaky-cleanness of the glass terminal.

They were both dressed casually now, Eurosporty, with tailored sport coats over Adidas tops, expensive jeans, and Chanel aviator sunglasses.

"Indeed," said Mr. Beckett as he pulled his rolling Gucci suitcase around a group of Africans and Western travelers sleeping and reading magazines in a row of pleather airport seats. He gazed up at the beams of light spilling down from one of the many overhead skylights.

"One might even call it a *momentous* day," he said.

They laughed together as they walked. Then Mr. Beckett yawned. He hadn't been able to sleep on the flight. Then he smiled again as he took a deep breath.

That was okay. He felt a second wind coming. One last sprint left for the final mile.

"Where is Katarina?" Mr. Joyce said as they approached the airport exit. "I specifically told her to be waiting for us up ahead, at the car-for-hire. I don't like this."

"Don't be paranoid, Mr. Joyce," said Mr. Beckett, grinning at his companion. "We're here. It's done. You need to enjoy it. In an hour, we call Armenio, who will rig the detonator. All we need to do now is go to the hotel and order Champagne. We dial the number and sit back on the seaside balcony and watch."

"Watch the fun?" said Mr. Joyce.

Mr. Beckett nodded vigorously.

"Yes. There'll be so much fun the entire world won't know what to do."

"For Mikhail?" said Mr. Joyce, looking at his partner.

Mr. Beckett agreed with a solemn nod. "All for poor Mikhail." They were near the exit, and Mr. Beckett was turning his phone off airplane mode, when a plain, petite, dark-haired woman in chic business wear and heels burst through the terminal's entrance and made a beeline for them.

"Katarina! What is it? What's wrong?" said Mr. Joyce.

"Everything!" Katarina said, swallowing. "Everything is wrong!"

# Chapter 91

"SLOW DOWN, KATARINA, before you run us off the road," said Mr. Beckett as they sped out of the airport in her tiny pale-green Fiat.

"I've been calling you since this morning," she cried. "It's a disaster!"

"Slowly, Katarina. What happened?"

"What happened? I should be asking you that," she said. "You said this would be discreet and that no one would ever know. Why did you contact the authorities? You never said anything about a ransom."

"A what?"

"A ransom! Don't give me that. Like you don't know! It's all over the news! The BBC! Where have you been?"

"We've been out of contact on an airplane,"

said Mr. Beckett. "What's all over the news?"

"You really don't know? They're evacuating New York!" she shrieked.

Mr. Beckett and Mr. Joyce looked at each other in horror.

"No," Mr. Joyce groaned. "Not now. We're so close."

"You said a ransom. What ransom?" said Mr. Beckett.

"The BBC said the Americans said they were evacuating New York and the Eastern Seaboard because of a tsunami warning," Katarina said as she screeched around a traffic circle, nearly on two wheels. "But the BBC said that was an unlikely story and that there were rumors about an impending terrorist attack and a ransom demand."

"We didn't ask for a ransom," Mr. Joyce said. "Who would do that if we didn't?"

"Two words. Dmitri Yevdokimov," said Mr. Beckett after a long thirty seconds.

"That son of a bitch we bought the aluminum dust and the pump trucks from?" said Mr. Joyce.

"He's the only one clever enough," Mr. Beckett said, looking out at the passing island countryside. "Besides, he's a computer expert. I knew I shouldn't have given him my fucking e-mail. He must have hacked us—saw our plans and the video we were going to show after. He put two and two together, copied the video, and tried to pull a ransom deal."

"I'm going to handcuff him to a radiator and snip out his liver with a pair of kitchen scissors!" Mr. Joyce said, screaming, as he punched at the door of the car. "He ruined our entire plan!"

"It gets worse!" Katarina yelled. "The fucking Americans are here! Armenio texted me two hours ago with this," she said, handing Mr. Beckett her phone.

American soldiers just arrived in the village. I will do my best to keep them away but I will set it off manually if I can't. Whatever happens the deal is still on.

"I keep trying to call him back, but he doesn't respond. He must be under arrest by now. Or dead. It's over. What are we going to do now? I'm all over Armenio's phone. We need to get out of Cape Verde now."

"It doesn't matter. Nothing matters," said Mr. Joyce, starting to cry in the backseat.

"Katarina, stop the car!" said Mr. Beckett, suddenly clutching his chest. "I'm not kidding. My chest. I'm having chest pains! I need my medication! In my bag in the trunk. Pull over! Please! Oh, it hurts!"

Katarina pulled over on the side of the deserted two-lane country road beside a stubbled field with baby sheep and goats roaming over it. Mr. Beckett stumbled out onto the shoulder and went to the trunk.

"Katarina! Help me—over here!" said Mr. Beckett a second later.

When she arrived at the trunk, Mr. Beckett without preamble smashed Katarina in the face with a tire iron. Blood poured out between her fingers, clutched to her face, as she began immediately to backpedal.

He hit her again in the back of the head as she turned, then she fell backwards into an irrigation ditch filled with muddy rainwater that ran parallel to the road.

She was beginning to crawl back up onto her knees when Mr. Beckett arrived to finish up. Right there in broad daylight, with three more blows to the head, he beat her to death with the tire iron as the baby sheep looked on.

A minute later, he was back on the road next to the car. He wiped the tire iron with a thin pink sweater that had been draped on the back of the driver's seat before he chucked it back in the trunk, tossed the sweater in after it, and closed the lid.

Crushing her cell phone under his heel, he found and pocketed its SIM card before he checked his watch. Then he got into the driver's seat and made a U-turn back toward the airport.

He wriggled his wet toes in his muddy shoes as he drove. He'd have to hit the gift shop for some socks.

He hadn't killed Katarina because she had disappointed him. On the contrary, she'd been loyal and competent to a fault in helping to set everything up. He'd even been good friends with her father back during the Cape Verdean revolution he'd helped bring about.

He killed her simply because he always covered his tracks. That's why he had been in business for so long. It was the secret of his success.

In the backseat, Mr. Joyce was still sobbing.

"I know it's disappointing after all our hard work," said Mr. Beckett. "All the money, all the planning. We got rooked—they were ahead of us by a few measly hours. It was the ambitiousness of the plan. The more people, the more moving parts, the easier for one to malfunction."

"But that city! That city deserves to be destroyed! What about Mikhail? What about Mikhail?!" sobbed Mr. Joyce.

"This isn't over. Not by a long shot," Mr. Beckett said reassuringly. "We need to regroup and go to the backup plan. We're still ahead of them. We'll use the Dutch passports and be back in New York by tomorrow."

Mr. Beckett looked up at the narrow-bodied DC-9 airliner on takeoff that roared low over their car as they turned into the airport access road.

"There is more than one way to skin a cat, my son," he said.

# Chapter 92

"I HAVE TO admit, Mike, the homebound leg of this trip is starting to grow on me a little," Emily said, yawning, as she placed her seat in the way-back position on the other side of the maple-paneled cabin.

"I'll say," I said, swirling the glass of Pinot Noir in my hand. "You think Yelp has a corporate jet section? I don't know about you, but I'm giving this puppy five stars all the way."

Things were looking up, for a welcome change. The mayor was so pleased with our finding the explosives that she insisted on sending her personal aircraft to give Emily and me and the two geophysical experts a lift home.

And what a plane. It was a sleek, brand-new eighty-million-dollar Bombardier Global 7000, with a custom interior that looked like a Park Avenue apartment. There were built-in flat screens everywhere, an Irish linen–covered dining table, Oriental rugs.

I couldn't tell which was softer or more soothing, the classical music playing on the overhead speaker, the heated leather seat, or the dimmed lights. I yawned, too, and wriggled my aching shoeless feet against the expensive carpet as I drained my glass.

I'd actually buzzed back my own seat to catch a little sleep when my aggravating brain started bringing stuff up. Stuff like how though we'd finally put some points on the board, this wasn't over. How it wouldn't be over until the bombers were dead or behind bars. Mostly I couldn't stop thinking how my kids, along with everyone else in New York, were still extremely vulnerable, and soon my finger found the seat switch and I was heading back into the upright position again.

I asked the flight attendant for some coffee and took out my laptop. A moment later, I had my e-mail open and for the tenth time started reading through the detailed brief that the excellent Cape Verde Judicial Police had put together about the island guide Armenio Rezende.

Police divers had found Rezende dead in the

surf on the southwest side of the volcanic island about three miles away from the cliff he'd jumped off, and what they recovered from his pocket chilled me every time I thought about it.

Four twelve-volt garage door opener batteries.

So our theory was actually true: Rezende had tried to set off the bombs. He'd been dead set on killing himself and all of us there.

And only the Lord knew how many other innocent people would have died had the entire mountain shaken loose and crashed down into the sea.

I thought about the 2004 Indian Ocean tsunami that had killed 230,000 people. Five Yankee Stadiums of human beings, old and young, innocent after terrified innocent, suddenly caught in the flood. Schoolchildren washed out of their desks and drowned in their classrooms. Commuters on trains looking up from their papers to see the ocean coming in the window. Mothers made to watch as their babies were whisked away in the flood or crushed by debris.

And someone wanted that? Rezende wanted that? I thought as I glanced out the dark circle of the plane's window. He wanted countless homes and factories and churches and cities and towns destroyed? He wanted 230,000 last gulps of breath from people he didn't even know? How? Was Rezende a space alien? A zombie from a crypt? Because it didn't compute, that much hate. Not in human terms. How could a human be okay with a quarter million murders on his soul?

Yet it was true. Rezende did want it. Had in fact died trying to make it happen. Rezende had wanted it, along with whoever else was involved.

Because it was obvious that Rezende wasn't the mastermind. We'd sat down with the Cape Verde cops before we left, and they told us Rezende didn't even have a passport and that he had never been anywhere—let alone New York City.

No, Rezende was low-level, I thought, going over the report. He had several assault arrests as a young man, some domestic violence incidents, a 2010 burglary charge that didn't stick. He definitely didn't have any industrial or military experience with explosives.

What he did have, though, was a recent radical conversion to Islam. On his computer, they found records of time spent on jihadist websites. Time spent in chat rooms known to be frequented by people from al Qaeda and ISIS.

I thought about the low-level American criminal turned to Islam who recently beheaded a woman in

Oklahoma. Maybe that was where all the hate was coming from. Islamic jihad was certainly no stranger to inhuman acts of barbaric violence these days.

That wasn't all. What was even more curious was the fact that Rezende had an uncle on his father's side who was one of the most violent of the revolutionaries during the Cape Verde independence movement.

In the late '60s and early '70s, Cape Verde, along with the African continental nation of Portuguese Guinea, fought for independence from Portugal in a bloody jungle guerrilla war that many people called Portugal's Vietnam. The Marxist rebels, led by Amilcar Cabral, had about a third of the troop strength that the Portuguese had, but the rebels were heavily supported by the Soviet Union with supplies and weaponry, including jet aircraft. We'd learned from the Cape Verde cops that Rezende's late uncle, Paulo Rezende, who raised him, was a colonel in that rebel army and was actually trained to fly MiGs in Russia.

The Russians again, I mumbled at the screen. It keeps coming back to the Russians.

"Who am I kidding?" Emily said, suddenly sitting up across from me. "I can't sleep, either, with these maniacs still running loose out there. Is there any coffee left, Mike?"

# Chapter 93

"LET'S RUN THROUGH it again from the very beginning," I said after the flight attendant, Patricia, had poured a coffee for Emily.

"Okay," Emily said, tucking her stockinged feet underneath her. "We land at Rezende's village."

"We land at Rezende's village," I repeated with a nod. "What I don't understand is, if he was planning to detonate the bombs by the deadline, why wasn't he on Árvore Preta already?"

"That's an excellent point, Mike," Emily said. "According to the deadline described in the video threat, he should have had all the batteries in place already—had everything ready to go."

"But he didn't," I said, drumming my fingers along the edge of my Toshiba laptop. "We definitely seem to have surprised him. His attempt to manually set off everything with the batteries proved that. All the meticulous planning and money and expertise required to wire up the mountain came down to some sloppy and desperate last-ditch ploy to insert the batteries? No way. That doesn't make any sense."

"So what happened? Rezende was definitely involved in the planting of the explosives," Emily said, biting her lip. "Did he wake up late? There was some communication screwup? Why the hell was he surprised if the deadline was only two hours away?"

"Maybe . . . ," I said, tapping my forehead as I stared down at my socks.

"Maybe what?" Emily said after a moment.

I snapped my fingers as I looked up.

"Maybe the people who set the bombs up weren't the ones who called for the ransom. Maybe we're looking at two different groups."

"What do you mean? How? The guys on the phone actually sent a video of the bombs being set up."

"True, they *sent* a video, but did they *make* the video?" I said.

"You're losing me."

"I keep thinking about our initial read that the

bombing campaign is the idea of one person—one very angry, very motivated, very meticulous person—who is solely out to terrify and to destroy the city. That still makes the most sense to me."

"Me, too," Emily said with a nod. "The first thing the Unabomber told us out in Colorado was spot-on: 'They're going to destroy New York City—you know that, right?'"

"Precisely," I said. "The ransom-money play never corresponded to that. What if someone found out about the plot, found the video of the real people setting it up, and decided to try to make money off of it?"

"A piggyback!" Emily said. "That's entirely possible. Someone co-opting it."

"Somebody Russian or who runs around in Russian circles," I said.

"You're right," Emily said, putting her coffee down. "The mayor's sniper had Russian ties, there were Russian explosives on the island, and now the direct Russian connection to Rezende through his uncle."

I glanced out at the cloudy night rushing past the large porthole window beside me again as I racked my brain. Then it hit me. Right between the eyes, forty thousand feet above the dark Atlantic.

"Dmitri Yevdokimov!" I yelled, suddenly sitting up. "The Russian we had in custody. Not only can we place Yevdokimov at the drop where the video was picked up, he's also a computer expert."

"That's it," said Emily excitedly. "Yevdokimov must have hacked the real Russian bomber, copied the video, and cooked up the ransom deal!"

"Yevdokimov's the link. We needed to find him yesterday," I said as I almost knocked over my china coffee cup while fumbling out my phone to call New York. "He's the only one who knows who the real bombers are."

# Chapter 94

THE LINE OF massive steel pylons forming the truck-bomb barrier were built directly into the asphalt across the width of Broad Street. They glinted dully in the morning sun as we pulled up in front of them eight hours later.

Beyond them to the north, up the man-made slot canyon of Broad Street, you could see the reason for all the security—the iconic columned edifice of the New York Stock Exchange.

We were down here in lower Manhattan's Canyon of Heroes territory not for a ticker-tape parade or to engage in insider trading but to head into the new FBI headquarters across the street from the exchange, at 23 Broad.

The whole block around the exchange already had incredible security, so it was a no-brainer after the fall of 26 Federal Plaza for the FBI to rent out space at what had to be one of the safest blocks in the entire city, if not the planet. Still, as we waited for our turn at the checkpoint, I frowned at the oak-trunk-thick steel rods that formed a line across the street. There was something depressing and barbaric about them, something medieval.

"You know you're living in some interesting times," I said to Emily, riding shotgun, "when they've actually brought back the drawbridge."

The pylons retracted into the street after we showed our creds to federal cops manning the checkpoint, and we drove up and parked in 23 Broad's underground lot. We'd been able to catch some sleep and actually shower on the mayor's incredible plane, so we weren't looking too bad as we rode the fancy financial building's mirrored elevator up to the thirty-first floor.

I looked down at my suddenly vibrating phone to see that Fabretti was trying to call me. He'd texted me earlier to try to coordinate a media strategy, of all things. The raid on the island had been leaked to the press, apparently, and they wanted details. Leaked by whom? I wondered. I hadn't texted him back, nor did I answer his call. He didn't seem to understand that we were still very much in the middle of this. It wasn't mission-accomplished time.

Emily smiled at me in the elevator mirror as I looked up. We held eyes for a moment. Then two moments. Her eyes were nice to look at.

"What?" I finally said.

"Your kids," she said.

"Oh, them," I said, smiling back.

After we'd gotten off the plane, we'd been by my apartment to squeeze in a happy-reunion-slash-power-breakfast with my kids. Seamus had done God's work by having piles of scrambled eggs and toast and Irish sausages hot and ready for us. As we devoured them, the gang had regaled us about their incredible failed *Escape from New York* odyssey in the van. I laughed the hardest when they said they had to practically carry poor Martin, completely exhausted, into his dorm room back at Manhattan College.

He was probably still sleeping, I thought. Or looking for a new job.

"What about my little tykes?" I said to Emily as we ascended. "What did they do this time? Was it Eddie?"

She shook her head and smiled. "They're just terrific. All of them. So alive and funny and happy and good. They actually care about each other. No one even has kids anymore, and you have ten. Ten! That's a lot of love. They're so lucky."

"I'm the lucky one," I said. "They practically take care of *me* now."

Off the elevator in the hall on thirty-one, there was an incredibly stunning airplane-like view of the city. Outside the floor-to-ceiling glass on the east side, you could see the arches of the Brooklyn Bridge, and down the corridor was a clear shot of the gleaming Freedom Tower and Lady Liberty out in the harbor.

"This city doesn't quit, does it?" Emily said, walking over and pressing her forehead to the glass like a little kid.

"All the people and motion and money and work and art and history. Dizzying, jaw-dropping sky-scraper after dizzying, jaw-dropping skyscraper every-where you turn. I mean, look at it. It's . . . a wonder."

"It sure is," I said, looking down with her at the slants of light on the buildings and the ant-size people on Broadway. Out in the wide, sparkling bay, a bath-toy tugboat was drawing alongside Liberty Island, chugging earnestly toward Bayonne.

"But you know what the bigger wonder is?" I said after a beat.

"What's that?"

"Why all these losers keep lining up to destroy it."

# Chapter 95

I FOLLOWED EMILY around a corner, where she pressed some buttons on an electronic keypad beside an unmarked door. On the other side of it was a huge busy bull pen of desks and cubicles with phones ringing and FBI agents tapping at computers and running around.

Without saying anything to anyone, Emily guided me through the office maze and around another corner to another unmarked door beside another keypad. She typed in another combo, and then we were in a cramped, too-bright windowless room where there were rows of servers on shelves and wires on racks and eight or nine people typing at computer terminals.

Emily introduced me around to the agents of the FBI New York office cyber investigative squad.

CIS supervisory agent Chuck Jordan was a young, intense, clean-cut guy who, in his sharp Tiffany-blue button-down dress shirt and gray slacks, looked more like a young finance guy than a cop.

Jordan had called Emily as we were finishing breakfast. He said he might have found a possible lead on Yevdokimov's whereabouts.

"So you think you have something for us, Chuck?" said Emily.

Instead of saying anything, Chuck handed us a photograph. It was a shot of a cluttered table with papers and books piled on it. There was a pair of glasses, a magenta Sharpie, and a crumpled napkin on an egg-crusted paper plate. Beyond the messy table was a room with bare, paint-chipped plaster walls and dirty hardwood floors. The space struck me as vaguely industrial.

In the top left-hand corner of the photo, you could see a shadeless window. In the window was the stone edifice of an old office building on the other side of a narrow street.

"This is the PC where the ransom demand originated from," Chuck said. "This shot is from the PC's webcam."

"Where is it?" I said.

"That's the rub," Chuck said. "We don't know.

They sent the signal through Tor, the underground computer network. It bounces things around so you don't know the actual physical location or owner of a particular computer. Basically, we can find the original computer. Unfortunately, we just don't know whose it is or where it is. That's why we turned on the PC's camera to get a clue from the room."

"You turned on the camera on the bad guy's computer? How?"

"After the judge gave us a warrant, we sent in our Trojan horse," Chuck said.

"Trojan horses are the investigative malware we use," Emily explained. "It looks like a regular program on the surface, but behind the scenes, it's secretly able to contact the PC's internal controller to allow backdoor access to the target PC."

"Like a virus or something?" I said.

"Technically, no," said Chuck. "Technically, a virus attempts to inject itself into other files. A Trojan is its own file."

"But how do you get in?" I said. "What about firewalls and stuff?"

"Most people have one or two popular antivirus programs, so we usually send the Trojan through a pretend update to one of them," Chuck said. "But in this case, the target didn't seem to have an antivirus program on the list, so we used an exploit in their browser's PDF parser."

"A what in the what?" I said.

Emily rolled her eyes.

"Does it matter, Mike? They went around it with some computer stuff. Bottom line, we can look at a bad guy's files, even turn on his webcam and microphone, which is what they did here."

"And you searched their files?" I said to Chuck. "Did you find the ransom video?"

"No, it's not there. They must have removed it," he said, squinting.

"What about encryption? This guy is a hacker himself," I said. "He has to use encryption, right?"

"He had layers upon layers of it, but we looked at the PC's recorded keystrokes and got the passwords to the encryption software he used."

"Got it," I said, gazing at the picture again.

I concentrated on the building beyond the window. It had setbacks and some fairly elaborate ornamentation in the stonework. Some stone wreaths and a lot of fleurs-de-lis. Where was this building? It definitely seemed familiar.

"Hey, wait. Did you get any audio?" Emily said.

"I thought you'd never ask," Chuck said with a

mischievous smile as he clicked a terminal's button.

"We picked this up just three minutes ago," he said. "This is a live feed. Listen carefully."

We did. There were sirens and traffic, and then we heard it. A soft, rhythmic buzzing sound.

"No," I said. "That's not what it sounds like, is it?"

"Oh, yes, it is," said Chuck, rubbing his hands together. "Someone is close to that computer, and they're snoring. We heard a door open ten minutes ago, then somebody creaking down onto what has to be a bed or something."

"Yevdokimov! Has to be!" Emily said. "He's there right now!"

"Wherever the hell 'there' is," I said as I gazed at the photo again. "This building in the window here. I feel like I know it. I just can't place it."

"It's definitely in Manhattan, definitely some-where below Ninety-Sixth Street," Chuck offered.

"Old, dirty, once-grand office buildings. Where in the city do you have these old, dirty buildings? Basically all over the damn place," I said, thinking out loud.

"Tribeca, maybe?" Chuck said. "Or SoHo?"

"Yes, kind of," I said. "But in SoHo, the buildings are usually older and have elaborate fire escapes and all that painted cast-iron cladding. With all these setbacks, this building is prewar—classic-*Superman* era."

"It looks huge," said Emily.

"It also looks high up," Chuck said. "Ten or twelve stories, maybe."

"Wait. I got it!" I said, violently shaking the photograph. "The fleurs-de-lis!"

"The what?" said Chuck.

"The fleurs-de-lis. The intricate stonework design here under the windows. And the setbacks. I used to work in Midtown South. I know where this is!"

"You know the building?" Emily said.

"No, but I know the neighborhood. It's the garment district. The West Side below Times Square," I said, ushering Emily to the door. "Tell your buddies downstairs to lower the drawbridge, because we need to get uptown and pop this Russian clown before he wakes up and we lose him again."

# Chapter 96

SIREN CRANKING, WE raced up the West Side Highway all the way to midtown. I got off at 34th and gunned it five blocks to Macy's. The light was red on Eighth Avenue, but there were no cars coming from the east or south, so I hooked a shrieking, fishtailing left around a shocked-looking DOT parking-ticket lady standing in the intersection.

I'd turned off the siren by the time we arrived to a skidding stop six blocks north, at 40th Street and Seventh Avenue. If Yevdokimov was in the area and still sleeping, the one thing I didn't want to do was wake him up.

We parked by the southeast corner of the intersection, where the statues were. One was a bronze eight-foot structure called *The Garment*

*Worker* that depicted a sad, old-looking, wrinkly guy in a yarmulke bent over a sewing machine, working on some fabric. Next to him was a gigantic button with a needle stuck through it. Between the two sculptures stood a dozen NYPD uniforms from the Midtown South task force, whom I'd called for help in finding Yevdokimov's hideout.

We rushed over to them, and I quickly took a radio from the task force sergeant, Rowe, before handing out photographs of both Yevdokimov and the building in his window.

"Remember, guys. You need to look up," I said. "This fleur-de-lis architectural design on the building we're looking for is going to be on the tenth floor or so."

We sectored out the district and split up on foot into two-person teams. Emily and I walked south down the east side of Seventh Avenue. We passed a gimcrack tourist gift place and a seedy-looking barbershop with a sign that said it bought gold. Fifth Avenue this was not.

As we walked, we looked east and west, up and down the side streets. Every one of them was extremely congested. Double-parked delivery trucks in the streets, loading and unloading. Guys on sidewalks pushing racks of plastic-wrapped clothes. It was coming on the lunch rush now, and clusters of workers were spilling out of the old buildings and jamming up the already crowded dirty sidewalks.

"These buildings are tremendous," Emily said as we walked with our necks craned and eyes up, like Iowa tourists fresh off the farm. "They almost look like a cross between art deco skyscrapers and factories."

"That's exactly what they used to be," I said. "All these buildings are mostly offices now, but back in the old days, they were vertical clothing factories. The art deco–like setbacks were required so workers on the upper stories would have light and air.

"It's hard to believe, but before manufacturing went to Asia, New York City was an industrial powerhouse. In the thirties and forties, seventy-five percent of women's clothes in the country were made right here between Sixth and Ninth Avenues, from Forty-Second down to Thirtieth. They were stitched up and put on racks and then rolled over to Macy's on Thirty-Fourth for sale. Everything was centered around Penn Station, so people from out of town could come in and shop. The garment district here is why New York's fashion industry still leads the world and Seventh Avenue means fashion."

"But if these were just factories, why so elaborate? Why all the architectural stuff, especially on the upper floors? You can't even really see it from down here," Emily said.

"The people who built them were poor Lower East Side Jews who came up out of the sweatshops and made good," I said, remembering something I'd read. "They wanted to make their mark by building factories that had over-the-top class. Also, they had a heart and wanted the mostly female workers stuck in the buildings all day to have something pretty to look at out the window, hence the stringcourses and volutes and egg-and-dart molding on the upper floors."

"How do you know so much about all this?" Emily said, giving me a baffled look.

"I'm not all brawn. I actually have a library card," I said with a shrug. "I also used to walk an evening beat here when I was fresh out of the academy, and I used to wonder about the buildings, so I did some homework. You quickly run out of things to look at after all the pretty secretaries go home."

We were at 36th Street, staring up at the

setbacks of an old telephone-company building, when Chuck Jordan called.

"Mike, we've been monitoring the room, and it sounds like the person snoring just woke up and left."

"Is the laptop still there?"

"Yes," Chuck said. "No change with that. Maybe it's nothing. Maybe he just went out to get something to eat."

I'd just hung up with Chuck when one of the uniforms hailed me on the radio.

"Hey, Detective. This is Sergeant Rowe," he said. "I think you should head over here to Thirty-Seventh Street near Eighth. I'm not positive, but I think I found that doodad you're looking for on a building about a quarter of the way toward Seventh."

"Good job, Rowe," I said as I grabbed Emily's arm and immediately started hustling her west toward Eighth Avenue. "We're about a block away. Don't leave yet, and try to stay out of sight. Keep your eyes peeled for Yevdokimov coming out of the building across the street. It looks like he's on the move."

We heard the yelling right as we made it to the corner of Eighth.

A block to the north, at the intersection of 37th, there was some kind of commotion in the street between a guy in a car and some guys on a motorcycle.

The car was a silver Mercedes double-parked beside a sidewalk construction shed, its bald driver half out of its window as he yelled. The two guys on the motorcycle beside him were dressed in black and wearing black full-face helmets. The big glossy orange Japanese motorcycle they sat on was so close to the Benz it seemed to be leaning on its left rear quarter panel.

Had the bike tapped the Benz? I thought, staring, as I started crossing 36th. A fender bender?

As I reached the other corner of 36th, the motorcycle's engine suddenly screamed as it roared away from the Benz like a rocket east up 37th.

*East* up *westbound* 37th! I thought as the driver threw open his door.

"Down!" I yelled as I dove to the ground.

I was just able to pull Emily down on top of me on the sidewalk when the Mercedes exploded with a blast of light and a deafening boom.

# Chapter 97

I GOT UP off my knees a disoriented moment later.
I stood there with my hands over my ears, waiting
for them to stop ringing, before I realized the
ringing was the piercing blare of a stuck car horn.

I looked north and saw that the sound was
coming from the half-blown-apart Mercedes.
Through what looked like billowing white smoke,
I could see the car up on the sidewalk, its front end
wedged under the wreckage of the now-collapsed
sidewalk shed.

I called in the description of the motorcycle
over the radio as I ran toward the wreckage,
pushing through an already clustering crowd on
the sidewalk and street. I squinted against the
nasty tang of burned metal as I began pulling
away the aluminum poles and wooden sheets of

the destroyed construction shed, trying to get access to the car.

As I peeled away the last couple of splintered plywood sheets, I saw that some type of tarp from the shed had fallen perfectly over the side of the car, like a showroom cover. Then I pulled the cover away, and I got my first good look at the damage.

The car's hood was folded in, and its front and rear windshields were completely shattered. All the interior air bags had gone off, and all the tires were blown flat.

I had to move one last sheet of wood to get a look at the driver. He gasped as he sat in the driver's seat of the ruined car, clutching the wheel with his right hand. The driver's door was missing. So was the driver's left arm below the elbow. His striped polo shirt was scorched and sliced to tatters from bomb shrapnel, and when he turned, I could see a still-smoking piece of metal the size and shape of a Dorito embedded in his right cheekbone.

"You're going to be okay," I lied to him. "Just sit tight. What happened? Did you see who did it?"

He didn't say anything. I watched his jaw suddenly clench and his lips begin to tremble. His whole face started shivering, like he was suddenly freezing. I was looking into his blue eyes when they glazed over and he stopped moving. I stepped back in startled horror, looking away. I knew I'd just watched him die.

I recognized his face when I peered back at him a split second later. It was Anatoly Gavrilov, the other Russian we'd brought in during the Bronx arrest of Yevdokimov.

Yevdokimov! I thought as I quickly looked past Gavrilov's body to the passenger door on the other side of the car. Shit! It was open, and there was blood on the passenger seat and in the footwell.

"Yevdokimov!" I yelled to Emily as I scrambled out of the wreckage and headed into the street around the destroyed vehicle's trunk. "He was in the car. He's hurt and on foot. The real bombers must have tried to hit him. C'mon, he can't have gotten far."

Around the other side of the car, there was an actual blood trail on the sidewalk. A lot of blood. Yevdokimov was obviously hurt very badly. It was like we were tracking a gut-shot deer up Eighth Avenue.

"Back out of the damn way!" I said to all the looky-loos, trying to preserve the crime scene.

We turned the corner, and the trail ran smack-dab into a tall West African street vendor who was crouched down, picking up iPhone covers out of the gutter.

"Hey! Anyone come past here bleeding?" I said.

"Yes! A white man. A crazy white man," said the vendor in a musical voice. "He had blood on his arm and pouring off his chin. I tried to get him to sit, but he pushed past me and knocked over all my stuff. He got into a taxi not a minute ago."

I couldn't see any taxi on 37th when I stepped into the street, so I radioed it in.

Officer Rowe and his buddies had arrived and were surrounding the scene when we went back around the corner to the wreckage. There had to be about a thousand people standing around now. Cars stopped in the street. Everybody had their phones out, immortalizing our bombing scene for the folks at YouTube to instantly globally disseminate.

"Fuck the police!" someone in the crowd threw out over the still-wailing horn to get a laugh. He got several, unfortunately.

"Isn't this great? We're going viral," Emily said as we stood there gaping at the still-steaming, torn-apart car.

"Of course we are," I said. "Who wants to watch Times Square Elmo beat the crap out of Times

Square Spidey when you got a real live blown-up guy in a car?"

"So I'm going to take a wild guess and say we're not the only ones looking for Yevdokimov," she said, raising an eyebrow.

"Guess not," I said as I moved back through the crowd into the street. I walked around Rowe and crawled back toward the front of the car and reached in over the dead Russian and found the keys still in the ignition.

People in the crowd actually booed as I finally cut the car's engine and the horn.

"That's all, folks," I said.

# Chapter 98

"SO . . . ANYTHING YET?" I said for the twentieth time over Chuck Jordan's shoulder as he sat at the desk, tapping at Yevdokimov's laptop.

"Oh, plenty, Mike, but I'm keeping it to myself," the young agent said, rolling his eyes.

"Why don't we give Chuck a little space to work, Mike?" Emily said, yanking me out into the hallway.

We were in Yevdokimov's flop now. We'd found it soon after the bombing. Sergeant Rowe had been spot-on. The building was just where he said it was, down the block from the bombing off Eighth Avenue on the north side of 37th. Yevdokimov's crash pad was on the tenth floor, and it was filled with me and Emily and about twenty FBI agents who were scouring every nook and cranny for some sign of who the real bombers could be.

We still were unsure of Yevdokimov's whereabouts. We'd told all the hospitals to be on the lookout for him, but so far, nothing was shaking. The good news was that we'd actually found three computers, which Chuck Jordan and his guys were now poking through.

"This isn't exactly what people have in mind when they think 'New York loft,' is it?" Emily said, looking at the moldering plaster and probably asbestos-covered overhead pipes. "What did the building manager say? This used to be a sewing machine factory? Wasn't there a famous fire in a sewing machine factory in New York in the eighteen hundreds or something? Because this place definitely looks haunted."

"You're thinking of the Triangle Shirtwaist Fire," I said. "That was down in the Village. After the fire started, more than a hundred garment workers died. People were jumping out windows. Because the kindly owners had gated and locked the exit stairwells to keep the workers on task.

"Some good actually came out of it, though, because the public went nuts, and it led to fire safety laws and sprinkler systems and fire escapes and the forty-hour workweek."

"You're just a walking Ken Burns documentary, aren't you?" she said.

"Yes, and my fee for this extended walking tour is the capture of a Russian homicidal bomber in handcuffs with a big shiny bow on his head."

"Get in here! I think I found something," Chuck Jordan bellowed.

We went back in. On the screen was a picture of three fat kids in an aboveground pool. It took me a couple of seconds to see Papa Yevdokimov sitting behind them on the pool ladder holding a Super Soaker water gun.

"These are Yevdokimov's personal photographs. There are about a hundred that show him at the same seaside cottage," Chuck said.

"It's his dacha," Emily said.

"His what?"

"I worked a Russian organized crime case a couple of years ago. Dachas are Russian vacation houses. All the mobsters have them back in the old country," she said.

"So are we going to try to peg the location from the background again?" I said.

"No. These shots are JPEGs with Exif file formats, which means that they were taken with a smartphone. Smartphone cameras record GPS locations of where each picture is taken in a process known as geotagging. Give me a second," Chuck said, clicking open some new screens.

"Here it is. The latitude and longitude," he said a second later. "It's Eleven Roseleah Drive, Mystic, Connecticut."

"That's where he's headed—has to be," said Emily.

"What are we waiting for, then? Let's roll," I said.

# Chapter 99

WE WERE BACK in the dingy building's hallway, getting a move on so we could head up to Connecticut, when the elevator opened and Chief Fabretti appeared.

"There you are, Bennett. I've been trying to call you," he said with an agitated look on his face.

"Sorry, Chief," I said, fishing my phone out of my pocket. "Oh, here's the problem. Left it on airplane mode."

"Stop screwing with me, Bennett," Fabretti said, pulling me over to a corner. "I've been getting calls from my bosses. Their counterparts over at the Bureau saw you traipsing around their new digs this morning. They said thanks but no thanks for your help. There's no more task force. The feds are taking over the investigation from here."

"What do you mean?" I said, agitated myself now. "We're right in the middle of this. We're about to grab the only guy who knows who the real bombers are."

"No, Bennett. They're about to grab him. Not you. The feds want to nail the bastards who blew up their building all by themselves."

"What about the college kids who died on the train and the mayor and the people who died in the EMP attack? They were New Yorkers, right? The people we're supposed to protect."

"It's already been settled. The FBI is going to get the credit for this."

"They can have the damn credit, and if there's any left over, you can have it. I'll leave before the reporters show, I swear. C'mon, Chief. We've got a beeline on this guy. We just need to find this bastard now before the real bombers take him out."

"It's over, Bennett. So stop arguing," Fabretti said, glaring coldly at me. "You're off the case, and that's an order. There were about a hundred robberies during the evacuation. We have plenty of work for you to do. Now drive me back to One Police Plaza."

"Mike?" called Emily from down the hall, where all the FBI agents were packed into the elevator.

"Go," I said. "Get this guy. It's up to you now. Don't lose him!"

"That's the spirit, Bennett," said Fabretti as the elevator door rumbled closed.

# Chapter 100

FABRETTI INSISTED ON buying me a coffee at a Times Square Starbucks before we headed way back downtown to One Police Plaza.

"See, Mike? I'm not such a bad guy," he said, tipping his non-fat latte at me as I chauffeured him down Broadway. "Listen, I know you've been neck-deep in this from the beginning, but this is coming from up high. The mayor—hell, the senior senator—is involved. We're just small potatoes."

"You're right," I said.

"Exactly. I'm doing you a favor. I heard the mayor sent her plane for you. That had to be sweet. A real ride on the gravy train. Or should I say 'the gravy plane'? Honestly, you play your cards right, Mike, you keep playing ball, retirement is going to be smooth sailing for you."

"Sure, definitely," I said, checking my phone to see if there was anything from Emily.

After another excruciating twenty minutes of Fabretti's pep talk, I dropped him off at the door of One Police Plaza. I told him I was going to park and meet him up at his office, but instead I actually squealed out of the lot and got immediately on the northbound FDR Drive.

I called Emily as I punched it.

"Where are you?" I yelled.

"We just crossed the Connecticut border, but we're still about two hours away. Mystic is practically in Rhode Island. We have a team of agents out of New Haven almost at the house. What's your status?"

"I'm on the highway about half an hour behind you."

"What about Fabretti?" Emily said. "Aren't you off the case?"

"I never heard him say that," I said. "My ears are still ringing from that car bomb."

"Mine, too, Mike," Emily said with a laugh. "See you there."

I hung up and asked Siri for directions and proceeded to put the pedal to the metal. I took the Robert F. Kennedy Bridge into the Bronx, then took the Bruckner to I-95.

It was coming on rush hour when I crossed into Connecticut and hit traffic. It was stop-and-go past Stamford when I saw the Chevy's tank was almost empty, so I got off at the next exit and pulled into a BP gas station and filled up.

As I stood squeezing the nozzle, I looked at my phone and laughed when I saw that Fabretti had left twenty angry texts. Where the f are you? came his latest.

Taking a ride on the gravy plane, I texted back. My phone rang a moment later.

"Hey, Robertson," I said.

"Mike, big news!" he yelled. "We just got a bead on two Russians that might be our guys. Brooklyn and I have been going bonkers with these flight manifests, but we have two Russian immigrants who have been back and forth to Cape Verde from the States six times over the last year.

"Their names are Vladislav and Oleg Filipov. They're father and son. Turns out they flew to Cape Verde out of Miami, not New York."

"Miami?"

"Yes. The father, Vladislav, ran a brutal Russian prostitution and drug-dealing crew there for most of the eighties and nineties—allegedly,

432

at least, since he never got caught for a damn thing. No fixed address."

"What about the son?"

"We don't have anything on him in terms of a record. He had a house in Queens up until six months ago, but since then, nothing. No address. No job. No visible means of support. I'm e-mailing you their photographs from their driver's licenses as we speak. They could definitely be the guys on the video. One older, one younger. They're looking good on this!"

"Sounds great," I said. "Yevdokimov will be able to ID these guys once we catch up to him. Really good job, Robertson."

I hung up and looked at the pictures of the two Russians. They didn't have goatees in the pictures, but they both had lean, pale faces with sharp features and the same strong nose.

I left the pump still going and went inside to grab a Gatorade and some Pringles when I saw the clerk at the back of the store by the restrooms, standing with a mop by a pool of something that had spilled. I stopped in my tracks by a rack of magazines when I saw *what* he was mopping.

It looked like blood.

"Hey, what's up, kid?" I said, rushing over. "Is that blood?"

"It ain't tomato soup!" the blond college-age clerk said with a disgusted face. "Some guy was just in here, and when he leaves, the next customer comes out white as a ghost, screaming, 'Ebola! Ebola!' It looks like somebody hemorrhaged in here. I told my boss, and he said I should start mopping, but I don't know. You think I should call the cops?"

"This bleeding guy, when was he here?"

"About ten minutes ago."

I grabbed the mop out of his hand as I took out my shield.

"I am the cops. Show me the camera now!"

# Chapter 101

"EMILY, LISTEN!" I screamed as I roared along the shoulder on I-95, scanning the stop-and-go traffic. "I just saw him! I just saw Yevdokimov on a gas-station video. I'm about five minutes behind him. He's in a white Nissan Altima on Ninety-Five outside Stamford, heading north past exit ten. He's probably heading toward you. New York plates two seven eight FRG. He's bleeding heavily, and—"

I dropped the phone as I suddenly saw a white Altima ahead in the left lane. I drew alongside it across two lanes of traffic. I checked the plates. It was him.

"I see him!" I said to Emily as I snatched up the phone. "I'm on him. We're between exits ten and eleven."

"Stay on him, but wait for backup, Mike, before you try a traffic stop. Chuck's on the horn with the Connecticut troopers. Hang back. We're coming to you."

A horn honked as I cut back into traffic, then Yevdokimov turned and saw me. He had some kind of bandage on his chin.

He immediately gunned it. He got out of the left lane ahead of the SUV in front of me. A second later, I saw him flash into the right lane and onto the shoulder, going for the exit ramp we were already passing.

At first it looked like he was going to make it, but then at the last second, he sideswiped the yellow water-barrel divider that cordoned off the exit ramp from the highway. I watched as he spun and hit the concrete divider on the other side of the exit with a horrible crunch of metal.

I got over to the right and braked and skidded to a stop on the shoulder and ran back toward the turned-around Altima, now almost completely blocking the exit.

I thought Yevdokimov was most certainly dead after this second incredibly violent incident of the day, so I was surprised when the passenger door opened and he staggered out.

"Down!" I yelled over the honking horns as I pointed my Glock at his head.

Because he was bleeding, I probably shouldn't have cuffed and moved him, but we were in danger from the traffic, so I had no other choice.

I had him in my Chevy, down on his stomach in the backseat, while I was in the front passenger seat rifling through the glove compartment for the first aid kit, when the truck rear-ended us.

The passenger door was open, and I was thrown from the vehicle. It was the weirdest sensation of my life. One second I was sitting there reaching into the glove compartment, and the next I was out in the air banging the crap out of the back of my head as I skidded across asphalt.

I eventually ended up on a berm of newly mowed grass beside the shoulder. My head was ringing. I must have had a concussion. I felt numb as I lay on the grass facedown, not moving. I was definitely in shock.

Eventually I turned to look at my car.

We'd been hit by a big pickup, a Ford Super-something truck with an extended cab and a push bar in front and six wheels. Everything on it was black. The big tires and rims; the body; the tinted windows.

The two guys who climbed out of it were in black as well. They had ski masks on, and they rushed over and pulled Yevdokimov none too gently out of my smashed Chevy and put him into the cab of the truck.

Behind them, cars were just driving past normally. Some horns honked, but that was it. I couldn't believe this was happening in broad daylight.

When I looked again, the guys in the ski masks were heading in my direction. That's when I saw the guns they were carrying strapped over their shoulders—the nasty little black Heckler & Koch submachine guns that ESU guys have. I reached for my service weapon and drew air. That was not a great feeling. My Glock must have skidded loose when I was thrown.

I started backing up, scrabbling weakly on my unsteady feet on the grass. I couldn't get my bearings. I felt off balance and floaty, like I was standing at the bottom of the deep end of a swimming pool.

I thought that was it. They'd just shoot me. But instead they grabbed me and threw me back down onto the grass. I almost laughed. It was like we were all kids again, and they wanted to wrestle or play football right there on the side of I-95.

I didn't feel like laughing anymore when one of them hit me hard across the side of my head with the metal top of the gun.

One of them was holding me down in a headlock and the other one was fishing for something in the pocket of his leather coat when the Connecticut state trooper vehicle skidded to a stop behind the truck.

"No!" I yelled as the two guys let go of me and without delay opened up on the gray police car.

I sat frozen, eyes closed, palming my ears as the two deafening Heckler & Kochs went off a foot from my face. When the gunfire ceased, I looked and saw that the patrol car's windshield was now a smoking sheet of holes from the fifty rounds that had ripped through it in the space of five seconds.

As I tried to get up, they got me in a headlock again and slapped a wet cloth onto my face. It was really wet and clingy, like an antibacterial wipe. They smothered me with it. Stuck it in my nostrils. It felt like I was drowning. The smell of it was heavily astringent, medicinal, the scent of rubbing alcohol and something vaguely bitter.

The drug, whatever it was, was powerful. Almost immediately, I felt light-headed. The sky and traffic started fading in and out, like my eyes were on a dimmer switch some kid was playing with.

It took me a second to realize that I was being lifted again. I hardly felt it when my face slammed against the dirty carpet of the pickup a second or two later. I looked up at Yevdokimov sitting in the backseat above me with his eyes closed. Then I turned and, in my swimming vision, saw that my phone had fallen out of my jacket and bounced loose under the seat.

It felt like it was ten pounds as I pulled it out and looked around. There was a little alcove with a drink holder and maps in it beside Yevdokimov's feet on the seat above me.

The front doors were popping open when, with my last bit of strength and consciousness, I reached up and dropped the phone in there and passed out.

# Chapter 102

I WOKE SOMETIME later. I was on my back on a cold, hard floor. I felt hungover, nauseated—that bitter alcohol scent still coating the insides of my nostrils. When I opened my eyes, the light was agonizingly painful, and when I tried to move, I got the spins. So I closed my eyes and lay still. After about ten minutes, I opened my eyes again in little slits, giving them time to get used to the idea.

After a minute or two, I made out that I was in a cramped room with rough stone walls and a raw-drywall ceiling. It was lit by a shop light on the floor whose cord snaked along the ground and out under a cheap wooden door. Across from me along one wall was a huge, cheap-looking leather couch, above which hung a big plastic roll of what looked like industrial Hefty bags on a cylindrical metal holder attached to the wall.

What the hell is this place? I thought groggily. A crash hangout for a janitor?

There was a strong musty smell in the air, which could only mean a basement. It comforted me somehow as I lay there. It was a happy smell. Suburban families, popcorn and videos on sleepovers, board games on a rainy day.

Those visions imploded as I heard the horrendous screams start in the distance. There were three in a row. Three impassioned shrieks of someone in hysterical, unholy pain.

*Get out now!* I told myself. But as I jumped up, it was like my feet had been pulled out from underneath me. I smacked the left side of my face pretty good on the concrete. What the hell? I thought. Then I looked down and felt like letting out some unholy screams myself as my mind kicked straight into adrenaline-pumping animal panic.

My left leg was handcuffed to an old galvanized steel heating pipe that was embedded in the concrete floor.

The door shot open. One of the ski-masked guys walked in. He had his jacket off and was wearing a black long-sleeved T-shirt. Behind him came a second ski-masked guy wearing an army-green long-sleeved T-shirt, dragging something heavy.

He was dragging Yevdokimov, I realized a moment later. The Russian was naked and very dead. I don't think I'd ever seen anyone more dead. His face and arms and chest looked like they'd been worked on by a very motivated demolition crew. There didn't seem to be a part of him that wasn't black or blue or covered in blood.

The second guy walked over and, with a squeak, wheeled off a huge sheet of plastic over the couch. He slit the plastic off the roll with a box cutter that he pulled from his pocket, then the two of them lifted Yevdokimov up and tossed him onto the plastic-covered couch, wrapping him up like the largest, sorriest fish in the history of the world.

They taped the ends with a roll of duct tape they produced from beneath the couch, and when they were done they lifted him up like a rug and dropped him on the floor. The black-shirted guy sat down on the couch and put his feet on Yevdokimov like he was an ottoman. Then his buddy joined him.

Robertson was right, I saw as they peeled off their ski masks. It was Vladislav and Oleg Filipov.

I'll have to congratulate Robertson, I thought. If I ever see him again.

Father and son Filipov sat there staring at me with their pale, sharp, nasty-looking faces and their feet up on Yevdokimov, not saying anything. Staring back, I'd never been so afraid in my life. My heart beat against my chest like that of a rat trapped in a corner, and when I swallowed, I realized that I didn't have any saliva in my mouth.

# Chapter 103

THE OLDER GUY started laughing.

"And how are you?" he said in a deep Russian accent as he laboriously stood up. "Here. I have something for you."

The old man took something out of his black cargo-pants pocket. It was a two-foot piece of flex pipe with a sharp-looking fist-size chunk of metal on the end of it. The metal part was a heavy brass hose bibb, I realized as he came forward and whipped me over the top of the head with the metal flail.

As I sat up, I felt a trickle of blood drip down from my scalp, a warm rivulet that fell over my forehead, along the side of my nose, over my closed lips, and off my chin. "Do you like my cop-be-good stick?" he said as I sat there in agony. "It's the whipping action of the flex pipe that really delivers the groceries. I also love the way it smashes and cuts at the same time. All without putting too much strain on my wrist. I'm older and must consider such things. You will cooperate with us now."

I glanced into my tormentor's cold brown eyes as my skull throbbed.

"So here we are," said the cruel prick as he sat down and crossed his legs on Yevdokimov's body. "You wished to find us, yes, Mr. NYPD? Well, be careful what you wish for."

"Aren't you going to ask us who we are?" said the younger guy—the one in the green T-shirt— who, unsurprisingly, had a Russian accent as well.

"You're the bombers. The terrorists," I finally said with slow deliberation as I continued to bleed. With the drugs and the pain and the fear, it wasn't easy to keep my voice steady.

"We are the bombers. This is true," said the old man. "But we're not terrorists."

"No. More like pissed-off citizens, you could call us," said the younger Russian, cutting in. "What's the word? Disgruntled—that's it. Call us disgruntled immigrants."

"But enough about us," said the old man, slapping the flail into a palm. "Let's see what you know, okay? Question one."

He lifted his booted foot over Yevdokimov and brought it down hard.

"Do you know why we killed this piece of shit?"

"The ransom," I said carefully. "He found your video and tried to make money off it."

The old pig looked surprised. "That's right. Yevdokimov and I were associates. We actually used to work together in the KGB a lifetime ago. I contracted out a job for him, but he made a mistake. He tried to turn the tables.

"Now," the old man said, stomping the body again with his combat boot, "Yev *is* my table."

"When you were in the KGB, you worked with Rezende's uncle," I said, putting the pieces together. "In Cape Verde, to overthrow the Portuguese."

"You know a little history, I see," the old man said. "Which is saying a lot for an American. That's exactly where I met Paulo Rezende and his tool of a nephew, Armenio. Paulo was there when I came up with the tsunami project back in 1971."

Now I was confused.

"Yes. Surprising, isn't it? This plan has been in the pipeline since before you were born, cop. The bureau called it Krasnyy Navodneniye."

He smiled.

"Operation Red Flood," he said.

# Chapter 104

"IT STARTED OUT as a lark, really," the old man continued. "One night, Paulo and I came back from a bombing run and were listening to the BBC news. A story about the latest volcanic threat on Árvore Preta and a geologist who speculated that one piece falling off the volcano might be a titanic tsunami threat to the United States.

"That got me thinking. Why not just get some dynamite and give that cliff a push? I put it over the wire back to the big boys in Moscow, and they just ate it up. A month later, they sent out a team of engineers and surveyors who concluded that it could be done. They commissioned and typed up a plan for exactly how to do it, down to the last detail. I actually got a promotion for think-tanking that attack. And why not? It was genius."

"Why didn't they do it?"

"They were thinking about it in late 1980, I heard. There was some seismic activity, so they were going to make it look like an accident, but then Reagan got elected, and they thought if the truth ever came out, he was just crazy enough to let the nukes fly."

"Why now, then?" I said. "Why destroy New York now? Does Russia want to bring back the glory days and start World War Three?"

"No," said the old man. "We have no political agenda. I gave up all that political shit years ago. I've been a good honest crook for the last twenty years."

He looked over at the younger Russian.

"I did it for my son here," said the old man, patting the other guy on the back. "For him and for my grandson."

"Your grandson?" I said, panicking, thinking there was still another nut out there we hadn't found yet.

"My son, Mikhail," the younger Russian said, staring almost sadly at me. "We did it for Mikhail."

# Chapter 105

THE YOUNGER RUSSIAN took a photo out of his wallet and walked over and crouched beside me.

"Do you recognize him?" he said.

The picture was of a pale young teenager with a slightly misshapen shaved head. His eyes weren't exactly level with each other. He was more than a little loony-looking, but I kept that to myself.

"No. Should I know him?" I asked.

"Yes. He was on the cover of the *Daily News* last year."

Too bad I read the *Post*, I thought, not knowing where this could be going.

"Did something happen to your son?"

"I'm a thinker, an introvert, a shut-in, some might say," the Russian continued. "I like books. Math, physics, mechanics, engineering, abstract things. But back in my twenties, I was a little more outgoing, and I had a dalliance with a stripper."

"One of my workers," said the old man. "I owned four clubs in Miami at the time. It was his twenty-first birthday. The least I could do."

Father of the year, I thought.

"So she got pregnant, and Mikhail was born. He had problems from day one. Birth defects, then a diagnosis of autism, then schizophrenia. All these stupid diagnoses just to say he was mentally not okay."

"Years of psychologists and medication and my favorite—therapy," said the old man, disgusted. "Bullshit! All of it!"

"They wanted to institutionalize him," the son continued. "But I said no. I knew there was somebody in there. Somebody smart who could be funny and who just needed to be watched over. So I took care of him. I raised him by my side; he was with me all the time. He was a big pain in my ass, but he was smart. We would play chess and cards. He was so good at cards. Could add in his head almost as fast as me."

The son looked down at the floor wistfully as he took a breath.

"In 2012, he was doing okay enough that I was

able to leave him with an aide every once in a while. The aide, I thought, was a good man, but he turned out to be not so good. Because he smoked dope and fell asleep one morning while I was at an engineering conference in Philly, and Mikhail left the apartment alone.

"He got on the subway, and I don't know what happened, but that morning in upper Manhattan, he pushed a woman in front of the number one train."

"At a Hundred and Sixty-Eighth Street," I said, vaguely remembering the case now. "That's why you blew it up."

"Yes," the son said. "You're catching on. See, Mikhail was taken into custody. I'm away. Mikhail has no one, no ID. He can't speak for himself, but he was obviously mentally sick. They should have taken him to a hospital, yes?"

"No," said the old man bitterly. "Turned out the Manhattan DA knew the female victim and pulled strings to have Mikhail booked, put immediately into the system. Without learning the details about Mikhail's condition. Without thinking about any of the consequences. Do you know the name of the man who was the DA at the time?"

"Mayor Carl Doucette," I said.

He nodded, smiled.

"The *late* mayor Carl Doucette," he said.

"So Mikhail is booked, and there's no room in Central Booking to hold him, so they send him over to Rikers," the son said. "My son cannot cope with this. He's mentally sick, like I say, so he starts freaking. A corrections officer puts him in a room they have in the basement for people not cooperating. This room was over a hundred degrees. They said it was some boiler problem.

"It sure was a problem for Mikhail. They left him there for two days—my son. They forgot about him. My poor Mikhail. New York City boiled my mentally ill son alive."

# Chapter 106

"WHY DID YOU EMP Yorkville?" I said.

"Mayor Doucette had his mother at Sloan Kettering hospital," said the old man, smiling again. "The precious old girl didn't make it during the evac. Shame."

"And Twenty-Six Federal Plaza?"

"The corrections officer who locked up Mikhail got a new job on the maintenance crew there," said the old man. "I would have taken down an airliner if he was one of the passengers. To hell with him for slaughtering my grandson and to hell with this city and America. Oh, how you crowed when the Cold War was over; how much greater your country was than ours with your freedoms—or so you thought.

"And now look at yourselves. You have the

freedom to land planes at the wrong airports, the freedom to shunt downtown trains onto uptown tracks, the freedom to kill prisoners by accident. Why? I don't know. All I know is that you're a pack of fools, and a fool and his civilization are soon parted.

"Because this isn't over," he said. "If it takes us twenty years, we're going to make you bastards pay. I ran the Russian mob in Miami. I have millions of dollars and contacts and access to many interesting things. If you think Krasnyy Navodneniye is the only recipe in the old Soviet book of dirty tricks, think again. You should have thought twice before you fucked with my family!"

"I hear you," I said, trying to buy some time. "I'm a father myself, and I can't imagine how horrible it's been for you. How angry you must be. What happened to Mikhail was a disgusting travesty that deserves justice. But think about all the other Mikhails out there who are going to die over this. You're right about this decadent Sodom-and-Gomorrah direction we've taken of late. But there are still some good people out there."

"What's this? A Bible-thumping cop?" said the old man. "Spare the city for the sake of a few good people? Where are they? Who's good? Wait. Let me guess. You?"

"Sure. I'm not so bad," I said with a shrug. "Spare it for me. Why not?"

The old man dropped the flail and took out a Glock and pressed it to my forehead.

"If I were God, I might be tempted," he said as he cocked the hammer. "Too bad for you: I'm the other guy."

# Chapter 107

THAT'S WHEN WE heard the noise. A heavy crunching sound followed by glass shattering.

It was coming from upstairs.

The old man still had the gun to my head as the two Russians stared at each other. The old man looked down at me with hate in his eyes, pressing the barrel hard against my head, but then there was another creak of wood. It was a footstep in the room directly above, and the younger man put a finger to his lips and the cold metal lifted away.

He cut a piece of duct tape and wrapped it around my mouth before the two of them went out the door. The massive shoot-out erupted thirty seconds later. Automatic gunfire in the next room starting and stopping and starting again. I hit the deck just before a round ripped a hole in the cheap wooden door.

Twenty seconds after that, I heard it. The three words I'd been praying for.

"He's in here!" Emily said.

"How'd you find me? My phone?" was the first thing I said.

She nodded, smiling.

"That find-your-friend app comes in damn handy!" she said, smiling, as she unlocked my cuffed ankle.

"I'm glad we're friends," I said, finally standing. "There was an old guy and a younger one. Russians, like we thought. Did you get them?"

"The Filipovs. We heard. We got the younger one. He got hit and they found him a block away. They'd bugged out of a cellar door we missed."

"What about the old bastard? He said he was KGB. Evil as a snake."

"Not yet. But we have the whole neighborhood surrounded. He's on foot."

Emily handed me my Glock and I stumbled up the basement stairs behind her. Golly tamale, did it feel good in my hand at that moment. I could have kissed both it and her. They must have found it at the crash scene.

We went outside through the front door. I was shocked to see that the building was a small brick house at the dead end of a leafy residential street. To the right of it was a huge school or something— several dark buildings with a large empty parking lot beyond the guardrail at the end of the street.

"Where are we?" I said.

"Brooklyn. Manhattan Beach, Brooklyn. That's Kingsborough Community College right there. We think he ran in there. Don't worry, we're on it. A dozen agents are on his tail. We're going door-to-door."

I immediately hopped the guardrail and started running across the parking lot.

"Mike, stop! What are you doing?" Emily yelled at my back. "You need a doctor."

I didn't have time to explain. I was probably still half in shock or something after the accident and beating, but wherever he was I had to find the crazy old evil prick. There was nothing this guy wouldn't do to get away—no depths he wouldn't stoop to. He had no qualms about killing another innocent person. I had to find him if it was the last thing I did.

I passed a guard shack and came down some steps and was running past a building when I noticed one of its doors was slightly open. I creaked it open some more, then I heard feet pounding on the stairs inside.

I ran in and up and got to the second floor just as the person left the stairwell onto the third floor. I was coming through the third floor's swinging door into a dark hallway five seconds later when I felt something on my face, and a wire was tightening around my neck.

I was just able to get my hands in as the old bastard tightened the garrote. It was a steel wire, incredibly fine, like titanium dental floss. Blood squirted as it slid deep into the edges of my palms above my wrists.

I bulled back into him. We went through the swinging door into the stairwell and tumbled backwards, banging down the stairs. The garrote slackened as I fell on him on the landing, and I ripped the wire away from my neck with a hiss of breath.

I crawled to my feet, blood freely pouring from the cut meat of my palms. I turned as the old Russian was taking something out of his pocket. It was a straight razor.

Before he could cut me again, I kicked him in the right ear. I center-massed my size-11 Nunn

Bush wingtip oxford right in his ear. Hard. I booted him like I never kicked anything in my life. His head slammed back at the crushing impact and bashed off the radiator with a low gong as the straight razor went flying.

As he was sitting there, stunned, I lifted him by his lapels with my bloody aching hands, yanked him up and off his feet, and with every nanoparticle of panicked strength I had in me, threw the evil old prick as hard as I could backwards down the next flight of stairs.

He was facedown when I got to him, his nose bleeding. I lifted him up again. I thought of all the people he had come a hairbreadth from wiping out, people like my kids. How he'd tried to kill me a split second before.

I was about to send him flying down the stairs again when Emily and two other agents came running up.

"Mike, we got him! You got him!" she said. "It's over!"

# Chapter 108

IT WAS AROUND midnight when Emily and I arrived back at the Broad Street FBI building, across from the stock exchange. We were in the underground lot, and about half a dozen New York–office FBI guys were taking the old KGB bastard who'd just tried to kill me none too gently out of one of the other cars.

"Mike, you want to help book and interview this guy? You're the one who found him," Emily said.

"Nah, you guys take it," I said, holding up my bandaged hands. "I've spent enough time with him. Believe me. Besides, I told Fabretti that I'd disappear before the reporters showed. He's all yours. Tell the FBI they can't say I never gave them anything."

"You want me to drive you back to your apartment?"

"I'll catch a cab. You need to debrief that snake."

"You sure? You've been through hell today, Mike. It's okay to have some help. Or at least some company."

I went over and gave her a hug.

"Don't worry about me," I said in her ear. "You've done enough already, friend."

I came up out of the ramp of the garage onto shadowed Broad Street. I made a drunk guy walking past in a suit laugh as I saluted the flag on the stock exchange and then the statue of George Washington on the steps of Federal Hall. Then I proceeded to walk past Wall Street to Chinatown and then Little Italy until I found the Bowery.

It was a gorgeous night. It had rained a little as we were coming back from Brooklyn, but it was clear now. The neon signs in the bar windows and brake lights up the avenues were vivid as high-def against the night.

I walked through Nolita and smiled as I arrived at Astor Place, where I used to get New Wave haircuts with my buddies. Afterward we'd go to the pizza place on the corner, which had the greatest slices known to man. I remembered being a teenager, standing out on the plaza where the cube sculpture was, smoking cigarettes with my goofball friends, staring down the punk rockers as we tried to get girls' phone numbers. The few numbers we'd scrape together we'd scrawl on scraps of paper and napkins and keep under our mattresses like precious medals.

All those years ago, I thought, smiling. It really was a wonder, like Emily had said. This city. How many ghosts? I wondered. How many memories and dreams and aspirations packed in and out of how many walls? Who knew what would happen tomorrow? But I was glad I'd been part of keeping this old wonder rolling for at least another day.

I went left on 14th Street to Union Square and walked through some skateboarders rolling around the empty farmers' market and past the closed doors of the Barnes & Noble. I found Broadway and pushed north.

It was coming on 2:00 a.m. by the time I got to my building on West End Avenue and stepped off the elevator onto my floor.

I truly was bamboozled by all the noise coming from behind my closed apartment door. There was laughing and distinct whooping.

A party? I thought. Who was old enough to

party till 2:00 a.m.? Seamus was *too* old, I thought as I turned the lock and pushed open the door.

"Michael! You're home!" Mary Catherine said, standing there wide-eyed on the front-hall carpet, surrounded by the kids.

I stood there, stunned frozen, with my fingers still on the key in the lock.

How? I thought. *Wasn't she still in Ireland?*

Then I wisely dispensed with all that and did the only sensible thing.

I let the door bang closed behind me as I slammed into Mary Catherine and hugged her for all I was worth.

"I love you, too," she finally whispered in my ear.

# THIS HOUSE WILL COST YOU... YOUR LIFE.

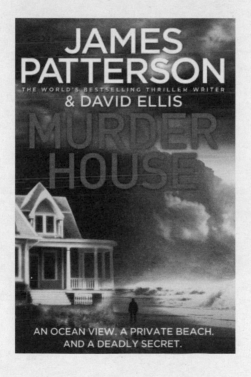

THE FUNERAL FOR Melanie Phillips is heavily attended, filling the pews of the Presbyterian church and overflowing onto Main Street. She was all of twenty years old when she was murdered, every day of which she lived in Bridgehampton. Poor girl, never got to see the world, though for some people, the place you grew up *is* your world. Maybe that was Melanie. Maybe all she ever wanted was to be a waitress at Tasty's Diner, serving steamers and lobster to tourists and townies and the occasional rich couple looking to drink in the "local environment."

But with her looks, at least from what I've seen in photos, she probably had bigger plans. A young woman like that, with luminous brown hair and sculpted features, could have been in magazines.

That, no doubt, is why she caught the attention of Zach Stern, the head of a talent agency that included A-list celebrities, a man who owned his own jet and who liked to hang out in the Hamptons now and then.

And that, no doubt, is also why she caught the attention of Noah Walker, who apparently had quite an affinity for young Melanie himself and must not have taken too kindly to her affair with Zach.

It was only four nights ago that Zachary Stern and Melanie Phillips were found dead, victims of a brutal murder in a rental house near the beach that Zach had leased for the week. The carnage was brutal enough that Melanie's service was closed-casket.

So the crowd is owed in part to Melanie's local popularity, and in part to the media interest, given Zach Stern's notoriety in Hollywood.

It is also due, I am told, to the fact that the murders occurred at 7 Ocean Drive, which among the locals has become known as the Murder House.

Now we've moved to the burial, which is just next door to the church. It allows the throng that couldn't get inside the church to mill around the south end of the cemetery, where Melanie Phillips will be laid to rest. There must be three hundred people here, if you count the media, which for the most part are keeping a respectful distance even while they snap their photographs.

The overhead sun at midday is strong enough for squinting and sunglasses, both of which make it harder for me to do what I came here to do, which is to check out the people attending the funeral to see if anyone pings my radar. Some of these creeps like to come and watch the sorrow they caused, so it's standard operating procedure to scan the crowd at crime scenes and funerals.

"Remind me why we're here, Detective Murphy," says my partner, Isaac Marks.

"I'm paying my respects."

"You didn't know Melanie," he says.

True enough. I don't know anyone around here. Once upon a time, my family came here every summer, a good three-week stretch straddling June and July, to stay with Uncle Langdon and Aunt Chloe. My memories of those summers—beaches and boat rides and fishing off the docks—end at age seven.

For some reason I never knew, my family stopped coming after that. Until nine months ago when I joined the force, I hadn't set foot in the Hamptons for eighteen years.

"I'm working on my suntan," I say.

"Not to mention," says Isaac, ignoring my remark, "that we already have our bad guy in custody."

Also true. We arrested Noah Walker yesterday. He'll get a bond hearing tomorrow, but there's no way the judge is going to bond him out on a double murder.

"And might I further add," says Isaac, "that this isn't even your case."

Right again. I volunteered to lead the team arresting Noah, but I wasn't given the case. In fact, the chief—my aforementioned uncle Langdon— is handling the matter personally. The town, especially the hoity-toity millionaires along the beach, just about busted a collective gut when the celebrity agent Zach Stern was brutally murdered in their scenic little hamlet. It's the kind of case that could cost the chief his job, if he isn't careful. I'm told the town supervisor has been calling him on the hour for updates.

So why am I here, at a funeral for someone I don't know, on a case that isn't mine? Because I'm bored. Because since I left the NYPD, I haven't seen any action. And because I've handled more homicides in eight years on the force than all of these cops in Bridgehampton put together. Translation: I wanted the case, and I was a little displeased when I didn't get it.

"Who's that?" I ask, gesturing across the way to an odd-looking man in a green cap, with long stringy hair and ratty clothes. Deep-set, creepy eyes that seem to wander. He shifts his weight from foot to foot, unable to stay still.

Isaac pushes down his sunglasses to get a better look. "Oh, that's Aiden Willis," he says. "He works for the church. Probably dug Melanie's grave."

"Looks like he slept in it first."

Isaac likes that. "Seriously, Murphy. You're looking for suspects? With all you know about this case, which is diddly-squat, you don't like Noah Walker for the murders?"

"I'm not saying that," I answer.

"You're not denying it, either."

I consider that. He's right, of course. What the hell do I know about Noah Walker or the evidence against him? He may not have jumped out at me as someone who'd just committed a brutal double murder, but when do public faces ever match private misdeeds? I once busted a second-grade schoolteacher who was selling heroin to the high school kids. And a candy striper who was boning the corpses in the basement of the hospital. You never know people. And I'd known Noah Walker for all of thirty minutes.

"Go home," says Isaac. "Go work out—"

Already did this morning.

"—or see the ocean—"

I've seen it already. It's a really big body of water.

"—or have a drink."

Yeah, a glass of wine might be in my future. But first, I'm going to take a quick detour. A detour that could probably get me in a lot of trouble.

AS THE FUNERAL for Melanie Phillips ends, I say goodbye to my partner, Detective Isaac Marks, without telling him where I'm going. He doesn't need to know, and I don't know if he'd keep the information to himself. I'm not yet sure where his loyalties lie, and I'm not going to make the same mistake I made with the NYPD.

I decide to walk, heading south from the cemetery toward the Atlantic. I always under-estimate the distance to the ocean, but it's a nice day for a walk, even if a little steamy. And I enjoy the houses just south of Main Street along this road, the white-trimmed Cape Cods with cedar shingles whose colors have grown richer with age from all the precipitation that comes with proximity to the ocean. Some are bigger, some are newer, but these houses generally look the same, which I find both comforting and a little creepy.

As I get closer to the ocean, the plots of land get wider, the houses get bigger, and the privacy shrubs flanking them get taller. I stop when I reach shrubbery that's a good ten feet high. I know I've found the place because the majestic wrought-iron gates at the end of the driveway, which are slightly parted, are adorned with black-and-yellow tape that says CRIME SCENE DO NOT CROSS.

I slide between the gates without breaking the seal. I start up the driveway, but it curves off to some kind of carriage house up a hill, which once upon a time probably served as a stable for the horses and possibly the servants' quarters. So I take the stone path that will eventually lead me to the front door.

In the center of the wide expanse of grass, just before it slopes dramatically upward, there is a small stone fountain, with a monument jutting up that bears a crest and an inscription. I lean over the fountain to take a closer look. The small tablet of stone features a bird in the center, with a hooked beak and a long tail feather, encircled by little symbols, each of which appears to be the letter *X*, but which upon closer inspection is a series of criss-crossing daggers.

And then, *ka-boom.*

It hits me, the rush, the pressure in my chest, the stranglehold to my throat, I can't breathe, I can't see, I'm weightless. *Help me, somebody please help me—*

I stagger backward, almost losing my balance, and suck in a deep, delicious breath of air.

"Wow," I say into the warm breeze. *Easy, girl. Take it easy.* I wipe greasy sweat from my forehead and inhale and exhale a few more times to slow my pulse.

Beneath the monument's crest, carved into the stone in a thick Gothic font, are these words:

## Cecilia, O Cecilia
## Life was Death Disguised

Okay, that's pretty creepy. I take a photo of the monument with my smartphone. Now front and center before the house, I take my first good look.

The mansion peering down at me from atop the hill is a Gothic structure of faded multicolored limestone. It has a Victorian look to it, with multiple rooflines, all of them steeply pitched, fancy turrets, chimneys grouped at each end. There are elaborate medieval-style accents on the facade. Every peak is topped with an ornament that ends in a sharp point, like spears aimed at the gods. The windows are long and narrow, clover-shaped, with stained glass. The house is like one gigantic, imperious frown.

I've heard some things about this house, read some things, even passed by it many times, but seeing it up close like this sends a chill through me.

It is part cathedral and part castle. It is a scowling, menacing, imposing structure, both regal and haunting, almost romantic in its gloom.

All it's missing is a drawbridge and a moat filled with crocodiles.

This is 7 Ocean Drive. This is what they call the Murder House.

*This isn't your case,* I remind myself. *This isn't your problem.*

*This could cost you your badge, girl.*

I start up the hill toward the front door.

I'M TRANSPORTED BACK hundreds of years, to a time when you rode by horseback or carriage, when you lived by candlelight and torches, when you burned witches and treated infections with leeches.

When I close the front door of the house at 7 Ocean Drive, the sound echoes up to the impossibly high, rounded ceiling, decorated with an ornate fresco of winged angels and naked women and bearded men in flowing robes, all of them appearing to reach toward something, or maybe toward one another.

The second anteroom is as chilling and dated as the first, with patterned tile floors and more of the arched, Old Testament ceilings, antique furniture, gold-framed portraits on the walls of men dressed in ruffled shirts and long coats, wigs of wavy white hair and sharply angled hats—formalwear, circa 1700.

The guy who built this place, the patriarch of the family, a guy named Winston Dahlquist, apparently didn't have a sense of humor.

My heels echo on the hardwood floor as I enter the open-air foyer, rising up three stories to the roof. Every step I take elicits a reaction from this house, fleeting coughs and groans.

"Hello," I say, like a child might, the sound returning to me faintly.

The stairs up to the second floor are winding and predictably creaky. The house continues to call out from parts unseen, aches and hiccups and wheezes, a centuries-old creature drawing long, labored breaths.

When I reach the landing, it seizes me again, stealing the air from my lungs, pressing against my chest, blinding me. *No, please! Please, please, stop—*

—high-pitched childlike squeals, uncontrollable laughter—

*Please don't, please don't do this to me.*

I grasp the banister so I don't fall back down the stairs. I open my eyes and raise my face, panting for air, until my heartbeat finally decelerates.

"Get a grip, Murphy." I pass through ornate double doors to the second-floor hallway, where the smell greets me immediately, the coppery odor of spilled blood, the overpowering, putrid scent of decay. I walk along a thick red carpet, the walls papered with red and gold, as I approach the bedroom where Zach Stern and Melanie Phillips took their last breaths.

I step onto the dark hardwood floor and look around the room. Gold wallpaper is everywhere. Against one wall is a king-size canopy bed with thick purple curtains and sturdy bedposts. The bed is dressed in a purple comforter and ruffle with velvet pillows, some of which are still on the bed, some of which lie on the floor. The dark wood dresser holds two pewter statuettes that were probably bookends for the thick volumes of short stories that also now lie on the floor. The statuettes, as well as an antique brass alarm clock, are knocked to the side on the dresser.

Opposite the bed, made of wood that matches the dresser, is a giant armoire. And in the far corner of the room, south of the armoire and west of the dresser, is the bathroom.

I remove copies of the crime scene photos I xeroxed from the file. Zachary Stern was found lying facedown on the floor, his head turned to the right toward the door, his feet pointed toward the bed. Beneath him was a pool of blood and other bodily excrement from the horrific stab wound to his midsection. Several of his fingers were crushed as well. Melanie Phillips was found by the armoire opposite the bed, the back of her right hand touching the armoire's leg; she was lying on her stomach like Zach, her head to the left, her eyes open and her mouth frozen in a tiny *o*. She was stabbed more than a dozen times, in the breast and torso and then in the face, neck, back, arms, and legs.

Now back to the scene. The comforter on the bed has been pulled back on the left side, showing a large blood pool where Zach was first stabbed while lying in bed. There is blood spatter on the wall behind the bed, and a thick sea of blood embedded in the floor where he died. There is blood spatter on the armoire and all over the nearby floor where Melanie lay as she died.

Two more facts: Judging from the fresh semen found inside Melanie and on Zach's genitalia, it seems clear that the two of them had had sexual intercourse not long before they were killed. And as of now, barring DNA testing that is still pending, there is no physical evidence putting Noah Walker in this house—no fingerprints, no carpet fibers, no shoe or boot prints.

And now the theory the STPD and the district attorney are running with: Noah was obsessed with Melanie. He somehow learned of her affair with Zach and followed her here. We don't know how he got in. The front door should have been locked, and no damage was done to it. In any event, he lay in wait until they had completed their sexual intercourse, when they were relaxed, when their guards were down, to spring into the room.

Noah surprised Zach in bed, plunging his knife into Zach's chest and dragging the blade downward, causing a vertical cut of roughly five inches, tearing open the esophagus and stomach. At this point, Melanie, who was in the bathroom cleaning up, came out. Noah subdued her by the dresser, knocking over the books and alarm clock and stabbing her multiple times in the breasts and torso before throwing her to the floor by the armoire, where he continued to stab her from behind, slicing her cheek and ear and neck and then her back, arms, and legs. He then returned to Zach and threw him out of the bed and onto the floor, stomping on and crushing some of Zach's fingers in a blind rage.

I move to the corner beyond where Zach's body was found and squat down, trying to get the angle right and using the photos to make sure I'm accurate. Where Zach would have been lying on the floor, with his head to the right, his sight line travels beyond the edge of the bed to the armoire. I repeat the same exercise from Melanie's vantage point and get the same line of vision, from the opposite end.

I remove my compact from my purse and squat down by the leg of the armoire that Melanie's right hand touched. I curl the compact under the armoire and around the leg so I can see the back of it. As I thought, the wood is abraded—scraped and cut.

Ten minutes later, I'm walking on Ocean Drive toward Main Street, on my cell phone with Uncle Langdon. "Melanie Phillips was handcuffed to the armoire's leg," I say. "He made her watch the whole thing. This wasn't an act of blind rage, Chief. This was a calculated, well-executed act of sadism."

## Also by James Patterson

### ALEX CROSS NOVELS

Along Came a Spider • Kiss the Girls • Jack and Jill •
Cat and Mouse • Pop Goes the Weasel • Roses are Red •
Violets are Blue • Four Blind Mice • The Big Bad Wolf •
London Bridges • Mary, Mary • Cross • Double Cross •
Cross Country • Alex Cross's Trial (*with Richard
DiLallo*) • I, Alex Cross • Cross Fire • Kill Alex Cross •
Merry Christmas, Alex Cross • Alex Cross, Run •
Cross My Heart • Hope to Die • Cross Justice

### THE WOMEN'S MURDER CLUB SERIES

1st to Die • 2nd Chance (*with Andrew Gross*) •
3rd Degree (*with Andrew Gross*) • 4th of July (*with Maxine
Paetro*) • The 5th Horseman (*with Maxine Paetro*) •
The 6th Target (*with Maxine Paetro*) • 7th Heaven (*with Maxine
Paetro*) • 8th Confession (*with Maxine Paetro*) •
9th Judgement (*with Maxine Paetro*) • 10th Anniversary (*with
Maxine Paetro*) • 11th Hour (*with Maxine Paetro*) •
12th of Never (*with Maxine Paetro*) • Unlucky 13 (*with Maxine
Paetro*) • 14th Deadly Sin (*with Maxine Paetro*) • 15th Affair (*with
Maxine Paetro*)

### PRIVATE NOVELS

Private (*with Maxine Paetro*) • Private London (*with Mark
Pearson*) • Private Games (*with Mark Sullivan*) •
Private: No. 1 Suspect (*with Maxine Paetro*) • Private Berlin
(*with Mark Sullivan*) • Private Down Under (*with Michael
White*) • Private L.A. (*with Mark Sullivan*) • Private India (*with
Ashwin Sanghi*) • Private Vegas (*with Maxine Paetro*) • Private
Sydney (*with Kathryn Fox*)

For more information about James Patterson's novels, visit
www.jamespatterson.co.uk

Or become a fan on Facebook